DETROIT RIVER CONNECTIONS

*Historical and Biographical Sketches
of the
Eastern Great Lakes Border Region*

By
Judy Jacobson

CLEARFIELD

Printed for
Clearfield Company, Inc. by
Genealogical Publishing Co., Inc.
Baltimore, Maryland
1994

Reprinted for
Clearfield Company, Inc. by
Genealogical Publishing Co., Inc.
Baltimore, Maryland
2002

International Standard Book Number: 0-8063-4510-1

Made in the United States of America

Table of Contents

Acknowledgements

My mother deserves thanks for the stories of families from early Detroit that she passed down to me. Bruce Leopold deserves thanks for coming through whenever my computer failed me.

When I wrote the library in the Highgate, Ontario area, my letter was given to Frances Phillips, a local genealogist, to answer. To my surprise, I received so much more information then I could ever have expected. My thanks to Frances.

The books and archives at the Bentley Historical Library at the University of Michigan were so helpful. My thanks to the librarians there, especially for sending materials to me even after I had returned home from Ann Arbor.

My thanks to my children for it was because of them that I got started looking into their heritage in the first place. And they were the ones who live amidst the clutter of genealogy material and books.

But most of all I want to thank my husband for his patience, his encouragement, his editing skills, and his willingness to foot the bill for trips to the Library of Congress, National Archives, Michigan and Canada.

Preface

It's flag has been changed five times; it has been under three different sovereignties. It has been besieged by Indians twice, captured in war once, and burnt to the ground once. Yet, because of its strategic location- both militarily and commercially- the settlers just kept coming into the U.S. / Canadian Border Region and moved freely across the narrow straits dividing them.

Eventually Windsor became Canada's busiest point of entry. By 1870, 500,000 Canadians had migrated to the U.S. And it has been estimated the 90% of the Canadian population still lives within 200 miles of the American border.

The Detroit River drains Lake St. Clair east of Detroit and forms the international boundary between the State of Michigan on the U.S. side and the Province of Ontario on the Canadian side. This was where I grew up.

Actually, I grew up in Detroit. But three of my grandparents lived in Canada before emigrating to the United States. In fact, my grandmother was born and raised across the bridge in Canada, so I had relatives still living there while I was growing up. When I was teaching school in a Detroit suburb, another teacher in my school drove across from Windsor every day to her job. Detroiters went to Ontario for their Sunday drives. Detroit businesses readily accepted Canadian money and vice-versa.

That's the way it was. People moved freely across the border. They always have. This book is about those early families who lived on both sides - the French, the English, the Scots, the Irish - the people that were connected by that invisible border.

vi

In Explanation

Symbols Used

aft	after
b.	born
betw	between
bpt.	baptized
br	brother of
bur.	buried
c.	circa
Capt.	Captain
circa	approximately
con	concession
d.	died
dau	daughter of
Dea	Deacon
employ.	employed as or employed at
eng.	engaged to
est dvd.	estate divided
fthr	father of
grad.	graduated from college
lt	lot number
Lt.	Lieutenant
m.	married
Maj.	Major
mthr	mother of
nd	no date given
np	no place given
pos	possibly
prob	probably
repr	reprint
Sgt.	Sergeant
sis	sister of
son	son of
tw	twin
twp.	township
vol	volume
wid	widow or widower of
wll dtd.	will dated
wll pro.	will probated

Names

Since many of the families which settled in the Border Region of Michigan and Ontario were from France, many first names were of French origin. In the different sources examined, both French and English versions were used. In this text those names have been interchanged. Some examples of interchangeable names are

Andrew	Andre
John	Jean
Francis	Francois
Geneva / Genevieve	Geneveva / Genevieve
Baptist	Baptiste
Anthony	Antoine
Phylis	Felicity
Josephine	Joseph / Josette
Agatha	Agathe
Dennis	Denis
Stephen	Etienne
Mary	Marie
Lawrence	Laurant / Eustache
Philip	Phillipe
Margaret	Marguerite
William	Guillaume

Interchangeable names are also used for places, such as

Three Rivers   Trois Rivieres
Thames River
Riviere a la Trenche

According to Father Christian Denissen, there were a number of reasons for the double names found among early families of the Border Region. The reasons were

<u>a</u>. Owners of estates gave their holdings titles as did European nobility. And often it was the title that survived; e.g., Douaire de Bondy.

<u>b</u>. The custom of giving nicknames brought about some double names; e.g. Poissant = Poisson-La Sallene.

<u>c</u>. It was sometimes necessary to distinguish one family from another of the same name; e.g., Joseph Martin for Joseph Durocher, son of Martin Durocher.

<u>d</u>. Some sought to glorify the section of the country they came from by adding the name of the province, city, or town. This was a very common practice among the soldiers; e.g., Vale dit Versailles.

<u>e</u>. Sometimes nicknames originated from the peculiar circumstances of a person's birth; e.g., Nicholas Campau dit Niagara

<u>f</u>. At times the name was given by the Indians; e.g. Peltier dit Antaya.

<u>g</u>. Sometimes the Christian name by which a person was known in the community was adopted; e.g., Louis Villers dit St. Louis.

<u>h</u>. The name, or the double name, of the wife sometimes prevailed; e.g., Godet dit Marentette. Jacques Godet married Margaret Duquay dit Marentette.

Ecu, egret, and other pronunciation marks normally found on French words and names have been left off in this text.

Scottish names with the prefix Mac / Mc / M' meaning "son" were originally added without consistency. A surname that followed Mac was usually capitalized, as in MacDonald. Otherwise the "second" name was usually in lower case, i.e. Maclean. Prior to the 1600's, surnames were not used.

In this text a single spelling of a name was used throughout the text with the exception of in the beginning of a specific genealogy when variations were given, and within a quote from another source. In quotations names were spelt as they were in the original passage.

Also in this text, when a place presently in the United States or in Canada was given, only the city and province / state were listed. The country was considered to be understood. For places outside of Canada and the United States, such as France, the country was given when known.

Other

Several other terms found in the text need explanation. An "arpent" and a "perche" were French linear measurements.

1 arpent = 1.5 acres
27.5 arpents = 1 U.S. mile
1 perche = 19.188 feet

A "Concession" was a block of land granted by the King to a company or the church.

As for money, Halifax currency was worth less than British Sterling. New York was worth less than Halifax. In 1780, John Askin related that

Halifax currency = 75-80% Sterling
New York currency = 60% Halifax

A livre was a French unit of currency.

1 livre = 1 pound of silver

"Seigneur" was a title awarded a person of high rank usually giving him the authority of "lord of the manor" over the land and people in the area. "Sieur" was the early version of the word "Monsieur" and was used for a landowner who was not a "Seigneur".

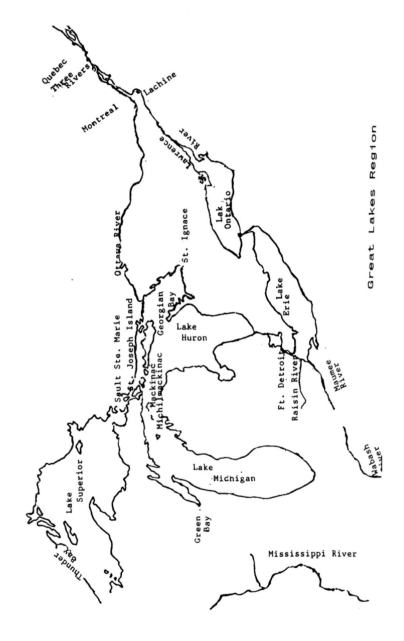

Great Lakes Region

Quebec

Three Rivers

Montreal

Lachine

Lawrence River

Lak Ontario

Ottawa River

St. Ignace

Georgian Bay

Lake Erie

Sault Ste. Marie

St. Joseph Island

Mackinac

Michilmackinac

Lake Huron

Ft. Detroit

Raisin River

Maumee River

Lake Superior

Lake Michigan

Wabash River

Green Bay

Thunder Bay

Mississippi River

x

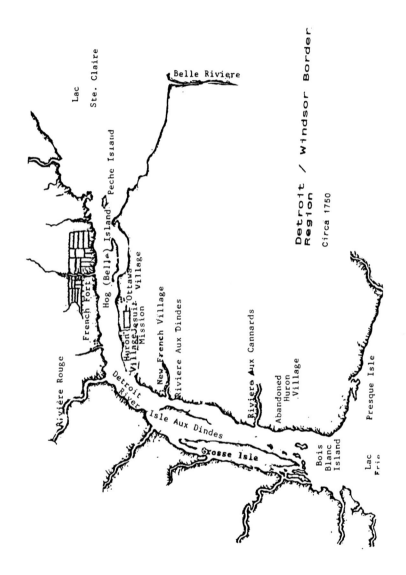

Detroit / Windsor Border Region Circa 1750

Lac Ste. Claire

Belle Riviere

Peche Island

Hog (Belle) Island

French Fort

Rivière Rouge

Detroit River

Huron Village

Jesuit Mission

Ottawa Village

New French Village

Riviere Aux Dindes

Isle Aux Dindes

Riviere Aux Cannards

Abandoned Huron Village

Grosse Isle

Bois Blanc Island

Presque Isle

Lac Erie

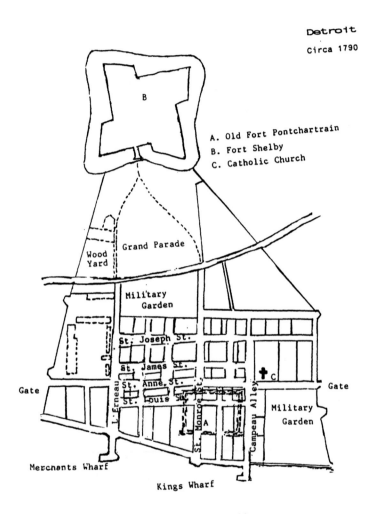

Detroit

Circa 1790

A. Old Fort Pontchartrain
B. Fort Shelby
C. Catholic Church

B

Grand Parade

Wood
Yard

Military
Garden

St. Joseph St.

St. James St.

Gate   St. Anne St.   Gate
        St. Louis St.
L'Erneau St.
St. Monroe
Campeau Alley   Military
                 Garden

Merchants Wharf

Kings Wharf

Detroit River

xii

History of the Border Region

Early adventurers may have probed the St. Lawrence - Great Lakes waterways in search of a route to China as early as the 1500's. Jacques Cartier entered the St. Lawrence in 1534, while the next year he sailed up the river for the first time. Through the next two centuries, the waterway lured French priests and explorers deep into the continent.

The Quebec area was the first settled. New France became a haven for the lower and upper classes of France: the middle class was practically non-existent. The French governmental system set up in Quebec was a feudal one in nature, not one overly attractive to those seeking economic and religious freedom. According to Lord Durham, the system was badly organized and repressive. In the beginning, the French were distributed along the St. Lawrence. As in France, seigneurs owned large parcels of land and rented small blocks of land to the lower class.

But the goal of the French government was to establish a series of forts between Montreal and New Orleans. And that they did, sending troops and settlers alike into the Michigan/ Ontario Border Region.

While adventurers like Brule and Champlain were the first Europeans to enter the area, it was actually the priests who first claimed the area for France.

On August 8, 1665; Father Allouez and six Frenchmen left Three Rivers near Quebec following more than 400 Indians who were returning "to their own country." According to his journal, Father Allouez's travels took him all the way to Lake Superior. Along the way three of the Frenchmen deserted the group and the "savages", believing that baptism caused the death of Indian children, abandoned Allouez on a deserted island when he endeavored to follow them.

Later, in 1669, Joliet traveled down the Detroit River and along Lake Erie's north shore. He met priests Francois Dollier de Casson and Rene de Brehant de Galinee along the way, and Galinee's journal described the new route they took at Joliet's urging. Galinee wrote that on the shore of the Detroit River, "six leagues above Lake Erie," they discovered a stone idol venerated by the Indians. The priests broke the idol into pieces and threw them into the river.

LaSalle and Father Louis Hennepin followed in 1679. Their primary purpose was to extend French Catholicism throughout the continent. In the late 1670's, Father Hennepin wrote of the area that

"the banks of the Streit (were) vast meadows and the prospect (was) terminated with some hills covered with vineyards... Groves and forests are so well disposed that one would think Nature alone could not make, without the help of art, so charming a prospect."

Sieur de Tonty wrote in his memoirs that LaSalle and he traveled as far as "Missilimakinak" where they crossed "two lakes larger then that of Frontenac (Lake Ontario)." Henri de Tonty was LaSalle's primary aide. He was also known among Indians as "Tonty of the Iron Hand" because as a young man he had lost his hand in battle and it had been replaced by an iron artificial one.

In Historical Geography of Detroit, Parkins quoted a 1690 map of unknown authorship, which revealed that all the country in the area of "Lake Terocharronting" (Lake Erie) had been discovered and explored. Erie was the 4th largest of the Great Lakes and had the modern day U.S. to the south and west and Canada to the north. The Detroit River was its inlet from Lake St. Clair and Lake Huron beyond, and the Niagara River was its outlet to Lake Ontario.

Since few Indians lived along the Detroit River, traders had not yet been drawn to the area. But then after King William's War (1689-1697), both the British and French considered setting up trading posts or forts in the West.

The fur trade began taking on increasing economic importance to the French. But in order to get into the interior to trade with the Indians, traders were required to obtain a French trade passport beginning in 1681. The system continued off and on until 1760. Through those years a number of the family names found among these genealogies appeared on trade passports; including Barthe, "Beaudry:, Bondy, "Campault", "Cullerie" / Cullerier, "Gaudent" / Godet, "Godefroy", Meloche, and Parent / "Parant"

Soon two countries, Britain and France, claimed the area. The British became interested in the area because of its millions of elk, deer, swans, geese and all sorts of fowl. So on July 14, 1701, the English received a deed from the Iroquois giving them the land east and west of Detroit.

Despite the English deed, Antoine de la Mothe Cadillac and his men took physical control of the Detroit site for France on July 24, 1701, and began to build a fort they named Ft. Pontchartrain. Cadillac founded Detroit on the river or strait as a means to check the English trade and any Iroquois advance. Just two days later, St. Anne's Day was celebrated at Detroit's first religious service.

Before founding Detroit, Cadillac had been stationed at Michilimackinac, between Lakes Huron and Michigan, where he learned the necessity of winning the confidence of the Indians. So when Cadillac arrived in the Detroit area, he attempted to attract various Indian tribes and form them into a local army. However, only the powerful Ottawas and Potawatomis of the Algonquian family of Indians, and the Hurons of the Iroquoian family came to establish villages near the French fort. Although the Iroquois were much more ferocious than the Hurons, Bougainville reported that the Hurons were a nation "always suspected and troublesome (who) have bad ideas in their heads."

Because of the closeness that developed between the missionaries and the Huron Indians, the Hurons also became an critical element of the fur trade. While linguistically the Hurons were related to the Iroquois, between 1648 and 1650 the relatively peaceful Hurons were driven from their lands in the Ontario lowlands by the fiercer Iroquois, who diverted the

2

flow of furs to the Dutch. During the winter of 1701-2, 6,000 Indians stayed at Detroit.

Cadillac's establishment of a fort at Detroit was just another move in the long chess match being played by France and England in the New World. The placement and movement inland of both countries' settlements were certain to lead to a clash and during Queen Anne's War (1702-1713) the area was in chaos.

The first large group of people arrived in the Border Region during the summer of 1706 and the settlers were granted pieces of land. But they were allowed to keep the land for only as long as they kept the land cultivated. Jean Fofard, an interpreter, received the first grant on March 10, 1707.

Relationships with the Indian deteriorated. In 1712, three hundred Sauk, Fox, and Missauka Indians prepared to attack the thirty-man garrison at Fort Pontchartrain. The garrison's Indian allies arrived in time and, after a nineteen-day siege, the French and their allies were winning. The battle continued for another four days at Grosse Pointe, nine miles northeast of Detroit on Lake St. Clair, before the French became totally victorious.

Then, during the French and Indian War, the Border Region furnished the French with supplies and allies. In 1757, Bougainville reported that French troops in Detroit hoped to persuade the Choctaws to fight the English, leaving the Catawbas as the only western Indian nation allied with the British.

But the English won and British Major Rogers was sent to Detroit, Michilimackinac and points farther west into the Northwest Territory to collect arms and administer the oath of allegiance.

The Northwest Territory was the name the British gave to the area laying between western Pennsylvania and the Mississippi River, from north of the Ohio River into the Great Lakes. Major Rogers took control of Detroit in November, 1760, and Capt. Donald Campbell became first post commander there. Upon arrival they found 500 men who could be used to defend the area and a total of 2,500 people living on the two sides of the river. There were 300 whitewashed cottages erected continuously along eight miles on either side of the river. The fort along the river front was
> "enclosed by a picket fence about twenty-five feet high, with a bastion of eight artillery at each corner and a block-house over the main gate way. It contained a barricade, quarter for officers, a council house, and a church, and also enclosed about one hundred small houses."

The stockade was 1200 yards in circumference. According to Russell's The British Regime in Michigan, Campbell found the people in "want of everything," but that the fort was in good repair. At Campbell's request, Col. Bouquet sent two Dutch traders loaded with supplies for the area.

After supporting the French, obviously, the Indians were not thrilled with the arrival of the British. The English reputation for seizing Indian land was notorious. In addition, wherever the British went, hoards of settlers and acquisitive adventurers followed.

Pontiac was an Ottawa chief born circa 1720 in the Maumee River region who would lead the Indians against the English. His mother was probably from another tribe and Pontiac may have grown to become a medicine man who, according to The History of Wayne County, had a "threatening hatred" for the British. He commanded the Indians in defense of Detroit in 1746 and against General Babcock in 1765. In 1763, as principal chief of the Ottawas, Pontiac led a confederacy of Ottawas, Potawatomis, Ojibwas, Chippewas, and others to check the English and drive them from Indian land.

The British, of course, believed the French were the instigators. All forts in the area, including those at Presque Isle and Mackinac, fell; and traders and full garrisons of men were killed. But Detroit survived Pontiac's attempted massacre of the garrison there. At the time there were also 33 French families, with their 41 children and 60 slaves living inside the fort.

With Indians hiding on marshy and forested islands ready to attack, traveling along the Detroit River was dangerous at the time. In May, 1763, ten ships were attacked and eight were captured near Detroit. But in July, re-enforcements with provisions made it through and the siege at Detroit was ended. The loss at Detroit discouraged Pontiac and, by October, he had quit fighting.

In 1769, during an Illinois Indian council, Pontiac was assassinated. In his Wayne County history, Burton added that in one version, because Pontiac had been cruel to his Peorie wife, her tribe had murdered him. As punishment, the Ottawas exterminated the guilty tribe.

It has also been claimed at various times that Pontiac was killed by an Indian spy or a British sympathizer. In another version he was killed by an English trader as he wandered drunkenly through the forest. And yet another account had Pontiac being killed by a Kaskaskia at a drunken orgy.

When the American Revolution began, many inhabitants of the area attempted to remain neutral. But it eventually became evident that the Americans were going to take control of Detroit, and the British living there realized they would have to choose between becoming Americans or remaining British.

The 1783 Treaty of Paris stipulated that the border between the United States and Canada would follow the St. Lawrence River through the Great Lakes and beyond. However, the British continued to maintain forces at Detroit and Michilimackinac and controlled the fur trade throughout the Great Lakes Region. While a number of English and Scotch merchants from Detroit moved to the south side of the river, many British remained in Detroit. Even the Indians were confused as to which country they lived in.

Then, as tensions grew in the early 1800's, movement between the United States and Canada grew more difficult. As

early as August, 1807, James Askin wrote his brother Charles that another war between the British and the Americans was expected at any time. The calvary was patrolling every night and the militia was practicing frequently. That October, Isaac Todd wrote to John Askin, Sr. that
"the Americans has themselves to blaim that neither Indians nor the Inhabitants of Detroit St. Lewis &ca. like them as they unjustly want to deprive them of lands..."
In fact, in a July, 1808 letter, John Askin, Jr. wrote from St. Joseph's to his father that he was disappointed with his brother-in-law Elijah Brush of Detroit for not smuggling cider to him. John wrote "He could as well Smuggle cyder to our side as wine to his."

During the War of 1812, the Border Region faced more divisions. America had fifteen as many citizens as Canada and the U.S. clearly coveted Canada. In addition to battles along the Atlantic seaboard, war was also waged in the Great Lakes area. General Hull appealed to Canadians to join the Americans by saying
"You have no participation in (Great Britain's) councils nor interest in her conduct. You have felt her tyranny; you have seen her injustice ... Many of your fathers fought for the freedom and independence we now enjoy..."

American troops from Detroit covered an area as far south as Monroe, Michigan. With its isolated position, Detroit fell. But Ft. Malden on the Canadian side was isolated too, cut off from all communication and supplies via land. Then the September, 1813 defeat of the British fleet at Put-in-Bay Harbor, east of Toledo, made it easier for the Americans to reclaim Detroit. McNaught claimed that Canada might have fallen to the Americans but for
"the loyalty of French Canadians and 'late Loyalists'; the superior training and tactics of the small British regular force; and the almost total incompetence of the American generals."

On the Michigan Side of the Border

Russell, in <u>The British Regime in Michigan and the Old Northwest 1760-1796</u>, used the word "Michigan" to designate "a small part of the western territory ceded by France to England in 1763." During both the French and British rules, Michigan was the area within the present-day state of Michigan; plus much of Wisconsin, and parts of Indiana and Ohio.

When the Articles of Agreement were signed on September 26, 1795, early Michigan was defined as
"Situated on the Lakes Erie, Huron and Michigan, & Bounded by a Line commencing at the Miami Village, thence down the River of that name (later Maumee River), till it falls into Lake Erie, thence along the said Lake up the Channel of the river of Detroit through St. Clair, up the Channel of the River St. Clair, thence along Lake Huron to Old Michilimackinac, and thence along Lake Michigan on a south-Westerly direction to Chacagou, thence across the Portage there, and down the Illinois River, 'till a line drawn due East from the said River strikes the Miami Village aforesaid, Comprehending all the Lands, Island & water within the said Boundary line."

In the 1800's, Michigan advertized free land grants and lumbering jobs in Ontario newspapers in an attempt to attract Canadian settlers. Soon Canadian visitors to the U.S. began to realize democratic reform was lacking on the Canadian side of the border, while economic conditions improved on the American side. After the American Civil War, young Canadian farm workers moved back and forth between Ontario and Michigan, making use of the two seasons to increase their income.

Bass Islands

The three Bass Islands are actually in northern Ohio's section of Lake Erie, west of Toledo. North Bass Island is a 1 1/4 mile long island originally the site of the village of Isle St. George. Middle Bass is 3 miles long. South Bass Island is 3 1/2 miles long. It's Put-in-Bay Harbor was the scene of Perry's 1813 naval battle.

Belle Isle

Walter Romig reported that Belle Isle's first name was Rattlesnake Island. The name of the 768 acre island was changed to Isle au Cochon (Island of the Hog or Hog Island) after hogs were released to kill off the snakes. Clarence Burton speculated the island was at one time, common land used to confine hogs and other livestock of the citizens of Detroit to protect them from wild animals and Indians. A 1769 letter from the French citizens seemed to back up that belief.

The approximately 2 miles long by 1 mile wide, the Detroit River Island had a number of owners through the years. According to one letter, even Commandant Tonty attempted to appropriate it for himself, but the citizens petitioned against him. On June 12, 1752, Douville Dequindre received a grant to the island. Later "Mr. Campeau" farmed it.

When Chief Pontiac attacked the island in 1763 as part of his attack on Detroit, he killed James Fisher, his wife, and 1 child; and took three of the Fisher children, a soldier, and the Fisher's maid as prisoners.

Then during British control, the land was owned by several lieutenants and by George McDougall, a former lieutenant. After McDougall and his sons, Belle Isle passed to Macombs and others. James McIntosh, brother of Angus and William, represented William Macomb when Macomb purchased Belle Isle in 1794.

On November 23, 1836, two gentlemen from Amherstburg, Arthur Rankin and Henry Richardson, went over to Belle Isle for a duel that began with a bar room quarrel which Rankin won.

As the area's population became larger, the island was used for picnics and became more of a resort-type area. In 1845 the name of Hog Island was changed to the more pleasing "Belle Isle."

Bois Blanc Island

One of two Bois Blanc Islands in the Border Region, this island was located in the straits between Michigan's upper and lower peninsulas near Mackinac Island. When Mackinac was ceded to the United States, the Chippewa Indians voluntarily gave Bois Blanc as a gift. Point aux Pins was a settlement on the south side of the island.

The Indians had originally named the island Mikobiminiss ("white wood"), probably because of the prevalence of birch trees on it. When the French moved into the area, they probably merely translate the Indian name of the island into their own language. However, George Stewart claimed "bois blanc" was the French term for "basswood."

Detroit

Antoine de la Mothe Cadillac chose land on the river, off the northwestern end of Lake Erie to build his fort. He decided to name it Fort Pontchartrain after Count Pontchartrain, France's minister to Canada. That first fort - or more correctly called "stockade" - was constructed of wooden pickets around one acre of land. Inside the stockade, log houses and a chapel were built.

Originally, the group had considered building the fort fifteen miles south, on Grosse Isle. However, they were concerned that they would eventually run out of timber on the 8 mile by 1 1/2 mile island.

Madame Cadillac and Sieur de Tonty arrived in Detroit in 1703. When Marie Therese Cadillac was born in 1704, she became the first baptism in the settlement.

Actually, the first religious service had been held in Detroit, led by Father Constantine on St. Anne's Day (July 26), 1701. That was the beginning of St. Anne's Church. In 1703, Indians burned the first church. The new one built in

1708 was burned by residents in 1712 to keep attacking Indians from using it. A third Catholic church named St. Anne's was erected in 1723.

According to Parkins, by 1710, farms stretched six miles along the river and
"land within the palisade was two city blocks in length, and one block deep. This area was divided into lots and garden plots."
Most streets were ten to fifteen feet wide and houses were built of logs. Parkins wrote that
"some houses had brick floors, and these were considered so valuable that they were inventoried in the household effects of the owner."

Ft. Pontchartrain's relationship with area Indians was precarious. The settlement was frequently under attack. In 1712, while Sioux and Fox Indians attacked the fort, Hurons and Ottawas helped the settlers fight them off. Then, half a century later, the Hurons would turn against the settlers.

Fishing and hunting became the chief occupations of the people and the area became a headquarters for the fur trade. It was about that time that the village around the fort began to be called Detroit, because of its situation of the strait between Lakes St. Clair and Erie. Detroit simply meant "the straits" in French.

In 1749, engineer Joseph de Lery designed a plan for a city to be named Detroit. But only one road connected the houses along the shore and only Indian trails traveled into the wilderness. One Indian village was established near the mouth of the Saginaw River to the north and another was located beyond present-day Ypsilanti to the west. Ypsilanti named for Demetrious Ypsilanti - a Greek patriot in that country's struggle for Independence.

In 1750, de Bonnecamps described Detroit as "charming". The river ran right next to the long, square fort. The surrounding area was by vast plains waiting to be farmed. He added that Detroit should be considered "one of the most important posts of the colony."

In late September, 1756, Louis Antoine de Bougainville wrote in his journal that
"in Spring there are famous foot races at that place (Detroit). It is the New Market of North America. The bets are made with packs of furs by the Indians and merchandise by the French. Sometimes they have as many as two thousand indians there, some of whom come from six or seven hundred leagues. That is the way to build up a good wind."

But the 1760's brought serious Indian problems to the area. A Seneca and Huron plot to massacre the garrison at Detroit was thwarted in 1761. But Pontiac attacked in 1763 in a siege on Detroit that lasted from May through October. Actually it was not until 1766 that Pontiac gave his allegiance to the British.

But even after that problems with Indians were not over completely for a number of years. In fact, according to Vexler's chronology, Daniel Boone was held captive by Indians in Detroit as late as March, 1778.

The city was growing. In 1771/2 a shipyard was situated at Detroit. While it became of real importance during the Revolutionary War, the ships also played an important part in the trade in Detroit.

In 1776, the newly enlarged fort at Detroit was supposedly in fairly good condition. But by 1777, considerable damage was done by the weather, not the American Revolution. In 1778 it was decided that a new fort on higher ground was needed and it was constructed under the direction of Major Lernoult who named it Fort Lernoult after himself. It was later renamed Fort Shelby before being demolished in 1826.

During the American Revolution, according to Russell, the inhabitants of the fort were primarily "French, with thirty Scotch, fifteen Irish and a few English." Additional fortifications were reinforced, but the fort saw little action. At one point during the revolution, George Rogers Clark planned an attack on Detroit in an attempt to claim it for the rebels, but his numerous attempts failed to develop.

After the war, the British claimed Detroit for the Canadian district of Hesse; while in the Northwest Ordinance of 1787, the United States also claimed it. In 1791, all of Michigan was "incorporated" into Upper Canada. In fact the British continued to claim Detroit until 1796. In that year, Catholic jurisdiction of the city also was transferred from Quebec to Baltimore. The American flag was raised over the city at noon, July 11, 1796.

In 1795; the Ottawas, Chippewas, and Potawatomies deeded all land between the Raisin River and the Huron River (later the Clinton River) of Lake Saint Clair except for a few parcels they had deeded previously, to Jonathan Schieffelen, Jacob Visger, Richard Pattinson, and Robert Innis. The grant included the city of Detroit, all land fronting the Detroit River and Lake St. Clair between present day cities Mount Clemens and Monroe and extended 18 miles inland. It was merely a reiteration of grants made earlier.

Jacob Lindley who visited Detroit in 1793 wrote in his journal that one-seventh of all lands belonged to the Crown and one-seventh by the Anglican Church. By the late 1790's, Detroit was the largest town in the Northwest Territory. In his book, Parkins told of an Irish traveler named Isaac Weld who described Detroit as standing
"contiguous to the river on the top of the banks, which (were) here about twenty feet high. At the bottom of them there (were) very extensive wharfs for the accommodation of the shipping, built of wood."
The city consisted of several narrow, unpaved streets which turned to mud whenever it rained.

The city of Detroit was destroyed on June 11, 1805, by a fire which was started by a baker's assistant. It spread rapidly and by noon the entire central village was in flames.

That year Detroit was made territorial capital. It remained the capital of the territory, and then the state, until 1847.

Despite its new status, Detroit was still a rough town. Indentured John Askwith (see Appendix) wrote from Detroit "I wish my time was out tomorrow I wou'd immediately go on board the last Vessel that sails, as this is at present perhaps the most miserable place ... I never detested any place so much ..." on December 31, 1812; Elijah Brush wrote to John Askin, Jr. "I do not think there is (any) place on the continent of America of the size of Detroit and number of its inhabitants that has produced so many drunkards, I shall try to hurry my children of it before They ever learn the use of this poisonous liquid." Many died in a cholera-like epidemic in 1813 and Indians attacked the city the next year. A peace treaty with the Indian council was not concluded until 1816.

But eventually civilization came to the city. Ordinances were passed in 1818 providing public whipping for of petty thievery, wife-beating, disorderly conduct, and public drunkenness. By 1818, with the uncertainties of the War of 1812 over, with "The Detroit Gazette" newspaper recently started, and with steam navigation beginning on Lake Erie; the region began to expand. A land office was opened that same year. And regularly scheduled ferry service between Detroit and Windsor was started.

The population of Detroit soared by over 300% between 1830 and 1840. But then the alarm brought by the Black Hawk War in Illinois and Wisconsin checked emigration to Michigan. On July 4, 1832, a steamer arrived with 370 soldiers, one of whom died of cholera upon landing. Although the ship was quickly sent on its way, many soldiers made it back to Detroit and citizens began to die. By mid-August, ninety-six residents of the Border Region had died.

Detroit Population

Source: *Historical Geography of Detroit* and *The British Regime in Michigan* and *History of Wayne County and the City of Detroit Michigan*

Year	Population	Notes
1707	270	25 families
1760	600	100 families
1770	2000	572 within the fort in 1768
1778	2144	
1780	2309	included 175 slaves
1788	4000	
1816	1650	
1820	1422	formal census
1830	2222	formal census
1834	4973	
1840	9102	formal census
1850	21019	formal census

Grosse Pointe

Grosse Pointe, a residential area northeast of Detroit, was named for a large jut or point of land extending out into Lake St. Clair. The area was first settled as early as 1701.

Grosse Isle

The Potawatomi Indians originally named the 8 by 1 1/2 mile island in the Detroit River Kitche-minishem. In 1740, Father de la Richardie proposed the Hurons be allowed to settle on Grosse Isle, which ran parallel to the western or U.S. shore. As a more peaceful tribe, it was hoped their separation from the Ottawas would make things less violent. Instead the mission and tribe were settled at Bois Blanc where they remained until the mission was moved to Sandwich.

Grosse Isle was closer to what would become the United States than to Canada. The island was considered government property and was about to be cultivated when the British took control of the area. In 1763 the Hurons, led by Pontiac, took over Grosse Isle and led attacks on boats taking goods destined for the besieged garrison at Detroit.

A deed that granted Grosse Isle to Alexander and William Macomb was signed by the Indians on July 6, 1776. The Macombs were traders and real estate dealers who subdivided the island and leased the land to farmers who built houses and otherwise improved the land. Early tenants included the surnames of Williams, Serret, Allen, Hicks, McCarthy, Anderson, Bariau, Johnson, Gill, Stoffer, Eiler, Horn, Jackson, Hoffman, Heacock, Chittenden, Monger, Mitchell, Myers, and McDulloach.

L'Arbe Croche

L'Arbe Croche, an Ottawa town twenty miles southwest of Michilimackinac, later became Cross City, Michigan.
Heldman related that the original Jesuit mission there was established in 1715 on a small piece of farm land in the middle of beaches and dunes. L'Arbre Croche was established circa 1742. But in 1763 Alexander Henry described the village of L'Arbe Croche as being
"At the entrance of Lake Michigan and at about twenty miles to the West of Fort Michilimackinac is the village of L'Arbre Croche is the seat of the Jesuit mission of St. Ignace de Michilimackinac and the people and the people are partly baptized, and partly not. The missionary resides on a farm attached to the mission and situated between the village and the fort ... The Ottawa of L'Arbre Croche, who when compared with the Chippewa appear much advanced in civilization, grow maize for the market of Michilimackinac, where this commodity is depended upon for provisioning the canoes."

Mackinac / Michilimackinac

In an attempt to strengthen the French position, De Louvigny re-established a post at Mackinac at the straits between the upper and lower peninsulas of Michigan. Actually when the English and French were there, the island and the area of land on either side of the straits between Lake Huron and Lake Michigan was known as Michilimackinac and had been ancient gathering place for the Indians of the Great Lakes region. It had first been visited by Jean Nicolet in 1634-1635. Capt. Jonathan Carver wrote that Michilimackinac meant "tortoise" in the Chippewa language.

Etienne de Carheil of Carentoir, France was ordained as a Jesuit priest in 1666. After serving in Quebec and Cayuga, de Carheil was assigned to the Huron and Ottawa mission at Mackinac in 1686. However, with the founding of Detroit in 1701, many of the Michilimackinac area Hurons were drawn there.

De Carheil and Antoine de la Mothe Cadillac did not get along. In a 1702 letter, the Jesuit complained bitterly to his superior about the "Commerce" in brandy and "savage women" conducted by the French soldiers. He complained that a public tavern at the fort even sold to the "savages" and that the women had discovered
"that their bodies might serve in lieu of merchandise and would be better received (at the fort) than Beaverskins."
This antagonism with Cadillac and fur traders, in general, brought about de Carheil's return to Quebec in 1703 and the practical abandonment of the mission at Mackinac.

Eventually another French post was constructed on the south side of the straits, at what would become Mackinac City. French soldiers remained there until the British took control of the fort in the Fall of 1761.

But the British garrison at Michilimackinac was massacred by Ojibwa Indians in conspiracy with Chief Pontiac in 1763. After the British took the fort at Michilimackinac, Capt. Jonathan wrote that the fort of the late 1760's was "composed of a strong stockade" with a garrison of 100 men. In addition, several traders lived within the fort.

The placement of the fort between Lakes Huron and Michigan made the area more important strategically. To demonstrate the area's importance, Bougainville, in his July 22, 1756 journal entry, described an alternate route between Montreal and Mackinac.
"At the Cascades the (St. Lawrence) river divides into two branches, the norther one called 'La Grand riviere' or 'River of the Ottawas' and is by following that one goes to Michilimakinac; the other branch leads to Frontenac and to the Illinois country by was of the lakes."
As Bougainville described, the Ottawa River, Lake Nipissing, Main Channel, Pickerel Inlet, and Georgian Bay did appear to lead from the St. Lawrence to Lake Huron, cutting a great deal of travel time. Michilimackinac was just beyond.

In 1780, the British sent Sinclair to rebuild the fort at Michilimackinac. He built it seven miles away on Michilimackinac Island, but soon had to turn it over to the Americans. When the British were forced out of the fort at Michilimackinac, they went to St. Joseph Island between Lakes Superior and Huron.

Since soil in the area was not very rich, many staples, such as corn, had to be brought in from Detroit. However, Father Payette at Michilimackinac Island had families from as far away as Green Bay (240 miles away) arriving to have him baptize their children. In 1810 only a few families were settled there. Then on July 16, 1812, the "Caledonia" arrived at Fort Mackinac with 250 agents (soldiers of fortune) for the Northwest Fur Company and 500 Indians. The 57-man American garrison was unprepared and surrendered. Except for during the War of 1812, the Americans have continuously controlled the fort.

Maumee / Miami

The city, named for the Maumee / Miami Indians who lived in the area, was just south of Toledo, Ohio. In 1680 it was the site of a French and, later, a British trade and military post.

The "fort of the Miamis" was located on the Maumee River, at the site of present day Fort Wayne, Indiana. The Miami Indians had moved east to the Maumee River by 1712 and the French erected the fort to protect trade with the Indians. The fort was captured and burned by Indians in 1747. But the fort was not abandoned at that time. In 1750, de Bonnecamps wrote that the French fort
"of the Miamis was in a very bad condition ... Most of the palisades were decayed and fallen into ruin. Within there were eight houses, - or, to speak more correctly, eight miserable huts ..."
The twenty-two Frenchmen living in the fort, including the commandant, were all ill.

The post was finally surrendered to the British in 1760. After General Anthony Wayne encamped there in 1794, the newly established fort was named after him.

The Maumee River was formed by the confluence of the St. Joseph and St. Mary's Rivers in Indiana. It floated East Northeast into Maumee Bay, an arm of Lake Erie, just northeast of Toledo. De Bonnecamps described his trip along "the river of the Miamis" as running through "vast prairies, where the herbage was sometimes of extraordinary height."

Although areas of the river were turbulent, making portaging necessary. However, at intervals de Bonnecamps found
"Beautiful reaches of smooth water, but they were few and short. in the last six leagues, the river is broad and deep, and seems to herald the grandeur of the lake (Erie) into which it discharges its waters."
Actually, the French called the Great Miami River, Riviere a la Roche (Rocky River) because of all the rapids.

Raisin River

The Raisin River south of Detroit ran 115 miles through Miami country. A town of the same name opened its first post office in 1807 and remained one of Michigan's ten largest settlements up until the War of 1812. During that war, the River Raisin Massacure took place for which Quaiffe reported Matthew Elliott was responsible.

The city of Monroe was built on the Raisin River and was named for President James Monroe. Monroe was the birthplace of George Armstrong Custer.

River Rouge

The Indian land which would become known as River Rouge was purchased in the late 1700's by the Navarre, Campau and a number of other French families. By 1808, thirty families lived in the area south of Detroit. Situated just below the Rouge River, it was named for its mucky reddish color.

On the Ontario Side of the Border

In 1641, the name "Ontario" was applied to the lake, possibly as a corruption of "Onitariio" meaning "a fine and beautiful lake" or "Kanadario" meaning "sparkling water". Later settlers called the land along the lake shore and then farther inland, Ontario. According to The MacMillan Book of Canadian Place Names, "Old Ontario" pertained to the southern section of the province. A confederation became the province of Ontario in 1867.

When Cartier first referred to "Canada" in 1535, it was just a little area around Quebec. English, French, Scottish, and native names were all among the names of the earliest settlements. But the French names played a much larger role in Canada then in the United States.

Actually the first European to visit Ontario may have been Etienne Brule, who arrived via the Ottawa River in the early 1600's. Then, in 1615, while accompanying Champlain, Brule first realized the extent of the Great Lakes.

After Canada was conquered by the English, it was ruled by a series of British Governors and was treated like a conquered nation. But then the Quebec Act was enacted in 1775 as a means of placating Canadians while colonists to the south were uniting against the British. The act extended Quebec's boundaries to the banks of the Ohio and the Mississippi Rivers and gave Roman Catholics the freedom to practice their religion.

After Amherst's victories, he obtained a promise from King George III that he would be given the estates of Canadian Jesuits following the Revolutionary War. Circa 1786, Amherst petitioned to have the pledge complied with. A commission to study it failed to reach a decision. In 1799, Amherst received a grant from the King which was good only upon the approval of the crown lawyers and governor. The governor opposed it. When the last Jesuit died, the Canadian government took possession of the land instead of Amherst.

At the end of the American Revolution, the treaty called for return of or compensation for the property lost by Loyalists during the war. Unfortunately the new government failed to keep that agreement. So the British began to subsidize resettlement of Loyalists in Canada. The British granted those who chose to move to Canada after the revolution were granted two hundred acres of land by the British, but these grants were not all given for perpetuity. Even then, much of what became Western Ontario, except for early settlements along southern boundary waters, remained closed Indian territory. W. Stewart Wallace claimed the Loyalists "changed the course of the current of Canadian history" ensuring British, rather then French control.

For instance, one of the first things Loyalists did was change the early French names to English ones. Fort Rouelle on the Hudson Bay became Fort York: Fort Frontenac became Kingston: La Grande Riviere de Canada became the St. Lawrence.

In addition, the first Loyalists to seek asylum in Canada were five women and thirty-six children who arrived at Fort George, Niagara, Ontario, in 1776. There were 1282 whites residing on the right bank in 1773. Between 1788 and 1812, Upper Canada's population increased by 75,000 people. Fred Landon claimed that one-fifth of them were Loyalists.

Actually, the American Revolution brought about the creation of two new English-majority provinces - Upper Canada and New Brunswick. These provinces not only had an English speaking population, they also had people passionately loyal to the British King. By 1784, most Loyalists who had fled to Quebec were repatriated to Upper Canada. It encompassed the peninsula between Lake Huron and the Ottawa River, north from the St. Lawrence River and Lakes Erie and Ontario. Kenneth McNaught described it as "thrusting" into what would become the industrial heart of America.

Although Upper Canada was supposedly created as a province as a home for Loyalists, actually it was formed because of Loyalists demands for a representative assembly like they had had in America. On July 8, 1792, Lt. Governor John Graves Simcoe declared that the Upper Canada constitution was the "most excellent that was ever bestowed upon a colony." The government was based on English common law, while the government of Lower Canada (Quebec) was more similar to the ancient feudal system.

The first attempted Loyalist settlement in Upper Canada was at Niagara, where Butler's Rangers, a Loyalist corps, wintered between 1778 and 1783. The assurance of the Ranger's protection encouraged Loyalist refugees to settle in the Niagara area. And after the division of the province, it became the capital of Upper Canada.

In the summer, 1780 settlers were given their lands rent free; and were given provisions, seeds, and farm tools for a year. McNaught related that each Loyalist received 200 acres, former officers received 3000, Legislative Counsellors received 6000.

In addition to the Niagara district, Loyalists were settled on the Detroit River and along the St. Lawrence, at Long Point on the north shore of Lake Erie. However, plans to establish a major loyalist settlement in the Border Region fizzled. In fact, according to Wallace, in 1791 there was only one Loyalist living at the post of Detroit. The Thames River (River La Tranche), thirty miles inland from Erie, took on a military and trade importance. The branches led off into remote areas of the province and the main river flowed into Lake St. Clair. Eventually London, Ontario would become the booming industrial and commercial center of the river valley.

Wallace reported about 200 acres being sold for a gallon of rum. Many Americans, posing as Loyalists, took advantage of the offer. In reality, many of the Loyalists were from humble origins and the Canadian government began to attempt to attract more well-to-do Americans with offers of free or inexpensive land.

Amherstburg

In order to continue to protect their lands, the British constructed new forts near the ones seized by the Americans during the Revolutionary War. When the fort at Detroit fell to the Americans, the British constructed a fort they named Fort Malden / Maldon, sixteen miles south of Detroit on the eastern side of the straits.

Captain Mayne of the Queen's Rangers, commandant "of the Post of Detroit River," called for sealed bids for equipment for construction of Ft. Malden on January 10, 1797. In June, 1798, William Backwell arrived to take command of the engineering department and to oversee erection of the fort. The British fort was established near the site of the Bois Blanc Mission at the mouth of the Detroit River. The mouth of the river was four miles wide there, but the only navigatable channel was between Bois Blanc Island and Canada proper. Bois Blanc was 1 1/2 mile long island in the Detroit River opposite Amherstburg and just east of Grosse Isle. The British built a block-house on Bois Blanc and were able to command from both sides of the only navigatable channel.

After the American Revolution, Henry Bird, William Caldwell, and other British army officers received a land grant of seven square miles at the mouth of the Detroit River near the site of Ft. Malden. Bird paid William Lee for clearing sixteen acres by giving him a "wench" named Esther. That land became the site of Amherstburg, named to commemorate Sir Jeffrey Amherst (1717-1797); the field marshall of the British Army, North American commander-in-chief, and the first English governor. He served from September 7, 1760 through November 16, 1763. The name Amherstburg first appeared on official records on February 9, 1797.

Caldwell received an additional four miles east of the mouth of the Detroit River and along fifteen miles of the north shore of Lake Erie. That area was settled by American Loyalists and was named New Settlement.

Although they were required to declare allegiance to one country or the other, British subjects were allowed to move back and forth across the border.

During the War of 1812, the British garrison at Fort Malden became a center of activity. The soldiers at Ft. Malden learned about the outbreak of hostilities between the Americans and the British on June 30, 1812. The first shots were fired in Detroit on July 5th of that year. And just as the British established forts on the Canadian side after the American Revolution, the Americans erected a temporary post they named Fort Covington outside Amherstburg.

Later, hundreds of runaway slaves fleeing the American South, moved to the Amherstburg area and formed a Black volunteer militia. Capt. Josiah Henson headed the Essex County Company of Blacks who assisted in defending Fort Malden from December, 1837 through Spring, 1838.

Amherstburg was incorporated as a village in 1851 and became a town in 1878.

17

Bois Blanc Island

One of two Bois Blanc Islands in the area, this was a 1 1/2 mile long island in the Detroit River opposite Amherstburg, Ontario, just east of Grosse Isle, Michigan.

A Jesuit mission conducted by Fathers de la Richardie and Potier for the Huron Indians remained at Bois Blanc until the missions removal to Sandwich. Actually, de la Richardie was the driving force of first establishing the mission. He was described by Burton as
"tall and gaunt, giving the impression of being hungary and ill fed. In his later days he wore glasses but let them slide so far down on his nose that he seemed to be looking over them rather than through them."
Then Potier replaced de la Richardie when he retired.

The mission included a farm and a trading post which sold flour, wheat, wine, brandy, tobacco, gunpowder, blankets, beads, and kettles; among other things. Actually, the trading post was established to attract area Indians to the mission and to protect Indians from unscrupulous traders. In 1749, Indian problems in the area caused the Fathers to close the farm at Bois Blanc. But fortifications remained.

With a block house constructed on Bois Blanc and Ft. Malden on the Canadian shore, the British commanded the channels of the Detroit River. However, in January, 1838, patriot forces occupied Bois Blanc Island opposite Amherstburg and began a miniature naval war.

Clear Creek / Clearville / Orford

A fortified neutral Indian village three miles up Clear Creek from Lake Erie was probably the first village situated near what would become Clearville, Ontario. According to Edward Bury's 1881 paper "The Early Settlement of Orford Township", before Bury's father settled in the Clear Creek area, he had visited settler's at Kettle Creek (Port Stanley), and with Col. Talbot at Port Talbot. Having looked at Point of Pines (Point aux Pins), having been stranded at Port Pelee, and having checked out Port Sarnia, Bury Sr. had decided that the mouth of the Clear Creek was where he wanted to settle. So in Spring, 1816, the elder Bury began to build a shanty for his family. When Edward Bury was born on August 31, 1816, he became the first white child born in what would become the township of Orford. Then in 1817, other families arrived in the Clear Creek area. William Bury had built a mill on Clear Creek by 1820.

By the late 1820's a number of other mills had been started but never finished. Others frequently ran low in water. So in 1834, Orford had only one sawmill and no gristmills. But by 1850 the township had two sawmills, two gristmill, and five taverns.

Orford was probably named for the oyster-fishing village on the Ore River in Suffolk, England, or for the town in Lancashire, England. As described by Hamil in The Valley of the Lower Thames 1640 to 1850, Clearville was developed along Clear Creek, between Talbot Road and the lake. It became a milling center and shipping port in the southeastern portion of Orford Township. David Baldwin established a tavern on Talbot Road as early as 1825. And Orford held its first township meeting in that tavern in 1828.

The first school in Orford Township met in David Smith's shanty on lot 57 south of Talbot Road. The rough benches were made of hewn logs and everyone had a different book. Bury remembered that "Some would have the Bible, another the New Testament, some had the alphabet and some spelling and so on." They always needed paper, but a few had slates on which to write. The school was open only in the winter and because of bad weather, the children couldn't get to school much of the time.

The area was still wilderness. According to Hamil, the Honorable David Mills wrote a letter in the mid-1800's which described the area as a place where
"wild cats, the lynres and the wolves were numerous and when the sheep had to be driven home from the fields before night and shut up in their folds till daylight to protect them. Cattle under two years were not allowed to run in the woods for if they were, they were not likely to be seen
again; they were pretty sure to be devoured by wolves ..."

Although Pioneers of the Eastern Townships presented the area as being full of wild animals and having "none of the resources for religious or intellectual improvement"; most of the settlers in the area had come from highly developed and civilized countries; and education was valued above everything except religious conviction.

Because Indians continued to be a problem, on January 7, 1828, laws were passed at a township meeting which decreed "flogging for anyone selling or giving whiskey to an Indian or squaw." Other laws provided for "the ejectment of Negroes, limitation of bits on horse-racing to twenty shillings and detention in the tavern-yard for sabbath-breakers."

Unfortunately, Clearville lost much of its importance as a shipping port when Canadian Southern built a railway several miles north of it in 1872.

Essex

The Essex area was named after the English shire by Lt. Governor John Graves Simcoe. The 18th Canadian county directly across from Detroit was described by David W. Smith on July 26, 1792 the area was bounded on the
"East by the Carrying place from point au pins, to the River la tranche (Thames) - bounded on the South by Lake Erie, & on the west by the River Detroit to Maisonvilles Mill; from thence by a line running parallel to the River Detroit & Lake St. Clair, at the distance of 4 miles, until it meets the River la tranche - thence up to said River to where the Carrying place from point au pins strikes the River."

The county's Lake Erie shoreline consisted of a hundred foot steep clay bank bordered at the lake by a narrow sand and gravel beach. Windsor was made the county seat.

Kingston

Originally, Kingston was an Indian village which grew because of its strategic location at the juncture of Lake Ontario and the St. Lawrence. It went on to become a French fur trading post and, finally, a British stronghold. The city even became capital of Canada for the short time between 1841-1844.

Ottawa Waterway

Actually the Ottawa Waterway was made up of a number of connecting waterways. Near Montreal, the Ottawa River met the St. Lawrence. The route continued from the Ottawa to the Mattawa River; to Lake Nipissing; to the French River, which emptied into the Georgian Bay section of northeastern Lake Huron.

Indians used the waterway for centuries before the appearance of the Europeans. Between 1611 and 1615, Indians guided Champlain's men on explorations along the Ottawa. Missionaries followed, fur traders arrived, military forces surfaced.

The area took on a great importance. Via Detroit and the St. Lawrence, the trip from Thunder Bay, Ontario on Lake Superior to Montreal, Quebec was 1,216 miles long. But via the Ottawa Waterway, the distance was only 934 miles long. In addition, the Ottawa Waterway route bypassed the Lachine Rapids south of Montreal. And during the American Revolution, the route went through strictly pro-British territory.

But on the other hand, the Ottawa Waterway also was the scene of a great deal of Indian unrest. Larger ships could not navigate the Ottawa: it had 36 portages. And the winter ice melted later in the Spring there.

But the importance could not be overlooked. And eventually, the Ottawa River became the dividing line between Upper and Lower Canada and the capital city of Ottawa sprung up on it.

Pain Court

In 1829 Charles Rankin surveyed the Pain Court block in Dover East for a group of French settlers. And about that time, roads were opened between the different townships. According to The Valley of the Lower Thames, until 1830, settlement was limited to
"the first three concessions on each side of the River Thames, to Talbot and Middle Roads, and to the Big Bear Creek region."
The town was just outside Chatham, Ontario.

Violent deaths were a matter of routine in the Border Region. One of the strangest was discussed in The Valley of the Lower Thames. Scotsman R. Scott lived alone in a shanty on

Pain Court Creek in Chatham Township. In 1834, a neighbor found Scott dead beside a fence having been accidentally hanged by a cord attached to a bag of wheat. The bag had slipped from the top of the fence while Scott was throwing down the rails.

Petite Cote

The word "cote" in French simply meant "coastline." In early Canada, the word took on a slightly different meaning. According to The Windsor Border Region,
"Strung bead-like along the river and linked together by a narrow road running along the edge of the water, ... farmhouses formed what was called in Canadian language a 'Cote'."
For instance, the area above the Huron Church was known as La Cote des Hurons. Even though the cotes were isolated, farmhouses were close, fostering interdependence within the community.

Petite Cote was an early settlement below le Ruisseau de la Vieille Reine - a settlement which later extended southward along the Detroit River to between the present North and South Essex. The Petite Cote area was described in the 1792 census as on the
"South Shore (of the Detroit River) below the Riviere a Gervais and bisected by the Riviere aux Dindes (Turkey Creek), opposite the northern 1/2 of Ile aux dindes (Grosse Ile) and North to the southwestern limits of the present city of Windsor, Ontario."

The French colony, the oldest white settlement in Ontario, was started there in 1749. And in 1789, six southern farm lots were granted to Indians. John Askin, Sr. was an early land owner there. A skirmish was fought there during the War of 1812.

Point Pellee

As early as the 1670's, La Salle, on board the "Griffin", passed Pointe Pelee while on a voyage from Niagara to St. Ignace. It was a ten mile long peninsula projecting into what would become southeastern Lake Erie. No township could be laid out along Lake Erie because of high banks between Long Point and Point Pelee and the land was inaccessible from the lake. In 1918, a national park was established on the headland.

Not to be confused with Point Pellee, Pelee Island, 8 miles to the southwest, was a nine mile long by four mile wide island in Lake Erie.

St. Joseph Island

After the 1649 destruction of the mission by the Iroquois and murders of fellow missionaries at Sault St. Marie, Father Paul Ragueneau wrote
"These poor distressed people forsook their lands, houses, and villages, in order to escape the cruelty of an enemy whom they feared more than a thousand deaths."

21

The surviving Jesuits fled to Saint Joseph Island between Lakes Huron and Superior where they were greeted by the friendly Hurons. Ragueneau went on to write

"Thank God, we found ourselves very well protected, having built a small fort according to military rules, which therefore could be easily defended ... Moreover, we set to work to fortify the village of the Hurons, which was adjacent to our abode."

However, despite the seeming security of their new surroundings, those living at St. Joseph Island were still in constant fear of an attack by the Iroquois. And the fear was well-founded, because on the afternoon of December 7, 1649, a band of Iroquois appeared at the gates of the mission. What followed was a massacre. Ragueneau reported infants being thrown into fires and mothers being beaten to death in front of their children. Many were taken prisoner. In order to make a rapid escape, the Iroquois killed all the elderly and the very young captives. Father Charles Garnier, the only Jesuit at the mission at the time of the massacre was also murdered.

In 1686, a white settlement was begun there when Daniel Deluth built a fort and trading post on St. Joseph Island.

In January, 1808, John Askin, Jr. wrote a negative description of the island to his brother Charles.

"Its an Island Abounding Wh Rocks & not a Deer Bear, wolf, & Racoon, Moose Cariboux or Muskrat about it. a few Hares is caught & pheasants. the Indians live entirely on fish. They even make their Mokasins with the skins of the sturgeon ... We have from 5 to 6 feet of snow in some places, but generally 4 feet in the woods, which has prevented the hawling of fuel ..."

But he had changed his view when, in 1810, Askin wrote to his father that if Capt. McKee applied for a position at St. Joseph

"he would live much better & have every article Necessary for his family as cheap as at Sandwich by importing them from Lower Canada. The country abounds in fish of a Superior quality Hares, Patridges & Ducks some Rein Deer & Bear. The Soil exceeding good for Raising Vegetables ..."

Years later, when the British were forced from Michilimackinac after the American Revolutionary War, they moved their fort to nineteen mile long St. Joseph Island.

Thamesville

Originally, Thamesville was named Tecumseh and, in 1818, it had a tavern and a store. Its name was changed to Thamesville in 1832, when it received a post office.

After 1834, William Grainger ran a tavern which was eventually taken over by Jacob Auberry. Norman L. Freeman of Thamesville was described in The Valley of the Lower Thames as a "Yankee tavernkeeper, schoolmaster, peddlar, and preacher." In 1846, when Freeman moved to Chatham, James Taylor took over the hotel. At about the same time, a two-horse covered coach ran from London to Thamesville travelled under six miles per hour.

Windsor (Ferry) / Sandwich

Missionaries arrived in the Border Region long before 1735, when Father de la Richardie claimed he converted six hundred Hurons in the area around Detroit. Using funds from the French government, he built a mission house, church, store, and warehouse on the site of Point de Montreal, later named Sandwich, on the east side of the Detroit River. The area was chosen to avoid problems of ecclesiastical jurisdiction with the Recollects across the river in Detroit.

A mission house and church were built. And eventually, the mission went on to own a blacksmith shop, farm, and sawmill.

It might have been the same settlement Capt. Jonathan Carver's journal referred to as an ancient Huron village that lay almost opposite Detroit on the eastern shore of the Detroit River. In the 1760's according to Carver, a missionary from the "Cartdusian" Friars was living among them.

In 1791, a surveyor named McNiff portrayed the land as "of no consequence being only a barren sandy plain." But in the summer, 1797, Peter Russell, executive council president, purchased the 1078 acre reserve at the Huron Church. Sixty-one acres on the river were set aside for the Hurons. More of this land "of no consequence" near the river was divided into one-acre lots. And the area was known as Assumption Parish.

Actual purchase of the townsite from the Hurons dragged on for a number of reasons, including the 1799 death of negotiator Alexander McKee. His son Capt. Thomas McKee finally executed the deed in September, 1800 for the cost of 300 pounds Quebec currency. And an 1800 report from the grand jury asserted that a number of Sandwich lots granted in 1797 were still unimproved, and only seven or eight houses had been built, impeding settlement of the town.

Sandwich was probably named for a city near the English Channel in eastern Kent. Originally the name of that English city meant "village in the sand;" according to Place Names of the English-Speaking World.

After the Americans took control of Detroit, the English at Sandwich decided they needed a clergyman of their own. They determined one of their own should take the position. So Richard Pollard was ordained in Montreal and returned to become the first pastor of St. John's Protestant Episcopal Church. However, that first church, a log building, was burned to the ground during the War of 1812. The second structure was erected circa 1816.

A number of influential men eventually lived and did business in the area. For example, John Askins lived in Sandwich for a while. George Jacobs was a merchant in Sandwich before removing to a farm on the Thames River.

23

In 1798, John Askin, Sr. was granted a liscense to operate a ferry from "the Landing to the Shore of the River Detroit." Illegal smuggling of American goods into Canada was widespread in these early years and that ferry area was a center of the illegal trade. So much so that in the early 1800's, when John Askin, Jr. held the position of customs collector; his father complained that John, Jr. spent most of his time watching for smuulers.

The Sandwich / Ferry area was renamed in 1834 for the city of Windsor, England. But actually the original English town was "Windlesore."

According to <u>Western Ontario and the American Frontier</u>, in December, 1838, a small steamboat loaded with Commander L.V. Bierce and more than one hundred men crossed the Detroit River to the village of Windsor. The small Canadian militia along with local blacks called in to help managed to defend Windsor. Forty-four of the invaders were captured and sent to London for court-martial where forty-three were sentenced to death. However, only six were actually hanged.

Transportation was an important factor in the development of Windsor. The city's shippers operated a number of schooners, steamers, and brigantines in the late 1830's. In January, 1842, there was a concerted effort to improve the road situation in the Windsor area. Because of its location on the Detroit River, it was considered of extreme commercial and military importance. And finally in 1846, a road from Windsor to Niagara was begun.

In fact, Windsor would eventually become Canada's busiest point of entry. Situated in Essex County in southern Ontario, Windsor also became Canada's most southerly city and the seat of Assumption College. It was incorporated as a village in 1854, a town in 1858, and a city in 1934; and was nicknamed the "City of Roses."

Askin / Askins Family

James Askin / Erskine Family

James Erskine / Askin
    m. Alice Rea / Rae, dau of Rev. John Rea of Dungannon,
    Ireland
    r. 1741; Loch Foyle, Ireland
    d. 1740's
    Children
        John (see below)
        Sarah - m. pos Campbell (d. by August 18, 1792) of
            Liverpool, England
        Mary
        Robert
        William

John Askin, Sr.
    b. 1739; Aughnacloy, County Tyrone, Ireland
    m1 Indian woman
    m2 Marie Archange Barthe, dau of Charles Andrew Barthe
    and Therese Campau; June 21, 1773; Detroit, Michigan
    d. 1818; Strabane, Windsor, Ontario
    bur. 1818; Assumption Church; Sandwich, Ontario
    Children by Indian wife
        John Askin, Jr. - b.c. 1762; L'Arbe Croche/Ottawa
            Town/ Cross City; Michigan
            m. Mary Peltier (d. Amherstburg, Ontario), dau
            of Jacques Peltier; October 21, 1791; Detroit,
            Michigan
            d.c. January 1, 1820; Amherstburg, Ontario
            Children by Indian consort
                Jean Baptiste/"Johnny" - b. April 10,
                1788
                    bpt. November 13, 1791; Detroit,
                    Michigan
                    m. Elisa Van Allen of Haldemand,
                    Upper Canada
                    d. November 15, 1869; London,
                    Ontario
                    Children (8)
                ?Julia - d. pos by 1820
                Therese (adopted) - m. Ensign O'Brien
                    d. pos by 1820
        Catherine - b.c. 1763
            m1 Capt. Samuel Robertson (d. 1782); 1779
            m2 Robert Hamilton
            d.c. 1796
            Children by Robertson
                William - b. by 1782
                John - b. by 1780
            Children by Hamilton
                Robert - b. 1786
                    m. Mary Biggar
                    d. 1856; Queenston, Ontario
                George - b. 1788
                    m. Maria Jarvis
                Alexander - b. 1792
                    m. Hannah Jarvis

25

Mary Madelaine - m. Dr. Robert Richardson (d.
1832); January 24, 1793
d. January 10, 1811; Amherstburg, Ontario
Children (see Richardson)
Children by Archange Barthe
James (see below)
Therese - b. February 10, 1774; Michilimackinac,
Michigan
bpt. September 20, 1774; Detroit, Michigan
m. Capt. Thomas McKee (d. Spring, 1815), son
of Col. Alexander McKee; April 17, 1797
bur. June 23, 1832; Assumption Church,
Sandwich, Ontario
Children (see McKee)
Archange - b. October 3, 1775; Michilimackinac,
Michigan
m. Capt. / Lt. Col. David Meredith (d. March,
1809; Halifax)
d. September, 1866; Bruges, Belgium
Children
Anne - b.c. 1792
David - b.c. May, 1793
Elizabeth - b. by 1800
John (tw?) -b. 1779 or 1783; Michilimackinac,
Michigan
bpt. September, 1780; Detroit, Michigan
d. September, 1780
Adelaide (tw?) - b. 1779 or 1783
m. Elijah Brush (b. 1772; Bennington, Vermont;
d. December 14, 1814), son of Nathaniel Brush
and Samantha Parker; February 17, 1802;
Detroit, Michigan
bur. July 20, 1859; Detroit, Michigan
Children (see Brush)
Charles - b. January 18, 1785; Detroit, Michigan
m. Monique Jacob, dau of George Jacob
d. 1862; Windsor, Ontario
Children
Mary Archange - b and/or bpt. February
25, 1823; Assumption Church,
Sandwich, Ontario
Elizabeth - b. and/or bpt. August 1,
1833; Assumption Church, Sandwich,
Ontario
Ellen Phyllis (Felicity Eleneora / Nelly) - b.
April 17, 1788; Detroit, Michigan
m. Richard Pattinson (d. by February 28, 1818;
Montreal, Quebec) of Sandwich; wid of Judith
de Joncaire dit Chabert; aft May, 1804
d. 1813; At Riviere a la Tranche (Thames
River), near Moraviatown, Ontario
bur. October 15, 1813; Assumption Church,
Sandwich, Ontario
Lt. Alexander David (Alick) - b. 1791; Detroit,
Michigan
d. shortly aft October 10, 1812

James Askin
b. November, 1786; Detroit, Michigan

m. Francis Godet dit Marentette (b. November 19, 1796),
dau of Dominic Godet and Mary Louisa Navarre; October 10,
1815
bur. December 7, 1862; Assumption Church, Sandwich,
Ontario
Children
    John Alexander - b. and/or bpt. March 7, 1817;
        Assumption Church, Sandwich, Ontario
        m1 Monique or Marie Navarre (b. October 13,
        1807, St. Antoine; bur. May 29, 1840; St.
        Antoine), dau of Isidore Navarre and Frances
        Labadie
        m2 Ann Mellany (Melinda) McCloskey (b.
        February 12, 1825; Detroit, Michigan; d. May
        20, 1908; Windsor, Ontario; bur. May 22, 1908;
        St. Alphosus Church), dau of James McCloskey
        and Susanne Godfroy; June 13, 1847; St.
        Antoine; River Raisin, Michigan
        Children
            Adelaide - b. May 3, 1838; St. Antoine,
                River Raisin, Michigan
            James Wallace - b. May 25, 1848;Sandwich,
                Ontario
            Ann Caroline - b. 1849; Sandwich, Ontario
                d. 1851; Sandwich, Ontario
            Henry - b. 1852; Sandwich, Ontario
            Alexander William - b. 1855; Sandwich,
                Ontario
            Mary Teresa - b. 1857; Sandwich, Ontario
    Mary Archange - b. November 24, 1818
        m. Henry Ronalds of England (d. by 1872)
        d. August 16, 1872; London, Ontario
        bur. Assumption Church, Sandwich, Ontario
        Children
            Lucy - m. George Beecher Harris of "Eldon
                House", London, Ontario, son of John
                Harris and Amelia Ryerse, grandson
                of Loyalist Col. Ryerse
                Children
                    Amelia Archange   H e n r y
                    Ronald
                    Edward Montgomery
    Charles David - b. July 3, 1820
        bur. February 15, 1838; Assumption Church,
        Sandwich, Ontario
    James - b. September 24, 1821
    Theresa - b. July 6, 1823
        d. unmarried
    Alexander - b. December 18, 1824
        bur. August 23, 1834; Assumption Church,
        Sandwich, Ontario
    Thomas Barthe - b. December 31, 1826
        bur. August 2, 1837; Assumption Church,
        Sandwich, Ontario
    Alice Rose - b. August 28, 1828
        d. unmarried; November 22, 1908; Sandwich,
        Ontario
        bur. November 24, 1908; Assumption Church,
        Sandwich, Ontario
    Helena Eleonora - b. September 30, 1830
        d. unmarried

27

Francis Ann - b. March 7, 1837
Margaret Jane - bpt. October 8, 1838; Assumption
          Church, Sandwich, Ontario
          m1 Daniel Murray of Toronto, Ontario
          m2 Edward Skal/Skae
          Children
               Edward

According to tradition, during Malcom II's reign a Danish
general named Enrique was killed at the Battle of Murthill.
The Scotsman who killed Enrique brandished the bloody head
stuck to the knife and declared "Eris skyne", which Sims, in
his book on the origins of Scottish surnames, related meant
"upon the knife." The Scotsman than added, "I intend to
perform greater actions then I have already done." At that,
King Malcom II gave the Scotsman the name Eriskyne. Erskine's
arms became a hand holding a dagger and the motto "Je pense
plues."

     According to Sir Robert Douglas, the family name more
likely came from the barony of Erskine on the Clyde, probably
in the family for many years (see Appendix). However, the
family crest was "a dexter hand, couped above the wrist
holding a dagar erect, proper, the pommel and hilt, or."

     John Erskine, the sixth Earl of Marr, was well-known for
his part in the 1715 Scottish uprising. Better known as
"Bobbing John", the Earl had been the Secretary of State for
Scotland and a staunch supporter of the Treaty of Union. Upon
Queen Anne's death, he wrote to the new King George to
ingratiate himself and appeal for re-appointment. When the
Hanoverian King refused to appoint him, Marr became a rebel
without a rebellion. He put out a call to arms to support
James III (the "Old Pretender"), then in exile. John led his
band of 14,000 Highlanders against a smaller group of King's
men led by the Duke of Argyll. They met at Sheriffmuir near
Dunblane and the troops of the inept Earl of Marr were
defeated.

     By the time the self-proclaimed James III arrived in
Scotland, it was too late to save the rebellion. Louis XIV of
France died and the rebels did not receive hoped-for French
support. James III and "Bobbing John" fled to France. Many of
their followers were taken prisoner, clans lost their estates,
and some were executed. Many sought refuge in Ireland.

     Many of the Earl's family also fled to Ireland and some
may have changed the name from Erskine to Askin at that time.
A number of Erskine families settled in America in the 1700's.
Most arrived from Ulster in Northern Ireland. Brothers
Christopher and Robert Erskine arrived in Massachusetts in
1719. Alexander Erskine, who arrived in Boston in 1746 from
Londonderry, Ireland, finally settled in Bristol, Maine.
Several Erskines resided in New York in the 1790 Census. A
John Erskine who became judge for the U.S. District Court in
Georgia between 1868 and 1883, was born in Tyrone County,
Ireland in 1813.

     Coincidentally, one of "Bobbing John's" sons or grandsons
was probably the James Erskine / Askin who settled near
Strabane in Tyrone County, Ireland. In a 1793 letter, John

Askin of this genealogy wrote that he and his father had both spelt their name Askin while his grandfather had spelt it Erskine. The Burton Historical Society claimed James Askin / Erskine resided in Loch Foyle, 60 miles west of Belfast, in 1741. According to the same 1793 letter, he was a shopkeeper. He married Alice Rea (see Appendix) and had what was considered a respectable Protestant family. They had three sons - John, William, and Robert - and two daughters - Mary and Sarah. James probably died shortly after the birth of his son John Askin / Erskine and John was raised by his maternal grandfather, John Rea.

John Askin (Erskine) of this genealogy was born in 1739 to James and Alice Rae / Rea Askin of Aughnacloy, Tyrone Co. In later years, he was described as having "a Hebernian cast, black curly hair, and an expression that denoted shrewdness, courage and determination."

Even though John was a native of northern Ireland; he was descended from Scots. In a May 26, 1801 letter, John Askin wrote to James Erskin of Drimcar near Dunleer Co., Leith, Ireland who was searching for his brother. John wrote
"I'm the son of James Askin of (Strabane, west of Belfast) in the north of Ireland neither him or any of his Family I ever heard of has come to this country & I'm sorry to say I fear they are all dead Except a Sister which I hear is in England I was brought up with my Grandfather John Rae within a mile & an half of Dungannon & on his Death came to this Country."

John Askin arrived in America in 1758 and enlisted in the British army to fight in the Seven Year's War. He may have been a volunteer in the first attempt to take Ft. Ticonderoga.

After that war, probably circa 1761 or 1762, Askin began to establish himself in the mercantile business in Albany, a major launching area for traders moving west. He had partners such as Maj. Robert Rogers, James Gordon, and Abraham Steele. His partnership with Rogers was a dismal failure which left him deep in debt. In fact Askin and Rogers had to file bankruptcy and their creditors weren't discharged until 1771.

During the siege of 1763, John Askin visited Detroit. Having heard of the city's need for provisions, Askin was able to deliver a fleet of boats through Indian lines. He had also become interested in the fur trade and became one of the earliest British traders.

It was during these year that Askin became the father of John, Jr., Catherine, and Mary Madelene by his Indian consort. John, Jr. was born in L'Arbe Croche, an Ottawa town twenty miles southwest of Michilimackinac. It later became Cross City, Michigan. Askin probably had a farm in the area as early as 1762. He had obtained title to the land by 1766.

John, Jr.'s mother may have been from the Ottawa tribe. But on September 9, 1766, after the children's birth; Askin manumitted (freed) a Pawnee slave named Manette / Monette who also may have been their mother. John Sr. wrote "I set at liberty and give full freedom unto my Pawnee slave Monette, which I had from Mons. Borussa." But on June 25, 1793 Askin was told that under a proposed law, when a free man who was married to a slave, his heirs would be "declared by this act to be a slave." Had Monette been the mother of John's children, they would have been slaves under that law. Whoever the mother of John Jr., Catherine, and Madelene was, she was out of the picture by 1773.

According to Heldman's Archaeological Investigations at French Farm Lake, in 1764, when the British returned to re-garrison the post, Askin became assistant commissary for the military garrison in Michilimackinac. In that position, John became both a private and government supplier of goods. His years in Mackinac brought him tremendous success and his business dealings with the Indians prospered so much, he opened a branch of his business at Sault Ste. Marie. He used his farm to experiment with plant cultivation and it flourished. He owned several vessels which he kept busy in Great Lakes trade and somehow managed to get around the rapids at the Sault into Lake Superior. Heldman called it a "flotilla of merchant sloops" which served settlements from Detroit to Grand Portage which was at the western end of Lake Superior.

At Grand Portage was a nine mile portage connecting Lake Superior with the Pigeon River above its falls. From the earliest days of the fur trade until 1801 when the American acquired control of the area, Grand Portage was an important stop in the British fur trade.

Askin imported goods from Europe and as far away as China. But most of the agricultural products he sold, Askin raised on one of his two farms in the L'Arbre Croche area.

While at Michilimackinac, Askin became the owner of two black slaves. He had already owned partial interest Jupiter and Pompey when he obtained full ownership from Abram Dow in 1775. Russell's The British Regime in Michigan and the Old Northwest related that Pompey was valued at 100 pounds in 1776, 116 pounds in 1779, and 150 pounds in 1789. Through the years, John Askin owned as many as six slaves who were valued at 390 pounds in 1779 and 680 pounds in 1781. At one point he sold a twenty-five year old panis named Susannah and her one year old daughter to George Jacob for 100 pounds. But that was after January, 1781 when Askin was listed as owning Jupiter and "Pomp", black men; Sam, a "Pani blacksmith;" and Susannah, a wench and two children."

It was probably the French who introduced enslaving Indians to benefit the white man. Under French law, "panis" were legal. Another term which appeared in a number of records was "esclave" which referred to both Indian and Black slaves.

In 1774 a French canoe handler indentured himself to Askin for 200 pounds and some clothing, as did Robert Nichol for 50 pounds in 1795. Nichol was to keep Askin's books and accounts. But while an indentured servant could earn his freedom, a slave could not.

According to Burton's history, while at Mackinac, John made a number of friends he would keep throughout his life. Primarily through the fur trade, he met James McGill, Isaac

Todd, and Alexander Henry. In 1806, Askin wrote to James McGill

> "was it not for your, & our most worthy Frind Mr. Todds ... generosity formerly and yours lately I must long since have seen myself & Family in real want ... I (never) receive a harsh nor unfriendly line from you, even when I owed you such large sums ... "

Col. Arent Schuyler De Peyster, commandant at the fort beginning in 1774, and other government agents also became his close friends.

In 1773, Askin married Marie Archange Barthe, daughter of Charles Andrew Barthe. The marriage was performed in Detroit, possibly by Maj. Henry Bassett. Several more children were born there. In his diary, Askin noted for April, 1774, that he "sowed some pease at the farm (and) the first Geese killed by (his) Brother." The brother in this case probably was really a brother-in-law since John had married Archange Barthe by that time. He wrote in 1801 that

> "I never have met with any Relati[ve] of mine in this country, Mr. Richard Rea an uncle of mine Excepted who died at New Yk several years ago."

When supplies dwindled in 1773, Capt. Vattas, commandant at Ft. Michilimackinac, wrote to General Thomas Gage

> "Mr. Askin Comisary & Mr. Ainse Indian Interpreter, have applyed to me for leave to enclose some few acres of land & build each a house within about three miles of the Fort, which I have OK'ed."

But it wasn't until July 7, 1774, that Capt. Vattas finally gave official permission to John Askin, the

> "Depy Commissary & Barrack Master of the fort of Missilimackinac to enclose from three to five Acres of Ground near a Spot called the three Miles pond from its said suppos'd Distance from the Fort & to build thereon a House with such other conveniences as He from Time to Time may judge ..."

However, John had not waited for permission before beginning to plant. According to Askin's diary, he had begun planting at the farm a full month and a half before receiving title from Capt. Vattas.

Heldman believed Askin established a second farm at Three Mile Pond (French Farm Lake) to make up for shortages in goods. The French Farm Lake name was derived from nineteenth century settlers. But in Askin's day the Three Mile Pond name was used. Its actual location was at T39N, R4W, Sec23, S 1/2 of the NE 1/4 in Emmet County.

Even though there was a house valued at 80 pounds in New York currency at the farm, Askin probably lived at the fort and merely worked the farm. He raised onions, beans, pumpkins, cucumbers, spinach, potatoes, clover, pigs, oats, rye grass, turnips, beets, lettuce, and barley on the farm. At the same time, according to his diary, John maintained a garden at the fort.

Things were going well for Askin. In May, 1778, he ordered 12 pairs of shoes for his wife and a "french fashion" wedding gown for his daughter "Kitty", his pet name for his daughter Catherine who was marrying Capt. Samuel Robertson.

But while things were good financially for Askin, those around him did not always profit. Circa 1778, Askin's clerk John Askwith (see Appendix) was in such financial trouble he had to auction off his wardrobe. In _History of Wayne County and the City of Detroit, Michigan_, Burton related that his wardrobe consisted of over thirty-five pairs of "breeches and trousers ... a dozen shirts, ten cravats, and fifteen coats.

Patrick Sinclair, who replaced De Peyster at Mackinac in 1779, did not get along with Askin. Perhaps he was jealous of Askin's close friendship with De Peyster. Or perhaps Askin's dislike of Sinclair stemmed from Sinclair's arrest of Samuel Robertson, Askin's son-in-law. Robertson died in Montreal in 1782, still awaiting trial. During the summer of 1780, Daniel Mercer, Askin's brother-in-law, was also arrested by Sinclair. Askin, Robertson, and Mercer were only three of the men Sinclair had serious problems with during his tenure at Mackinac.

Because of the new political environment at Mackinac, Askin moved his family to Detroit during the summer of 1780. However, on April 27, 1778 letter indicated he had considered the move as early as that, but had decided to wait until after the American Revolution was over.

It was not a wise move. In 1781, Fort Michilimackinac was purposely abandoned by the British and burned. Heldman related that Sinclair, the garrison, and any building that could be taken apart were moved to nearby islands. And most of the merchants and traders moved with them.

After setting up his fur business in Detroit, John was plagued by a number of set backs at first. His business was a gamble and it took McGill and Todd to save him from ruin. But eventually his financial situation stabilized and, according to Burton in his _History of Wayne County and the City of Detroit, Michigan_, Askin eventually became one of the most influential of the merchants of Detroit. In June 1796, Askin listed over 4675 pounds due him by September 30th of that year.

In addition to his other business dealings, Askin was granted a license in 1798 to operate a "Ferry From the Landing to the Shore of the River Detroit." That same year he sold the government 500 cords of wood. And in the early 1800's he ran a distillery (actually, a still).

The _Valley of the Lower Thames_ related that he sold goods to the Indians. In fact, missionary Gottfried Sabastian Oppelt complained the Indians had gotten themselves too deeply in debt to Askin and requested that Askin refuse them further credit. Askin agreed.

Askin also began to take part in land speculation and ended up claiming 5 million acres in northern Ohio. His son John, Jr., and other friends and in-laws, such as Richard Pattinson, Robert Innes, William and David Robertson, and Jonathan Schieffelin also took part. But Askin's land claims and Indian grants did nothing endear him to the American government. The Americans seemed to believe Askin was working for the British in an attempt to own land after they had lost sovereignty to it.

In one land deal, the Ottawa, Massassauga, and Chippewa nations deeded Askin and his associates land on Lake Erie between the mouth of the Cayuga River and the entrance of Sandusky Lake. But that grant was never confirmed by the U.S. government.

Burton's History of Wayne County and the City of Detroit, Michigan recounted that in 1795 John Sr. and Jr., and Alexander Henry received a land grant of a 720 square mile piece of land on the Huron River near the village of "Grosse Rock" from the Pottawatomi Indians. It was to be subdivided and sold to others. In another grant, Askin and his partners received nearly three million acres of land from the Ottawas and Chippewas. And John also offered to pay $5,000 for another twenty million acres in the area of southern Michigan, northwestern Ohio, northern Indiana, and northeastern Illinois.

In 1796 Askin purchased Presque Isle from fifteen Ottawa Indian chiefs. Presque Isle was the island on the north side of the Maumee River which in 1794 had been the site of the Battle of Fallen Timbers.

Also in 1796, because of financial difficulties, John needed to sell some of his land holdings. Sale he advertized to sell
- a "Large Dwelling House" in Detroit priced at 2000 pounds;
- one farm 2 acres wide by 80 foot deep with several rental houses and other outbuildings on it;
- a large vacant lot near his dwelling house;
- a house, shop, stable, and storehouse on a lot opposite his home;
- a 50 by 40 acre piece of land situated on either side of the Huron River, where the old Moravian Town originally was located;
- 33 by 120 acres of land with several houses, a windmill, a good road, and pasture land, 2 1/2 miles from Detroit;
- a large number of farms of various sizes on the Raisin River;
- 25 by 150 acres on either side of the Belle River;
- additional vacant tracts of land on both sides of the Detroit River.

But financial difficulties must have evaporated, because according to The Windsor Border Region, the next year William Smith sold John Askin, Sr. lots 8,9, and 10 on the west side of the Belle River. The lots were 200 acres each and cost Askin 60 pounds for all three.

In the 1792 Petite Cote census, John Askin was listed as a landowner, with no any family living on the land. He also owned lot number 128 of Assumption in 1793. And in 1797 he owned lot number 4 on the west side of Bedford Street in

Sandwich to others. So apparently he owned land in Ontario long before he moved there.

Although John Askin never renounced his allegiance to the British crown, he still served as a trustee of Detroit, a member of the land board, a local Justice of the Peace during the early 1790's, and an officer in Detroit's militia even after the American Revolution. In 1787 he was appointed captain of one of Detroit's two companies, with Jacques Baby and George Meldrum as his lieutenants. Then on October 23, 1795, he signed himself at Lieutenant Colonel of the north Essex Battalion of the Militia.

In the 1782 Detroit census John was recorded as having one married woman, four young or hired men, one boy, two girls, four male slaves, and two female slaves in his home. In September 1796 the Detroit census listed him as a man over 50 years of age with one white woman, six white children, three male slaves, and one female slave living with him.

Despite his marriage to a Catholic French Canadian, John Askin was a member of Detroit's Protestant Episcopal Church. According to Quaife. Rev. Philip Toosey was the first Protestant clergyman in the area. Then in 1787 John Askin gave 10 pounds to support Rev. George Mitchell and was appointed as a church vestryman along with James Abbot and George Meldrum. The next year William McComb replace Abbot.

On February 27, 1798, John Askin and Archange Barthe attested before Askin's friend William Harffy, that they married on June 21, 1773. But for some reason, the marriage was not registered until April 22, 1797.

In 1802 Askin moved to the Canadian (south) side of the Detroit River and settled there. The impetus for the move began with his receiving a commission as colonel of the Essex County, Ontario, northern regiment. Then in October, 1802, he was named a trustee for the newly organized town of Detroit. By taking the trustee position, Askin would have had to swear allegiance to the United States. Later he would write that he could "not comprehend how a man of honor & honesty can ever change his allegiance." So John refused the position and removed his family across the river to the Canadian side of the river. And after his arrival in Sandwich, John Askin was able to write he was "better in health and more contented in mind thank God than (he had) been for Thirty years past."

While living on the Canadian side of the river John's land speculations continued, frequently with his sons as partners. But while he appeared to be financially stable in 1805, he told his son-in-law Elijah Brush that he might have to sell the farm on which Brush and his family was living in order to repay James and Andrew McGill the two thousand pounds in Halifax currency that he owed them. Askin was unhappy he was in that financial predicament since the farm had originally been in his wife's family. Elijah agreed to purchase the farm from his father-in-law, thus keeping it in the family. And the farm became known as the Brush Farm.

Those financial problems of John's may have been related to a letter he wrote to Todd and McGill on July 22, 1805. In it he related that the U.S. government had declared only two English or French titles of land to be legal. Askin wrote he was trying to collect all the papers he could find in support of his grants to get a reversal. His only other hope was that the U.S. Congress would pass an act which might help and Askin told his friends he might have to take his case to the "Highest Court of the United States."

Although Askin had debts of his own, a number of people were indebted to him, He still worked in partnership with James McGill and Isaac Todd on a number of ventures. So he remained a influential man, able to arrange positions for his sons and sons-in-law, and powerful enough to back numerous political candidates.

Though John remained a Protestant in Canada, he did have some quarrels with the church. On June 1, 1807, he felt hounded for money by Rev. Richard Pollard when he wrote to Pollard that
> "I could not have thought that a Gentleman could have pressed an other as you have done me for 40 (pounds) which I did not contract ..."
Askin's bluntness continued even with the post script where he complained the clergyman owed money himself. However, in his June 1, 1807 reply, Pollard claimed he did not owe "one farthing."

Then later that year, Rev. Pollard rebuked Askin for calling a meeting of the militia at the same time as Sunday services. In his answer to Pollard, John Askin wrote sarcastically
> "All mankind by Your own Doctrine is Subject to error so is John Askin ... I respect all religion where the Serving of God is the intention and ... I have a Friendship for Mr. Pollard though he feels warmer in his Expressions than some others of the Gown on such an occasion."

The militia was important to Askin and he was pleased with their abilities. In 1807 he bragged that the militia "behaved remarkably well and fired like regular Troops." His full title was H.M.S. Col. Askin, Commandant of North and South Battalions of the Essex Militia. Even American slaves who had escaped to Canada were armed when tension between the U.S. and Canada worsened in 1807. However, on March 10, 1809, Major Hatton wrote to John that because of John's "infirm State of health" the Lieutenant Governor had judged it necessary "to place an Officer of more Personal activity at the head of the Corps (Askin had) lately commanded." With that, John Askin was relieved of duty as colonel of his beloved militia.

The War of 1812 was an trying time for the Askin family. The year before, Askin's wife Archange had been in a fire which had seriously burned her hands. In addition, because of his age and health, John Askin, Sr. was unable to participate in the war. And while all of his sons and a number of grandsons were in the British service; son-in-law Elijah Brush fought with the Americans and because of the war, a number of his children had to flee for their lives. Friends and family died.

On April 28, 1812, Askin wrote to his son Charles that there were preparations for war being made at Detroit and at Ft. Malden. Although Askin was doing a great deal of business with the military and was prospering, he still dreaded what was happening.

In July, the Americans took Sandwich, Ontario; but Askin related that General Hull treated them with respect and refused to allow his men to "take a Cherry, without the owners conser." In fact, Askin went so far as to write

"should it be our lot; to fall under any other Authority, I would not prefer anyman to the present General Hull; who I'm pretty sure will not only respect my property, but that of my Fri(e)nds, so far as he can consistan(t)ly do so, in which he will be Aided & Assisted, by the Talents & Interest of Mr. Brush, who now Commands at Detroit ..."

However, elsewhere he admitted that Hull did seize goods and building from Misters Baby, David, and McGregor.

John Askin, Sr. died at Strabane in 1818. Madelaine Askin wrote that her husband John, Jr. was "almost inconsolable." In his November 11, 1808 will, the elder Askin asked he be buried "avoiding all unnecessary expenses and vain pomp." He left all of his property to his wife Archange "during her widowhood and while she lives" to use as she saw best. Archange was also named executrix. At her death, the property was to be evenly divided among his children and, after them, his grandchildren.

John Askin, Jr., the eldest son of John, Sr. and an Indian woman, was educated in Montreal. After reaching adulthood, John, Jr. engaged in a variety of unsuccessful commercial gambles from which his father frequently saved him financially.

His land speculations proved somewhat more successful. On May 27, 1795, John Jr. joined in a partnership with his father and Alexander Henry of Montreal, Canada, to purchase Indian land on the Miami and Huron Rivers. He also joined his father and others in a variety of land purchases including the Cuyahoga Purchase.

As a member of Detroit's militia in 1790, he appeared as "John Askin junior Trader" on the June 7, 1791 roll of his father's militia.

Because of his Indian heritage and his friendship with the Chippewas and Ottawas, he was asked to interpret for the Indians at a meeting at Ft. Greenville in 1795. While there he attempted to dissuade the Indians from signing a treaty with General Wayne which gave land speculators too much of an advantage over the Indians. So General Wayne had him arrested as a spy and kept John, Jr. out of the way at Ft. Jefferson while negotiations continued.

Askin married Mary Madelaine from Detroit's Peltier family in 1791. But he already had a son, Jean Baptiste or Johnny, by a woman living in Indian country. Quaife related she might have been a white captive, but offered no proof.

On July 9, 1793, John Askin, Sr. wrote to Isaac Todd that he planned to take his "Son John into partnership ... for Ten Years, allowing him a third of ye Profits" in a business furnishing the post at Michilimackinac with provisions. He told his friend that John, Jr. was "perfectly Sober, honest, Industrious & Saving." Curiously the father added that his son's marriage had "cured (him of) the principal fault (he) Ever knew him to have." But he never said what that fault was.

Russell's book of Michigan showed "Jean Askin, Jr." as a man age 16-50 living at the time of the 1796 census in the Raisin River area with one white woman. Although Jean Baptiste would have been 8 years old, he was not listed. He might also have been with his grandparents.

In 1801, Gov. Hunter appointed John, Jr. as the Sandwich, Ontario customs collector. His father's friend Isaac Todd of Montreal helped him secure the position. But it was not much of a job and John Askin, Sr. wrote in 1802 that John, Jr. had "a great deal of trouble and very little profit as Collector, for his whole time almost (was) spent in watching the smuglers." He held the office until 1807 when he became an interpreter for the Indian Department on St. Joseph Island. Fort St. Joseph was the first white settlement in the area in 1686 when the fort and trading post was built by Daniel DeLuth.

It appeared that his father probably secured that position for him too. Isaac Todd revealed that John Sr. had first contacted him in an attempt to acquire the position, but that John Sr. had been erroneously informed that Charles Chaboillez had quit his situation as clerk and storekeeper at St. Joseph Island. But then in December, 1806, Todd wrote again that

"as St. Joseph (was) going to be the place of Depot & residence of the British Traders it (would) be more comfortable & better for Johnny if he gets the appointment of Mr. Chaboillez."

Todd wrote Askin that John Jr. should apply immediately to Governor Gore.

When John Askin, Jr. and family arrived at St. Joseph in June, 1807, he arrived he discovered that another interpreter had been hired so that his job was only a half-time one. He told his father that as soon as he had "accumulated sufficiency to Pay (his) debts & purchase a good situation" near his father, he intended to leave the job.

His financial situation must have improved because in 1809, John Jr. sent 25 pounds Halifax currency to help his sister Archange, when his father couldn't afford to help after her husband died leaving her penniless.

During the War of 1812, John's Indian parentage and influence made him useful for the British. In July, 1812, he led a combined Ottawa and Chippewa force to aid Capt. Roberts small garrison at St. Joseph to capture Mackinac. According to the History of Wayne County ..., John, Jr. managed to keep the Indians from committing any "depredations." Askin wrote he was

37

"happy ... for the Americans that they did not fire a shot, for had they fired and wounded any person, not a soul would have been saved from the hatchet."
Lt. Hanks and 58 of his American troops were freed and went to fight at Detroit. John, Jr. served at Mackinac until 1815 when the garrison removed to Drummond Island. He remained there until at least 1816. His wife wrote on August 4, 1815, that her husband had clothed 1500 Indians since they arrived "and still they come." She related that there were never fewer that four or five Indians at dinner each night.

John Askin, Jr. died at Amherstburg on January 1, 1820 and was buried in Sandwich two days later.

In several 1811 and 1812 letters from St. Joseph Island, John Jr. mentioned Madelaine, his wife; Therese; and Julia. Therese was an adopted daughter who was originally a member of the Roberts family. Julia was not identified. Neither Therese nor Julia appeared in John Jr.'s will leading Quaife to suggest that both had died by then. However, Therese did marry Ensign O'Brien of the Royal Newfoundland Regiment in 1815. So John might have no longer felt responsible for his adopted daughters.

Jean Baptiste Askin, the son of John Jr. and his Indian or white captive consort, was with his father on St. Joseph Island in 1810 when he accepted an offer to take part in the fur trade. Before that, John Jr. and Sr. were attempting to secure Johnny "the Situation of Asst. Comy & Bark Mast" (Assistant Commissary and Barracks Master) for the post at St. Joseph's.

After deciding to work in the fur trade, Jean Baptiste spent a winter at the St. Croix River. On September 18, 1811, his father recounted that
"Johnny remained with (him) about One Month & then went to winter on the heads of the Montreal River which emptied into Lake Superior."
Jean Baptiste received only 50 pounds Halifax currency in wages and his father did not expect him to do it again. However, the next year Johnny wintered at Lac du Flambeau in norther Wisconsin.

In the War of 1812, Jean Baptiste Askin served under Capt. Charles Roberts in the capture of Michilimackinac and then returned with the intention of leading Indians in a campaign at Detroit. However, he arrived after Hull's surrender.

After his marriage to Elisa Van Allen, the couple settled in Norfolk County, Upper Canada, where Jean Baptiste served as clerk of the peace, district court justice, deputy clerk of the crown, and issuer of licenses. When the district court was transferred to London, Ontario in the 1830's, Jean moved there and became the first court clerk.

In December, 1837, Jean Baptiste Askin began raising volunteers to suppress Mackenzie's Rebellion. For a short time he was given the command of a militia. However, his biggest battle during that time turned out to be the destruction of the press and type of a liberal newspaper.

Jean Baptiste was considered of high social standing and was head of a prominent London, Ontario family when he died on November 15, 1869.

His uncle Charles Askin was born in Detroit to John Askin, Sr, and Archange Barthe, but grew up at Michilimackinac. He married Monique Jacob, daughter of George Jacob of Detroit.

Charles trained for a business career and pursued his profession in Niagara, Upper Canada, and Mackinac. In a number of the mercantile dealings he acted as agent for his father. Then in 1806 he was acting as surveyor for his father. In 1809, according to John, Sr., Charles was offered the task of managing the estate of "the Late Mr. Hamilton" in Queenston and he accepted. During the War of 1812 Charles missed the Battle of Queenston when he was confined to bed for three days with boils and was "so ill with them that part of the time (he) could not even sit up in bed to eat." Then, when it became obvious the British were losing, Charles fled.

But he served the British with distinction and was present at the surrender of Detroit as captain of the Canadian militia. In one letter from "Dundass Mills Head of the Lake" on June 2, 1813, he described the loss of Fort George after only fifteen to twenty minutes. But Charles had "another fit of the ague" and sores were breaking out on his lips so he again could not fight. But he did keep his family appraised of the war.

In 1813, Charles was with the group who accepted the surrender of six hundred men under Col. Charles Boerstler of the 14th U.S. Infantry. Again at the "Head of the Lake" on October 23, 1813, Charles found himself with a number of Askin, McKee, Hamilton, and Richardson relations - all fugitives on the run from the Americans. But by December 14th of that year he was back getting food and supplies for the troops who were again on the move. And his letters home were an interesting documentation of the war in Upper and Lower Canada.

After the war, Charles Askin returned to the Canadian side of the border region where he managed the family estate and held a variety of public offices in the Windsor / Amherstburg area before his death. Charles resided at Strabane, the family home, until his death in 1862.

John Askin, Sr.'s daughter Archange was born in 1775 in Michilimackinac. She met and married David Meredith of the British Army's Royal Artillery while he was stationed in Detroit.

In 1792 the Merediths were stationed in Woolwich, near London, England. David wrote the elder Askin numerous letters telling them news from Europe and discussing his political opinions. Archange and their daughter Anne were in their own home so they would not be exposed "to the distress and miserry of a camp."

In April, 1793, Archange Askin Meredith wrote her parents that although many British officers were in Holland fighting the French, that Meredith had not been ordered there yet. She obviously loved her husband and told her parents that Meredith sacrificed "every thing for (her) comfort, and happiness."

Then on March 27, 1794, Archange wrote to her mother that David, Jr. had frequently been ill, but at the age of six months old had begun to improve. Nothing had been spared on his parent's part to make the child healthier. But in September, 1794, David Jr. was still not "strong enough to walk" even though he was sixteen months old. His mother blamed it on being brought up on cow's milk. By February, 1795 he was walking, but Archange complained in 1796 that he had become "delicate and spoiled" because of his illness.

Also in 1794, Archange was pleased that her daughter Anne could speak French, since parents wanted her to learn a second language young. In another letter that year, Archange wrote that Anne was growing "more amusing every day." Then in 1795, Anne's mother described her as "very delicate ... with a good appetite, and ... in perfect health." By 1796, Anne was reading.

The family went to Yarmouth where Archange finally learned to swim. But in Fall, 1796 the Meredith family was forced to move from the "extremely cold and damp" Yarmouth back to Woolwich because of David Meredith, Sr's ill health. Archange explained to her parents that he had diabetes, "a very uncommon complaint." Meredith was ordered to move by his physician and forbidden to exercise. The family was hurt financially by this turn of events and Archange resorted to asking her father for money.

By February, 1797, after a ten-month illness, Meredith had improved. But the military did not let him recuperate anymore than necessary. In April of that year he was suddenly ordered to Ireland, a country that Meredith wrote was in a "torpid state" and was supporting the French in their war against Britian. Meredith was sent so suddenly that his family could not accompany him. But at least the move saved him from having to serve in the West Indies.

While in Ireland, Meredith's health improved. By 1799, Archange had joined him in Ireland and she wrote that Meredith looked "remarkably well." Unfortunately in 1799 Meredith was moved back to England. In 1805 the family was in Portsmouth and Meredith was in "tolerable health but quite thin," according to his wife.

By 1807, the Merediths had finally returned to Canada. Although they had hoped to be stationed closer to Archange's family, the British Army assigned them to Halifax, and David had become Lt. Col. Meredith. David referred to Halifax as a "very ostensible Command." Both Anne and Elizabeth accompanying their parents to Halifax. David, Jr. was sent to the Royal Military Academy and was expected to be assigned to his father's command upon graduation. But that never came to be. David Meredith, Sr. was dead in March, 1809.

Both John Askin, Jr. and Sr. sent money to help Archange after her husband's death. On September 13, 1809, John Askin, Sr. wrote to Isaac Todd

"Lieut Colonel Meredith must have left little money & his
Funeral (which was expensive) must have taken a part of
that. (Archange) had during her stay to hire a House at
a high rate ... She was necessitated to go home (to
England) on account of her Son who had or soon was to get
his Commission ..."
In fact, in 1812, John Askin, Sr. wrote to Archange and told
her to return to Canada, that England had become too
expensive. But she did not return and lived another 57 years,
dying in 1866 in Bruges, Belgium. Isaac Todd once described
her as an "affectionate Good little Woman."

In this volume, with the exception of Archange, John
Askin Sr.'s daughters are discussed more thoroughly in their
husbands' genealogies.

John Sr.'s son James Askin first appeared in his father's
journal in 1798 when James was attending Matthew Donovan's
school in Detroit. Then in 1801, he was in Rev. David Bacon's
school. And just six years later, James Askin and his brother
Charles received six acres of river front property on the
south side of the River Raisin from their half brother John
Askin, Jr.

When ill feelings between the Americans and British were
intensified. James wrote to Charles that as a member of the
militia, James was discouraged with the lack of discipline.
During the War of 1812, James Askin served as captain of the
militia. While the Americans occupied Sandwich, James and
Alexander Askin were serving at Ft. Malden. On September, 16,
1812, John Askin, Jr. wrote to his father from Michilimackinac
that he had
        "heard a great deal of James and Alexander prvious to
        Genl Brocks arrival, they having been exposed several
        times at the different Skirmishes that took place at the
        Canard, Petite Cote & Moguagon Much praise (was) given
        them.
Then in 1813, James wrote to his father telling him about the
British victory at the Raisin River. They took 450 prisoners.
James added that the only relation of his that had been
injured in the battle was Robert Richardson who had received
a knee wound.

James made it through the war safely. On May 1, 1815,
John Askin, Jr. related to his father that
        "James wrote (him) from York that he intended to proceed
        to Sandwich for Mr. Pattinsons children ... He will be
        married to the Young Lady he so long has sigh'ed for."
That "young Lady" was Frances Godet dit Marentette whom James
married on October 10, 1815.

In 1806, Alexander Askin witnessed his father's sale of
the old Barthe family farm to his brother-in-law Elijah Brush.
Then on March 25, 1807, John Askin revealed to Dr. Richardson
that he had sent Alexander to the United States "to learn the
Profession of a Lawyer" from Elijah Brush. However, John was
concerned that Alexander would suffer having not studied in
Canada. He noted that Alexander was
        "an Officer in the British Militia and does his Duty as
        such & does all others as if residing on this (Canadian)
        Side & who has constantly refused several Offers made him

41

by the Governor on the other side [American] if he would become a Citizen."

Probably because of these concerns, in 1808, John sent Alexander to study with "Mr. Elliot, after having tried Mr. Dickson at Niagara, who had as many Clerks as he wanted." Elliott agreed to provide Alexander with room, board, and laundry; while his father agreed to clothe Alexander.His father felt that there was a good deal more to learn on Canadian side then on the American one, since there was more formality observed in a Canadian practice.

During the War of 1812, Alexander served as a lieutenant. James and Alexander Askin; and Captain Thomas, Theresa and Alick McKee fled east across Upper Canada as the American troops advanced behind them. On October 10, 1813, Theresa McKee communicated to her father back at Strabane that everyone was well except for her brother Alexander who had "the ague."

Ague was a catch-all term for symptoms of fever, chills, aches, cough, and sometimes a nosebleed. A person with ague might have been suffering from anything from a cold, to influenza, to malaria.

On October 23, 1813, Alexander Askin wrote to his parents himself that the McKees and his brother James and his nephew Johnny were at the "Head of the Lake." Also in the area were "all the Hamiltons and Robinsons" except for Jane Richardson and Nancy who had left for York two days before. Alexander added that none of them had suffered any hardships. However, his own healthy condition did not last. Whether it was from the "ague", a war wound, or something else, Alexander was dead shortly after his letter.

Askin Family II

William Askins Family

William Askins
  b. Canada
  m. Eliza Cassidy (b. Canada)
  Children
     Harriet Ann (see below)
     Hannah - m. Field
       r. Pontiac, Michigan

Harriet Ann Askins
  b. February 8, 1839; Ontario
  m. Joseph Sawyer Landon (1842-May 1, 1886), son of Truman
  and Caroline (Burns) Landon
  r. Pain Court, Ontario
  d. February 6, 1920; Gosfield Township, Ontario
  bur. February 6, 1920; Gosnell Cemetery, Highgate,
  Ontario
  Children
     See Landon

Truman Landon believed Harriet Ann Askins to be the daughter of John Askins Jr., granddaughter of John Askin, Sr. However, John Jr. was born in 1762. At Harriet's birth, he would have been 77 years old, had he lived. As it was, John Jr. had died 19 years before Harriet's birth. So if there was indeed a relationship between Harriet and John Askin, Jr., Harriet would have been a part of his granddaughter's or great-granddaughter's generation.

Civil registration of births did not begin in the area until 1868. So there was no birth certificate for Harriet. However, according to Harriet's death certificate (no. 1920-05-014485), Harriet was the daughter of William and Eliza (Cassidy) Askins. They had at least two daughters, Harriet and Hannah. They probably grew up in Pain Court, outside Chatham, Ontario.

Hannah Askins married a man named Fields and moved to Pontiac, Michigan. Her husband may have been a descendant of Daniel Field who owned land on the Thames River, Ontario, in the late 1700's.

Her sister Harriet Ann Askins married Joseph Sawyer Landon and they had eight children. According to the 1861 census, Harriet Landon lived on concession 1, lot 4. Forty-one of 155 acres were under cultivation and the land had a cash value of $2000.

In the 1871 census, Harriet was listed as a 28-year-old female, white Methodist who was born in Ontario, Canada and was able to read.

After her husband's death in 1886, Harriet shared her home with her mother-in-law Caroline Burns Landon. According to her death certificate, Harriet died in Gosfield Township on February 6, 1920. Her age was given as 81 years, 11 months, and 29 days. Her daughter Aleda Landon Miller was listed as informant on the death certificate.

Barthe Family

Andre Barthe
    m. Jane De Cosmesse of St. Jean Tarbe, Tarbe Gascogne,
    France
    Children
        Theophile (see below)

Theophile Barthe
    b. 1695; Tarbe Gascogne, France
    m. Margaret Charlotte Alavoine (b. 1695), dau of Capt.
    Charles Alavoine (bur. May 11, 1749) and Mary Geresa
    Machard (bur. October 10, 1728) of Rochelle, France;
    March 18, 1721; Ville Marie Montreal, Quebec
    Children
        Charles Andrew (see below)
        Pierre (Dr.) - m. Mary Charlotte Chapoton (b.
            November 21, 1737; Detroit,
            Michigan), dau of John Chapoton and Margaret
            Esteve; March 3, 1760; Detroit, Michigan
            Children
                Marie Felicity - b. January 20, 1761
                    bur. August 6, 1761; Detroit,
                    Michigan
                Pierre - b. April 11, 1762
                    bur. September 19, 1762; Detroit,
                    Michigan
                Charlotte - July 17, 1763
                    m1 Stephen Louis Reaume (December
                    27, 1748; Montreal-by 1784)
                    m2 Antoine Louis Descomps/Deschamps
                    dit Labadie (b. 1730 bur. December
                    17, 1807; Assumption, Sandwich,
                    Ontario), wid of Angelica Campau,
                    son of Peter Descomps/Deschamps and
                    Angelica Lacelle; October 18, 1784;
                    Detroit, Michigan
                    bur. February 11, 1849; Detroit
                    Michigan
                    Children
                        Eleonora - m1 J. Reed
                            m2 Jean Baptiste Piquette
                            m3 Thomas Sheldon
        Jean Baptiste

Andre Charles / Charles Andrew Barthe
    b. February 22, 1722; Montreal, Quebec
    m. Mary Teresa Campau (b. February 7, 1729; Detroit,
    Michigan bur. June 13, 1765; Detroit, Michigan), dau of
    Jean Louis Campau and Mary Louisa Robert; February or
    April 24, 1747; Detroit, Michigan
    d. March 14, 1786; Detroit, Michigan
    bur. March 16, 1786; Detroit, Michigan
    Children
        Louis Theophile (see below)
        Charles - b. April 15, 1748; Detroit, Michigan
            bur. May 14, 1748; Detroit, Michigan
        Marie Archange - b. March 13, 1749
            m. John Askin, Sr., son of James Askin and
            Alice Rae; June 21, 1773; Detroit, Michigan
            bur. November 25, 1820; Assumption, Sandwich

44

Children (see Askin)
Catherine - b. September 25, 1750
   bur. October 4, 1750; Detroit, Michigan
Charles Andrew - b. March 4, 1752
   bur. May 31, 1752
Jean Baptiste - May 4, 1753
   r. Sault St. Marie
   m. Genevieve/Geneveva Cullerier dit Beaubien
   (b. May 1, 1761; Detroit, Michigan d. Peck
   River, Ontario bur. July 14, 1847; Assumption,
   Sandwich), niece of French Commandant Picote
   de Bellestre, dau of Jean Baptiste Cullerier
   and Mary Ann Lootman dit Barrois
   bur. June 22, 1827; Assumption, Sandwich
   Children
      Jean Baptiste (Lt.) - b. October 10 or
        18, 1779; Detroit, Michigan
        d. 1812
      Theresa Victoria - b. 1794
        m1 Hubert Villers dit St. Louis (b.
        June 25, 1792 bur November 5, 1826;
        Assumption), son of Louis Villers
        dit St. Louis and Charlotte
        Reguindeau; November 24, 1818;
        Assumption, Ontario
        m2 Constant Gautier (b. St. Henry de
        la Mascouche, Lower Canada), son of
        Alexander Gautier and Cecilia
        Geoffrey; February 18, 1828;
        Assumption, Ontario
        bur. February 14, 1841; Belle River,
        Ontario
      dau - pos m. Robert Viller dit St. Louis
Mary Teresa - b. July 21, 1754
   bur. August 2, 1754; Detroit, Michigan
Bonaventure Anthony - b. March 6, 1756
Terese - b. March 25, 1758
   m. Alexander Grant (May 20, 1734;
   Glenmoriston, Scotland - May 8, 1813; Castle
   Grant, Grosse Pointe Farms, Michigan);
   September 30, 1774; Detroit, ,Michigan
   d. November 11, 1810; Grosse Pointe, Michigan
   Children
      Therese - b. February 13, 1776; Detroit,
      Michigan
      m. Dr. Thomas Wright (d. by 1801)
      d. 1801; New York of Yellow Fever
      Children
         Therese - b.c. 1797
         3 other - d. 1801; New York of
           Yellow Fever
      Jean (adopted) - b.c. 1778
      m. Judith Campau
      Nancy (Ann) - b. February 5, 1785
      m. Mayez / Maillet
      Archange - m. Thomas Dickson
      Phyllis (Felicity) - b. August 29, 1782
      m. Alexander Duft (d. June, 1809);
      Amherstburg, Ontario
      Isabella - b. December 20, 1783

m. Capt. William Bilkeson (1777-1833)
d. February 10, 1828; Glasgow, Scotland
Eleanor (Nelly) - m. George Jacob; October 31, 1820
Elizabeth - m. James Woods (1778-1828)
Mary Julia - b. April 4, 1796
m. Miles
Jeanne / Jane Cameron - b. August 29, 1799
m. William Richardson (b. January 7, 1801), son of Dr. Robert Richardson and Madelaine Askin
Children
James
Arabella
Eleanora
Marie Felicity (Phyllis) - b. December 18, 1762; Detroit, Michigan
m. Capt. Daniel Mercer (d. 1806/07)
Charles - b./d. October 18, 1765; Detroit, Michigan
Jean Baptiste - b. June 12, 1765; Detroit, Michigan
bur. November 13, 1765; Detroit, Michigan
Lavoine

In German the word "barth", meant " the man with the beard". However, the family who ended up in the Canadian border region apparently was descended from the ancient French house of Barthe, a family which originated as rulers of an area situated in the Pyrenee Mountains near the Spanish border. The first Vicomte de la Barthe was Auriol Manse from whom the Dukes of Aquitaine, Kings and Counts of Toulouse, and Counts of Aragon descended. Sevenus, Duke of Aquitaine, lived circa 600 A.D. Amant, his son, became the Duke of Novempopulanie and Captain of Gascogne and was alive in 620 and 627 A.D.

The family detailed in this genealogy could definitely be traced back to Andre Barthe who married Jane De Cosomesse of St. Jean Tarbe, Tarbe Gascogne, France. Their son Theophile Barthe was born in Tarbe Gascogne in 1695. He was the first of the family to emigrate to Canada where he worked as a gunsmith. Hall referred to him as "armurier du Roy." But Hall incorrectly claimed that Theophile married Margaret in 1781. He would have been 86 years old at the time. In reality Theophile married Margaret Charlotte Alavoine, the daughter of Charles Alavoine, a captain of the militia, in 1721 in Montreal.

They had at least three children, Andrew Charles, Pierre, and Jean Baptiste. Pierre Barthe became a doctor and, along with at least Charles, emigrated to the Detroit area. A J.B. Chapoton Barthe witnessed Chief Pontiac's grant of land to Alexis Masonville at Detroit on September 18, 1765. So the third brother might also have emigrated to Detroit.

In the area's 1762 census pieces of Barthe property appeared. The first piece of property was listed as "Barthe (supracit)" and had no one living on it. It was three acres on the north side of the Detroit River, northeast "to Grosse

Pointe on Lake St. Claire." There was a "Barth (supra cit.)" owning a 30-foot-wide piece of land inside the fort which also had no one living on it. And, finally, the 1762 census noted a 90-foot-lot inside the fort belonging to a Charles "Berthe".

Charles Andre or Andrew Charles Barthe, depending upon the source, was the eldest son of Theophile and Margaret. He was a "Grand Voye" or chief overseer of roads and, like his father, an "arqu" or gunsmith.

According to 1748 Jesuit documents "Sieur barte, armorer, at detroit," paid one of the Jesuit priests 312 livres to pay a debt owed to "sieive dumouchel, blacksmith" for a house in the fort he had purchased in 1749. But looking at Jesuit documents from the time, that could also have been Jean Barthe dit Belleville who arrived in Detroit in 1706. Then in 1750, Father de la Richardie paid "Barte" for repairing a gun and sold "Barte" 1/4 livre of borax.

Charles Barthe and his brother became wealthy fur traders who operated at Mackinac and on the Miami River, according to Jesuit documents edited by Thwaites. Charles Andrew Barthe, referred to as a gunsmith in legal papers, married Mary Teresa Campau in Detroit in 1747. They had 12 children. Through the marriage, Charles acquired a plot of land in Detroit from his father-in-law. Then he acquired more land in 1759 from the estate of Nicholas Campau. Charles and Mary Theresa lived on the farm in Detroit which would eventually go to daughter Marie Archange Askin, and finally to Marie Archange's son-in-law Elijah Brush.

On March 15, 1786, John Askin recorded "Mr Bathes" death which had occurred the day before, "after a sickness of about a month."

For a number of years, Charles' son Jean Baptiste Barthe lived at Sault Ste. Marie where he supplied the fur traders. Then he moved to Mackinac. When it appeared the Americans were about to attack Detroit, Jean Baptiste hurried there and married Genevieve Cullerier dit Beaubien.

In 1786, John Askin and Jean Baptiste Barthe hired William Robertson and Thomas Finchley to examine their accounts and "to settle some other points hither to desputable." Askin wrote to Todd and McGill that Barthe was "going to make his Residence at St. Marys for some years" and no longer wanted Askin to ship him any goods.

Jean Baptiste was listed in the 1796 census as a man aged 16-50, having 1 white woman, 1 male slave, and 1 female slave living northeast of the city of Detroit. But after the 1796 American occupation of Detroit, Barthe opted to remain a British subject. He was buried in Sandwich in 1827.

His son Jean Baptiste II was a lieutenant in the First Essex Militia who became an explorer. In <u>Michigan Voyagers</u>, edited by Donna Russell, "Baptiste Barte" was listed as employed by Jean B. Berthelot for a trip on the Mississippi River in July, 1816. Back then voyageurs were required to sign a formal contract before a notary.

47

Jean Baptiste Barthe II's daughter Theresa Victoria married Hubert Villers dit St. Louis. And Hall claimed another daughter married Robert Viller dit St. Louis, although he may have simply meant Therese marriage to Hubert. The Villers dit St. Louis family received their Sobriquet (dit St. Louis) from the Christian name of one of their ancestors, a Louis Villers who married Marie Josephine Morin.

Charles Andrew Barthe's daughter Therese married Alexander Grant, while daughter Mary Felicity married Daniel Mercer. When Mercer was stationed at Mackinac, he, like many others, fell into disfavor with Patrick Sinclair and was arrested during the summer of 1780. It was later, when he was stationed in Detroit, that Mercer married Felicity/Phyllis.

According to Hall, Louisan Theophile Barthe, eighth child of Charles and Mary Therese, married Madeleine des Ruisseaux de Bellecour, daughter of Francois and Madeleine Adhemar de Lusignan. It was more likely that Denissen was correct that Louisan married Mary Madelene Trotier dit Bellecour, daughter of Francis Xavier Trotier dit Bellecour and Mary Trotier de Lusignan. Louis Theophile and Mary Madelene were married at Fort St. Clair at the junction of the Pine and St. Clair Rivers.

Francis Xavier Trotier was descended from a family from Ige, France. Circa 1775 he "located at the pinery at the mouth of the Pine River" and by 1780 he was in charge of Gov. Patrick Sinclair's interest there.

In 1791 "Louis Barth Clerk" was on the roll of John Askin's militia company. Then, for a considerable period of time, Louis was employed in a pinery apparently as an employee of John Askin. On July 29, 1799, Askin wrote Barthe

"You are aware that the men I have at the Pinery are a great expense to me, therefore I have no doubt but that you have made every effort to have them work to the best advantage, that is, in hauling the logs, making roads, ets."

Lavoine Barthe was frequently connected with members of this Barthe family. However, an exact relationship has not been established. As early as 1778, John Askin was writing Commodore Grant about "Young Mr. (J.B.) Barth, LaVoine & Louisen (Barthe)." LaVoine was Jean Baptiste Barthe's clerk at Sault St. Marie beginning as late as 1776. In 1778, John Askin sold LaVoine a panis (slave) who Askin referred to as "too stupid to make a sailor or to be any good whatever."

Baudry dit Desbuttes dit St. Martin Family

Guillaume Baudry dit Desbuttes
- b. October 2, 1657
- m. Jeanne Soullard (b.c. 1666); July 13, 1682; Quebec
- Children (15)
    - Jean Baptiste Baudry (see below)

Jean Baptiste Baudry
- bpt. July 3, 1684; Trois Rivieres, Quebec
- m. Marie Louisa Dayon, dau of Nicholas Dayon; October 8, 1721
- Children
    - Jacques (see below)
    - Joseph Marie - b.c. 1725
        - m. Madeleine Paille; 1757; Detroit, Michigan
        - d. 1778; Detroit, Michigan
        - Louisa Margaret Desbuttes dit St. Martin - m. Louis Joseph Toupin (b. February 16, 1735; Quebec. bur. July 7, 1810, Raisin River), grandson of Jean Toupin, Sieur Dusault; January 11, 1762; Church of the Huron, Sandwich, Ontario
        - bur. July 19, 1766; Detroit, Michigan
        - Children
            - Jean Francis Toupin dit Dusault - b. August 11, 1762; Sandwich, Ontario
            - m1 Mary Jane Raoul, dau of Jean Baptiste Raoul and Mary Jane Prudhomme
            - m2 Mary Francis Davignon dit Beauregard
            - d. 1811; Detroit, Michigan

Jacques Baudry dit Desbuttes dit St. Martin
- b. August 23, 1733; Quebec, Quebec
- m. Marie Anne Navarre, dau of Robert Navarre and Marie Lootman dit Barrois; October 28, 1760; Detroit, Michigan
- bur. June 18, 1768; Detroit, Michigan
- Children
    - Marie Archange - m. Angus McIntosh (b. 1762; Inverness Scotland bur. January 25, 1833; Scotland), June 17, 1783; Detroit, Michigan
    - d. July 13, 1827; Canada
    - bur. Assumption Church, Sandwich, Ontario
    - Children
        - Duncan - b. September 24, 1785
        - Alexander - b. August 23, 1787
        - Anne - b. 1789; Detroit, Michigan
            - m. Henry Jackson Hunt; 1811
        - Archange - b. April 25, 1793
        - Isabelle - b. March 17, 1795

France produced a number of distinguished Baudry families. The Baudrys who had the Seigneur de Semilly en Normandy and Generalite de Rouen titles were headed by Guard Baudry de Semilly in 1645. In 1593, Nicholas Baudry was the Seigneur de Bretteville and advocate of the Parliament of Normandy. Simon Baudry was Maitres des Requites in 1344. Louis Baudry de Riencourt was Chevalier de Malte in 1612. And yet another Baudry family came from Bourgogne.

The Baudry / Beaudry dit DesButes / Desbuttes family was in Canada as early as the 1600's (see Appendix). On the Beaupre Coast in Chateaus-Richer, an Urbain Baudry was on record as baptizing Marie-Francoise, future wife of Nicholas Paquin. A Jane Baudry dit St. Martin married Jacques Duquay dit Marentette and had Margaret Duquay dit Marentette who married Jacques Godet in Trois Rivieres on November 4, 1698. And a Jacques Baudry de la Marche purchased Antoine de la Mothe Cadillac's rights in Detroit. He was baptized on September 13, 1676 at Trois Rivieres as the son of Urbain Baudry dit La Marche, a tool maker, and Madelene Boucher. Jacques eventually removed to France where he became attorney of the Charon brothers. He died in France after 1738.

Another of the earliest found in the New World was Guillaume Baudry dit Desbuttes who was born on October 2, 1657. Guillaume, Jane (b. prob. by 1660), and Urbain (b. prob. by 1655) with their connections with Trois Rivieres, Quebec; were in all probability related.

Guillaume Baudry married Jeanne Soullard, an armourer's daughter, in Quebec on July 13, 1682; when she was only 15 or 16 years old. They resided in Trois Rivieres and had 15 children. Guillaume received two grants of land from Rene Robinau de Becancour on March 4, 1689 and January 14, 1693.

Guillaume worked as a gunsmith, goldsmith, and silversmith. He engraved the lead plaque on the cornerstone of the Recollet Church. The cornerstone, which was laid on July 11, 1710; earned Guillaume 500 livres in 1713.

A son named Jean Baptiste Baudry dit Desbuttes (bpt. July 3, 1684; Trois Rivieres, Quebec) was also a gunsmith. He married Marie Louise, daughter of Nicholas Dayon on October 8, 1721 and moved to Detroit.

Jean Baptiste appeared in early records again on February 18, 1726, when he was summoned to court. A surgeon named Alavoine claimed Baudry owed him 175 livre. But Baudry won the case.

Jean Baptiste's daughter Louisa Baudry dit Desbuttes married Louis Joseph Toupin at the Church of the Huron in Sandwich, Ontario. Louis was the grandson of Jean Toupin, Sieur Dusault; and great grandson of Toussaint Toupin, Sieur Dusault (see Appendix).

Louisa and Louis had Jean Francis Toupin dit Dusault who was the subject of a February 25, 1799 letter from George MacDougall to John Askin. "Phenon Dusau" (Jean Dusault) of Raisin River had contacted George about a "disagreeable predicament" in which he found himself. Jean had "purchased with the Mill only twelve Acres, in lieu of (Jacques) Gailliards whole Farm." When he purchased the mill, Jean had believed he was purchasing Gailliard's farm and an additional 120 acres, along with the mill. Instead, he ended up with only 12 acres of land; not enough to furnish the wood he needed to heat and cook, to repair the mill, and to build fences and bridges. So MacDougall wrote to Askin for advice. In his February 26, 1799 answer, Askin suggested MacDougall and

50

Dusault become partners in the mill, with MacDougall supplying the timber.

Dusault's uncle and Jean's son Jacques Baudry Desbuttes dit St. Martin was Detroit's official interpreter for the Huron Indians, in addition to being a merchant there. According to Burton, Jacques and his wife, Marie Anne Navarre lived southwest of the fort before moving inside the town. Jacques might have been the "La Butte" in the 1762 census who had a 30-foot-wide lot inside the fort and a 50-foot-wide lot in the "Suburb of Ste. Rosalie." "La Butte" was listed in the census as "rich".

Marie Archange, Jacques and Marie Anne's daughter, married Angus McIntosh (see Appendix). According to Burton, Angus' father had been a supporter of Bonnie Prince Charlie and Angus' mother "had taken the field in person at the head of the clansmen and perpetuated the rout of Moy (the McIntosh ancestral home)." A number of sources claimed that after the rebellion failed, the McIntosh's lost their family estate and Angus emigrated to North America.

Whatever the cause of his emigration, in 1787 Angus was in Detroit, serving as ensign in the district militia. He married Marie Archange Baudry the next year and became a prosperous trader connected with the North West Company. But when the Americans took control of Detroit, Angus McIntosh moved his family to the south side of the river where he built a mansion he named Moy House.

Even though a number of sources claimed McIntosh had emigrated after the loss of the family estate, Burton claimed that in 1831, after Marie Archange Baudry Desbuttes dit St. Martin's death, Angus and his sons returned to Scotland to collect his inheritance, Moy Hall.

Ann McIntosh, daughter of Angus McIntosh and Marie Archange Baudry Desbuttes dit St. Martin, married Henry Jackson Hunt, the second mayor of Detroit.

According to _The Windsor Border Region_, a Marie L. Desbuttes and Jacques Godet had a daughter Madeleine Godet who was baptized on January 2, 1769 in Ste Anne's parish. Their son Joseph was baptized on February 19, 1775. But I have been unable to uncover the connection between Marie and the family in this genealogy.

Bondy Family

Thomas Douaire de Bondy I
    m. Barbara Regnier
    d. France
    Children
        Thomas (see below)

Thomas Douaire de Bondy II
    b. 1636; St. Germain, Auxerre, France
    m. Marguerite dit Chavigny (b. May 30, 1643, Quebec), dau
    of Frances de/des Chavigny and Eleonora de Grandmaison;
    July 26, 1656; Quebec
    d. 1667, drowned near Isle of Orleans
    Children
        Jacques (see below)
        Augustin - b. August 28, 1667; Quebec
            m1 Catherine Tetard de Folleville (April 18,
            1671, Montreal - January 25, 1746, Quebec),
            wid of Peter Pinquette
            bur. December 28, 1702; Quebec
            Children
                Joseph - b. February 5, 1700; Quebec
                    m. Catherine Raimbaut (b. January
                    12, 1699; Montreal), wid of Julian
                    Trotier; October 11, 1739; Quebec

Jacques Douaire de Bondy
    b. February 21, 1660; Quebec
    m. Magdeline Gatineau dit Duplassis (b. 1672), dau of
    Nicholas Gatineau Sieur Duplassis and Mary Crevier; 1697
    bur. March 25, 1703; Montreal, Quebec
    Children
        Joseph (see below)

Joseph Douaire de Bondy I
    b. February 27, 1700; Montreal, Quebec
    m. Marie Anne Cecilia Campau (b. June 21, 1707;
    Montreal), dau of Jacques Campau and Cecilia Catin; July
    28, 1732; Detroit, Michigan
    bur. April 6, 1760; Vercheres, Quebec
    Children
        Joseph (see below)
        Magdelene Elizabeth - b. December 19, 1736; Detroit
        Jean Baptiste - b. August 27, 1738; Detroit
            m. Elizabeth Coursol, dau of Michael Coursol
            and Mary Joseph Dion; January 16, 1764;
            Vercheres
        Louis - b. May 20, 1741; Detroit
            bur. November 2, 1755, Vercheres
        Mary Catherine - b. February 10, 1743; Detroit,
        Michigan
        Theresa - b. September 29, 1745; Detroit, Michigan
        Margaret - b. December 3, 1747; Detroit, Michigan
        Louis - b. January 11, 1749
            bur. April 27, 1749

Joseph Douaire de Bondy II
    b. 1733; Detroit, Michigan
    m. Marie Josephene Gamelin (b. July 23, 1741; Sandwich,
    Ontario bur. November 27, 1797; Sandwich, Ontario), dau

of Laurent Eustache Gamelin and Marie Josephene Dudeboir
dit Bonvouloir dit Lachene; August 7, 1758 Detroit
bur. November 18, 1802; Detroit, Michigan
Children
Joseph III - b. January 30, 1759; Detroit
m. Jeanne/Jane Meloche (b. January 18, 1761)
dau of Pierre Meloche and Marie Catherine
Guisgnard; October 8, 1781; Detroit
bur. October 1, 1805; Detroit
Children
Joseph IV - b. December 3, 1781;
Sandwich, Ontario
Mary Jane - b, November 15, 1783;
Sandwich, Ontario
m. Jean Baptiste Saliot; January 21,
1799; Detroit
d. June 6, 1815; Riviere du Portage
Catherine - b. November 20, 1785;
Sandwich, Ontario
m. Stephen Menencon (b. March 1,
1824), son of Stephen Menencon and
Mary Ann LeBlanc; September 21,
1802; Detroit
Anthony - b. January 10, 1788; Sandwich,
Ontario
bur. April 11, 1808; Detroit,
Michigan
Eustache - b. February 11, 1790
Peter - b. June 30, 1792; Sandwich,
Ontario
bur. March 14, 1807; Detroit,
Michigan
Angelica - b. November 2, 1794
m. Hyacinthe Riopel; April 26, 1813;
Detroit, Michigan
Basil - b. February 18, 1797; Detroit,
Michigan
Amable - b. March 4, 1799; Detroit,
Michigan
Mary Louisa - b. November 24, 1801;
Detroit, Michigan
bur. November 27, 1801; Detroit,
Michigan
Gabriel - b. October 23, 1762; Detroit, Michigan
m. Marie Archange, dau of Thomas Pageot /
Paget and Marie Louise Villers dit St. Louis;
November 17, 1787; Assumption Church,
Sandwich, Ontario
Children
Mary Archange	Joseph
Laurence	Gabriel
Anthony	Veronica
Thomas	Eustache
Anthony	Valentine
Frances - b. December 24, 1763; Detroit, Michigan
bur. December 18, 1766; Detroit, Michigan
Angelica - b. February 21, 1765; Detroit, Michigan
bur. July 8, 1765; Detroit, Michigan
Veronica - b. March 5, 1766; Detroit, Michigan
m. Bernard Campau (b. October 20, 1752;
Detroit, Michigan), son of Nicholas Campau and

Agatha Casse dit St. Aubin; February 23, 1784;
Assumption Church, Sandwich, Ontario
bur. November 27, 1819
Anthony de Pauda - b. November 14, 1767; Detroit,
Michigan
m. Jane Nipiaka, a Miami
d. 1821
Children
Josephine Teresa - b. December 13, 1811;
Ft. Wayne, Indiana
bpt. July 24, 1815; Detroit,
Michigan
m. John Connor (b. 1801), son of
Henry Connor and Teresa Tremblay;
October 16, 1835
bur. March 18, 1901; Mt. Clemens,
Michigan
Monica - b. September 6, 1819; Detroit,
Michigan
Catherine - b. July 14, 1769; Assumption, Sandwich,
Ontario
m. Anthony Alexis Baron dit Lupien (b.
September 28, 1769), son of Peter Baron dit
Lupien and Mary Ann Reaume; September 7, 1789
Laurant/Lawrence (Capt.) - b. March 21, 1771;
Assumption, Sandwich, Ontario
m. Magdelene Pageot (b. August 19, 1772;
Sandwich, Ontario), dau of Thomas Pageot and
Mary Louisa Villers; November 21, 1791;
Assumption Church, Sandwich, Ontario
d. Battle at "pied des Rapids de la Riviere
des Miamis"
bur. May 8, 1813; Sandwich, Ontario
Children
Mary Madelene - b. November 28, 1792
Laurence - b. September 14, 1794
Gabriel - b. August 18, 1796
Mary Ann Prisca - b. January 17, 1800
Edward - b. December 27, 1801
Florence - b. January 10, 1805
John Chrysostom - b. June 1, 1809
Mary Jane
Archange - b. December 5, 1772; Sandwich, Ontario
Mary Teresa - b. September 18, 1774; Sandwich,
Ontario
m. Gabriel Godfroy (b. November 10, 1758;
Detroit, Michigan bur. September 2, 1833;
Detroit), wid of Catherine Couture; February
14, 1795; Assumption Church, Sandwich, Ontario
Joseph - b. September 25, 1776; Sandwich, Ontario
m. Archange Godfroy (b. March 14, 1786;
Detroit - 1823), dau of Gabriel Godfroy and
Catherine Couture; March 1, 1810
bur. November 11, 1816; Detroit, Michigan
Children
Gabriel - b. January 8, 1811; Detroit,
Michigan
Laurence - b. August 6, 1812; Detroit,
Michigan

bur. November 9, 1812; Detroit,
Michigan
Gregory - b. August 31, 1813; Detroit,
Michigan
bpt. February 17, 1814; Detroit,
Michigan
Anthony - b. October 2, 1816
Dominic/Dennis - b. January 26, 1779; Sandwich,
Ontario
m. Teresa Saliot (b. September 9, 1782 bur.
January 8, 1849), dau of John Saliot and Mary
Magdelene Jourdain
bur. February 9, 1858; St. Francis Xavier,
Ecorse, Michigan
Children
Teresa - b. May 2, 1800
m. Jean Baptiste Godfroy (b. May 29,
1792), son of Gabriel Godfroy and
Catherine Couture; July 25, 1820
d. by 1823
Mary Magdelene - b. March 12, 1802
m. Peter Navarre, son of Peter
Navarre and Magdelene Cavalier dit
Rangeard; February 2, 1803
Dominic - b. November 9, 1803
Jean Baptiste - b. August 12, 1805
Anthony - b. April 10, 1807
m. Monica LeBlanc
bur. September 6, 1834
Mary Joseph - b. January 1, 1809
Hubert - b. January 22, 1811; Detroit,
Michigan
Emily - b. May 25, 1813; Detroit,
Michigan
Eulalie - b. January 13, 1815; Detroit,
Michigan
James - b. May 15, 1817; Detroit,
Michigan
Joseph - b. August 15, 1819; Detroit,
Michigan
Teresa Elise - b. May 28, 1823; Detroit,
Michigan
Elizabeth - b. April 15, 1826; Detroit,
Michigan
Charles - bpt. 1784; Assumption Church, Sandwich,
Ontario
Geneveva - m1 Stephen Nicolas Hunot (b. Reims,
France), son of Nicholas Hunot and
Geneveva Robert; October, 1798; Assumption
Church, Sandwich, Ontario

In Italian the name Bondi referred to a man who
habitually saluted "good day" to others. But with the family
of this genealogy, the title, Douaire de Bondy, originated
with an estate the family owned and, according to The Windsor
Border Region, the name was a title held by European nobility.

Thomas Douaire de Bondy II, the first member of the
family in the New World, was born in St. Germain, Auxerre,
France. He emigrated to Quebec, Canada, where he married

Maquerite de Chavigny in 1656. However, he was only about 31 years old when he drowned near the Isle of Orleans.

His son Jacques became a merchant in Montreal, Canada. Jacques Douaire de Bondy married Magdeline Gatineau dit Duplassis. Little else was discovered.

Jacques' son Joseph became a trader and became the first Bondy in Detroit. He was there in 1742, when account books at the mission noted that "Sieur bondi" owed the mission "60 Livres 10 sols".

In 1743, Father Pierre Potier conducted a census in which he listed "Bonde, Clean? Tonque". Editor Donna Russell speculated that that referred to Joseph Douaire de Bondy. Since I have not seen Potier's handwritten copy, I cannot determine what the entry read exactly. However, the "Bonde" does seem to be a Bondy and Joseph Bondy I did not die until 1760. But he might also have had siblings in the area. Could the handwritten "Clean" have been "Jean"?

Other early Michigan censuses did include Joseph Bondy. Since the name survived through at least four generations, confusion among them was easy. Although most references were to Joseph Douaire de Bondy II, a few of the later entries were probably Joseph III or Joseph IV.

Joseph Bondy I was definitely in Montreal in 1730, but had removed to Detroit by his July, 1732 marriage to Marie Anne Cecilia Campau. Although their children were supposedly born in Detroit, censuses placed his son's family in what would later become Canada, on the south shore of the Detroit River in the 1760's.

Quaife claimed that Joseph I returned to Vercheres, Quebec in 1748. However, in 1750, Joseph I witnessed a deed transfer in Detroit which was included in Quaife's book. Perhaps Joseph was just back in Detroit visiting when he witnessed the document. No matter when he returned to Vercheres, Joseph I was in Vercheres before his burial there on April 6, 1760.

The 1762 census listed a Bondy, but Joseph I had died by then. This Bondy was listed as owning a 40 foot lot, but was also listed as being "poor". On the January 23, 1768 census, a Bondy owned three acres of land, two of which were in woods on the south shore of the Detroit River.

Joseph II witnessed marriages in Assumption Parish on July 8, 1776 and February 27, 1781. In 1780, he witnessed a sale of land and The Windsor Border Region listed him about that time on a petition for a water mill on Turkey Creek as a member of the Assumption Parish. On July 28, 1781, he was a church warden of Our Lady of Assumption and, in November of that year and again in the next year, he signed parish account books.

The 1779 census listed a Joseph Bondy and wife with 1 man, 1 woman, 2 lodgers or young men, 4 boys, and 4 girls and 0 slaves. Then in the 1782 census, the family contained 2 men or women, 3 young or hired men, 2 boys, 5 girls, and 1 male slave. They were living on the south shore of the river in Sandwich, Ontario. The family fortunes had improved. The census reported the family owned 1 female slave, 5 horses, 6 oxen, 9 cows, 5 steer and heifers, 30 sheep, 7 hogs, 20 bushels of wheat, 40 bushels Indian corn, 22 sown arpents of wheat, 3 arpents Indian corn and 120 acres of cleared land.

Since Joseph II (at age 59) was possibly the eldest living Joseph Bondy in the area, he may have been the Joseph Bondy, Sr. listed in the July 27, 1792 minutes of the Board of Land of the District of Hesse as owning lot 16, but "being sick & incapable of attending" the board meeting and of discussing business.

On August 3rd, 1787, his son Joseph Bondy III (at about 28 years of age) was probably the "Joseph Bondi" listed as one of the

> "disbanded troops and Loyalists to be settled on the
> N. side of Lake Erie, from a creek 4 miles from the
> mouth of the River Detroit, to small creek about a mile
> and half beyond Cedar River."

As a Lieutenant in the Indian Department, Joseph III was given lot number 55. In a 1793-4 survey of Gosfield and Colchester Townships the lot was described as "along the shore" and next to "an old Indian entrenchment."

At the same time, Bondys were listed as owners of land in Petite Cote. Joseph's brother Laurant Bondy held lot number 1 and brother Gabriel owned number 3. Three lots; numbers 4, 16, and 51; were listed as belonging to a Joseph Bondy.

Joseph III was presumably the Joseph Bondy, Sr. in Petite Cote in the 1792 census along with Askins and McKees. He was listed as having 1 boy aged 15+ (Joseph IV would have been aged 15), 2 boys -15 (Anthony and Eustache), and 2 girls (Mary Jane and Catherine). Their farm was 3 arpents in front by 40 deep and Bondy was listed as commander in chief. In the same 1792 census, a Joseph Bondy owned land at Rivier Aux Dendes (Turkey Creek). Another Joseph Bondy, with 2 males under 15 and 2 females in his family, also had land there. And Gabriel Bondy had 1 male under 15 and 2 females living with him at Riviere Aux Dendes.

A 1796 census for the River Rouge and Ecorse River area showed a "Josh" Bondy aged between 16 and 50 had a family containing 1 white woman, no children, 4 male slaves and 3 female slaves. Joseph Bondy II would have had his wife at home and all of his children grown and gone, but the age would have been wrong. He should have been 63 years old, not between 16 and 50. Joseph III would have been the right age (37), but he should have had at least five children listed in the census as living with him. Joseph IV of this genealogy would have been only 11. However, others of Joseph II's sons also named their sons Joseph Bondy. In fact, according to Denissen's <u>Genealogy of the French Families of the Detroit River Region</u>... and other resources, Joseph II had two sons named Joseph born 27 years apart in 1759 and 1776, and died 11 years apart in 1805 and 1816.

Brush Family

Unknown
    Nathaniel (see below)
    Alexander - m. Ruth Fay Lyman (d. aft March 1, 1837), dau
        of Dr. Jonas Fay; April 20, 1780
        d. July 15, 1815; Madrid, New York
        Children
                Ebenezer - b. November 19, 1780; Bennington
                    Vermont
                    r. Potsdam, Franklin County, New York
                    m. Susanna Fay, dau of Dr. Jonas Fay;
                    August 18, 1805
                Mary - m. Meigs
    ?Josiah - b.c. 1747; Huntington, Long Island, New York
        r. April, 1777; Bennington, Vermont
        m. Betsey ____ (b.c. 1757 d. September 5, 1837);
        November, 1773; Bennington, Vermont
        d. August 11, 1832
        Children
                Ruth - m. Danforth of St. Albans, Vermont
                Betsey - m. Webster
                Esther
                Smith
                Eppenetus
                Joshua
                Josiah

Nathaniel Brush (Col.)
    m. Samantha Parker
    Children
        Elijah (see below)

Elijah Brush
    b. Bennington, Vermont; 1772
    m. Adelaide Askin (b. 1779 or 1783 d. July 26, 1859);
    February 17, 1802
    d. February 3, April 1, or December 4, 1814
    Children
        Edmund (see below)
        Charles - b. December 6, 1804
            d. February 7, 1807
        Charles Reuben - b. April 25, 1807
            bpt. August 1, 1807; Detroit, Michigan
            m. Jane C. Forsyth, dau of Robert Forsyth and
            Jane Little; October 15, 1833
        John Alfred - b.c. 1811
            bpt. February 23, 1816; Assumption Church,
            Sandwich, Ontario
        Archange - b. March 21, 1813
            bpt. February 23, 1816

Edmund Askin Brush
    b. November 21, 1802
    bpt. April 10, 1803; Detroit, Michigan
    m. Elisabeth Cass Hunt (b. August 20, 1825; Detroit,
    Michigan), dau of John Elliot Hunt and Mary Sophia
    Spencer; August 6, 1845; Maumee City, Ohio
    d. July 10, 1877; Grosse Pointe, Michigan
    Children
        Adelaide Mary - b. May 12, 1846

m. William G. Thompson (b. July 23, 1842;
Lancaster, Pennsylvania d. July 19, 1904;
Yonkers, New York bur. July 23, 1904;
Princeton, New Jersey); June 5, 1867
d. May 10, 1876
Edmund b. March 6, 1848
d. November 15, 1865
Alfred Erskine - b. February 14, 1850; Detroit,
Michigan
m. Isabella Rowena Hunt, dau of John Elliott
Hunt and Virginia T. Mitchell; April 17, 1878
d. November 14, 1903; Detroit, Michigan
Children
Virginia Heloise
Alfred Erskine
Elliott Hunt - b. October 21, 1852; Detroit,
Michigan
d. January 29, 1877; Santa Barbara, California
Elisabeth Cass - October 2, 1854; Detroit, Michigan
d. by 1877, Grosse Pointe, Michigan

In England, vast areas of open, uncultivated land, grown over with heather and brush, begat names like "Brush." The infamous Tory Crean Brush (see Appendix) from Pennsylvania could have been related to this Brush family.

Elijah Brush was supposedly born in Bennington, Vermont, in 1772, the son of Nathaniel and Samantha (Parker) Brush. But according to Records of the Governor and Council of the State of Vermont, Col. Nathaniel Brush did not arrive in Bennington until 1775. Most likely either the 1772 birth date was wrong, or Elijah was a small child when his parents moved to Bennington and it was not his birthplace.

There were other named Brush in Bennington at the same time. Nathaniel's brother and Revolutionary War soldier Alexander Brush (W 15825, BLW 19606-160-55) married Ruth Fay Lyman at Bennington, Vermont on April 20, 1780.

Another possible brother of Nathaniel's was Josiah Brush (b.c. 1747) who claimed in his Revolutionary War Pension application (W 20789) that he had moved to Bennington, Vermont in 1777 from his Huntington, Long Island birthplace. However, he supposedly had married in November of 1773 in Bennington. His 1837 application listed Ruth, Betsey, Esther, Smith, Eppenetus, Joshua and Josiah Brush as his children.

If Josiah was a brother, then the family was probably descended from Thomas or Richard, English sons of Thomas Brush. The brothers emigrated first to Southold, Long Island; and then, Huntington, Long Island (see Appendix). Many from this family were driven from Long island by the British because of their rebel associations during the American Revolution.

The town of Bennington, Vermont received its grant on January 3, 1748/50. It was the first town granted by Gov. Benning Wentworth of New Hampshire after it became independent from Massachusetts. Vermont has a Brush Stream in Chittenden County and a Brush Hill in Lamoille County. Both were named after early families in the area.

On August 30, 1777, "Colonel Brush" was in charge of a company at Bennington. Nathaniel Brush was the commander of the town militia for the Battle of Bennington, acted as probate judge a number of years between 1781 and 1794; and served as clerk of courts between 1787 and 1803. In Vermont records, Nathaniel declined a legislative appointment to the "committee of pay table" on December 19, 1781.

Elijah arrived in Detroit shortly after the British vacated it. In 1802, he married Adelaide (Alice) Askin, the only one of John Askin's children to marry an American. And because Elijah was an American, they lived on the Detroit side of the river.

The couple eventually purchased what would become known as the Brush Farm. According to Burton, the farm was a ribbon farm, a type of French farm that had a major influence on the eventual arrangement of streets in what would become modern Detroit.

The Brush Farm, legally known as "Private Claim 1", had a frontage on the river of about 386 feet and ran inland nearly a mile and a half. The farm laid immediately east of the Kings Commons.

Originally the front portion had been owned by the Eustache Gamelin who received it from the governor-general of New France in 1747 for military services. The rear concession was given to Jacques Pilet in 1759 for the same reason. Pilet then purchased Gamelin's portion. After Pilet's death, the Barthe and, finally, the Askin families became owners. When John Askin moved his family across the river to Ontario, his daughter Adelaide and her husband Elijah moved to the farm.

There were problems within the family. Commodore Grant wrote to John Askin that Askin's son-in-law Elijah Brush "took umbrage at Gross Point at Mrs. Grant (Adelaide's aunt) & cursed and sowrn at the Point some says at Mrs. Grant. She says (she) never showed more attention to any man than she did to him when there. Donovan was with him when there. I asked Donovan what could offend Mr. B. the only thing irritate him because there was not some fine cherrybounce Mrs. G. had formerly produced. last year the cherrys failed."

For a number of years the Brush family lived in the house at Brush Farm without actually purchasing it. On March 22, 1805, John Askin told Elijah Brush that he could not continue to make repairs to Elijah's farm. Askin continued, continue "I wish it possible for you to purchase the place for I fear unless something fortunate turns up in spite of all I can do I will have to sell it at last to pay Messrs. James & Andrew McGill 2000 (pounds) nearly Hfx Curcy. I owe them."
Askin had been paying 200 pounds annual interest and wanted to "get rid of the debt." But since the place had originally belonged to his father-in-law, John did not want the farm to leave the family. So although Askin had hoped to get 2000 pounds "NY Cury" for the place, he was willing to sell the place to Brush for 1000 pounds "Hfx".

In the return letter, Elijah explained to his father-in-law that he had
"Some Serious ideas of removing into the Ohio Country which (was) the reason I (had) never attempted a purchase before ... and (was) still under the impression that before long (he would) leave."
Elijah suggested he take over the 200 pound interest payment his father-in-law was making until Elijah decided whether or not to sell his Ohio Country property.

Askin apparently agreed to that arrangement and Elijah eventually made his decision. On July 5, 1806, Askin reported that Brush had "gone sometime ago into the States" in order to sell lands there that he owned. On October 31, 1806, Elijah finally purchased the farm from John Askin for $6000. The farm was described on the bill of sale as "lying mostly in what is now called the New Town of Detroit." Alick Askin witnessed the sale.

Elijah Brush owned extensive amount of land in addition to the farm abutting the Kings Commons and the land near the Ohio River. But in March, 1808, Elijah couldn't pay John Askin the $160 he owed him until Governor Hull paid Brush the $1420 he owed Brush. Then, in 1809, Elijah appeared to have more financial difficulties. Elijah apparently decided lots 13, 14, 15, and 16; which he purchased 4 years previously; were no longer worth the money and offered Todd and McGill, the previous owners, "new & unreasonable terms." In August, Todd and McGill made alternate proposals.

Elijah Brush was one of Detroit's first American lawyers. And in that capacity, he handled the estates of a number of area residents, in addition to representing his in-laws in various legal matters. Askin referred to his son-in-law as a "warm hearted fellow" and described Elijah as a
"regular, industrious man and except for improvements is by no means extravagant for a man who earns so much by his profession ... His practice is worth a great deal."
Askin frequently quoted Brush in his correspondence. In 1804, Elijah was handling debt collection for his father-in-law. Then according to an 1809 letter from John Askin, Jr., Brush managed to obtain 640 acres of land on the Michigan side for John Askin, Jr.

John, Sr. sent his youngest son Alexander David Askin to Elijah "to learn the Profession of a Lawyer." When questioned as to why, John Sr. answered he considered "Mr. Brush's professional knowledge at least equal to any Lawyer." But John did admit he was concerned because by not working for and learning from a Canadian lawyer, Alexander would not be able to plead cases in Ontario.

But Brush wielded a great deal of influence in the affairs of Detroit and of Michigan. He was elected trustee for Detroit in 1803 and served as Michigan's territorial treasurer beginning in 1806.

At the outbreak of the War of 1812, Elijah Brush had seven brothers-in-law and ten nephews fighting for the British. But Elijah became a Colonel in the First Regiment of Michigan Volunteer, the Michigan territorial militia. At the same time, there was a Capt. Henry Brush fighting with the Americans at the River Raisin, south of Detroit. But a relationship to Elijah has not been determined.

According to Burton, after the surrender of General Hull in February, 1813, Elijah was paroled and left for Ohio, leaving his wife Adelaide (Alice) and three sons with his father-in-law at Strabane. Burton claimed Elijah died in Ohio without his family ever seeing him again. But The Valley of the Lower Thames reported that Elijah took his family with him to Ohio for their protection.

To understand what really happened, information was gathered from letters written at the time by various members of the Askin and Brush families. That correspondence made the true story was clear. In an August 11, 1812 letter to John Askin, Sr., Elijah wrote
"I am going to send my family to reside at Mr. Meldrums. I know not what may be the destany of this country. my family are dear to my heart. will you received some money in Keeping for them. and if so, would you prefer to have it in bills on our Government, or Cincinnati Bank notes as to specie there is none here"
In July, 1813, Elijah's wife Adelaide Brush wrote to her mother that she was with "American friends."

In September, 1812, Elijah wrote to his father-in-law asking for advice about charges brought against him. He swore "there never was a greater falsehood." Supposedly the charges were that Elijah was "in favor of the capitulation" of Detroit.

In a March, 1813 letter, Charles wrote that Edmund Brush, son of Elijah, had told him that Elijah
"was obliged to go down to Kingston before he was allowed to stay at Queenston and go to Niagara when he pleased, and those who came down under similar circumstances were hardly allowed to walk the Streets of Niagara ... for what reason I cannot say."
Later in the letter, Charles suggested Elijah might not return to Detroit.

As early as July 31, 1810, the family had concerns about Elijah's health. At that time, John Askin, Sr. wrote
"Alice & child very well, but Brush not able to walk about from a severe fit of the gout - the rest of the family well."
Then either a new illness surfaced or the old one continued, because on December 26, 1812, Mrs. McKee wrote to her father that she hoped Brush was getting better. She added, "I pity poor Alice with my whole heart. I hope the children are well.

One year later, in December 1813, and after Elijah had been required to go to Niagara; he was again reported as seriously ill. And finally, on February 3, 1814, Isaac Todd wrote to John Askin, Sr. "you have lately felt ... the loss ... I am told (of) Mr. Brush."

A number of Burton's claims concerning Elijah's life and death were proven wrong by the Askin family correspondence during the time. For instance, concerning Burton's contention that after Hull's February surrender, Elijah was paroled and left for Ohio; Edmund Brush revealed that in reality his father had been sent to Kingston, then Queenston and, finally, Niagara by March 8, 1813.

Burton claimed that after Hull's February, 1813 surrender, Elijah sent his family to stay with John Askin. But in reality, Elijah had sent his family with the Meldrum family on August, 11, 1812. Then Adelaide wrote to her parents that she was with "American friends" in July, 1813.

And finally, Burton claimed that after February, 1813, Elijah never saw his family again. However, on November 12, 1813, John Askin, Sr. wrote that Brush, his wife and children contacted him every 2 to 3 days, suggesting that Elijah was with his wife and children.

After Elijah's death, the Brush family continued to prosper. The Valley of the Lower Thames reported that in 1832, an Edward P. Hall opened a private school "at Erieus in Raleigh" in a school building previously occupied by a Mr. Brush." So one of Elijah's children might have become a teacher.

Elijah named two sons Charles. The fate of the first Charles Brush was described in a January 31, 1807 letter sent from James Askin to Charles Askin at Queenston when Charles Brush was just three years old. James wrote
"Poor Nancy McKee and Charles Brush were much burnt, the former by her Cloaths taking fire & latter falling in a Kettle of Scalding Water. however there is no danger to their lives."
Although James had written there was no danger to their lives, on February 7, 1807, just eight days after James' letter, the first Charles Brush died.

Edmund was Elijah and Adelaide's eldest son, born just nine months after their marriage. He was educated at Hamilton College and, like his father, studied the law. While still a very young man Edmund assumed management of his father's estate. He managed to keep the farm in tact and leased out parcels to tenants. Through the years, Edmund served as Detroit's water commissioner (1852-68), police commissioner (1863-4), "grades" commissioner (1854-61), and city planner (1857-69). When Edmund died, he was worth several million dollars.

Burton described Edmund Brush as having "great will power and marked individuality of character and temperment."

He married Elizabeth Cass Hunt, niece of Governor Cass and they had five children. However, only one, Alfred E. Brush, survived his father.

Burns Family

A number of Byrn / Byrnes / Burn / Burne / Burns family members could have been related to the families of these genealogies. Most were Irish settlers who were attracted to the New World by posters stuck to cottage walls by passenger brokers. They sailed from Limerick, Galway, Cork, and even Liverpool to escape the famine. The final "s" was frequently added to short names to aid pronunciation or as a sign of plural.

In 1826, a Mary Burns married John Stone and an Ann Burns married Robert Stone. Both couples moved from Leeds, Canada to Orford, Ontario, near the Samuel Burns family of these genealogies.

Then, an Alexander Burns became the paymaster for the Queens Rangers on May 17, 1799. In October and November, 1801 Alexander was serving at Amherstburg.

And between 1791 and 1795, at the recommendation of Gov. Simcoe, David Burns served as surgeon for the Queens Rangers. By February 15, 1806, David had died in Toronto leaving "a considerable library".

The Captain Burns who fought with the Queen's Rangers and was wounded at the Battle of Brandywine could have been either Alexander or David above. Or he could have been the James Burns, a Loyalist who eventually received a soldiers land grant at Niagara.

Donald Whyte, in his <u>Dictionary of Scottish Emigrants to Canada before Confederation</u>, listed a different David Burn, a Northumberland County, Ontario merchant who died on March 2, 1840; and Rev. John Burns, a pastor who emigrated from Fenwick, Argyll, Scotland to Ontario in 1803.

According to Denissen, James and Mary Cowens Burns had a son named Hugh Burns who was baptized in Detroit in 1830. He also noted Patrick and Mary Delahanty Burns from Ireland who had a daughter named Catherine who was baptized in Detroit in 1818.

A William Burn managed Lord Selkirk's land in Canada. He had been sent from England in 1802 to head up the Baldoon settlement near present day Wallaceburg. However, sometime between a February 1, 1804 letter to John Askin and September 5, 1804, William Burn died.

Alexander Grant referred to a "Colonel Burns" in a May 6, 1808 letter he wrote to John Askin.

At least one Burns family settled in Chatham. In 1841 there was a Burns Boot and Shoe Shop. And in 1848, James Burns was the vice-president of Chatham's Temperance society.

Robert Burns, a clergyman from Borrowstounness, Linlithgowshire, Scotland died in Toronto in 1869. And yet another Robert Burns was a Canadian jurist who was born at Niagara in 1805.

Any of these might have been related to either of the two Burns families discussed here. The proof of relationship has not been uncovered.

Burns Family I

Samuel Burns Family

Samuel Burns I
    b.c. 1784
    m. Ann (pos) Sawyer (d. betw 1851-1861)
    d. betw 1861-1871
    Children
        Caroline (see below)
        Elizabeth - b.c. 1828
          m. Arnold
        Samuel II - b. 1830
          m. Catherine Johnson/Johnston (1838-1906; Windsor, Ontario, Canada) dau of Francis and Sarah (Chittick) Johnson/Johnston of Enniskellen County, Fermanagh, Ireland
          d. 1890's
          bur. Trinity Anglican Church, Howard Township, Ontario
          Children (10)
             Maggie - m. Galloway
        Nancy - m. Jacob Ward; November 28, 1844
          d. aft 1896
        Margaret - m. William Teetzel; January 14, 1846

Caroline Burns
    b. July 29, 1818; Orford; Upper Canada
    m. Truman Landon (c. 1810-1856), c. 1840
    d. June 2, 1906; Highgate, Ontario
    bur. Gosnell Cemetery, Highgate, Ontario
    Children
        Joseph Sawyer - b. 1842
          m. Harriet Ann Askins (1839-1920)
          d. May 1, 1886
             Children (see Landon)
        Margaret - b. 1843
        Edna - b. 1845
          d. aft 1896
        William - b. 1850
        Nancy - b. 1853
          m. Charles H. Holman (c.1847-1930)
          d. 1910
          Children
             Ann - m. Charles Forsyth of Rodney
               r. Aldborough Twp., Elgin County, Ontario
             Edna - m. Thomas Ford of Duart, Orford Twp., Ontario
               Children

Neil	Althea
Pearl	Clifford
William	?Joyce?
Lila	

             Thomas - r. Highgate, Ontario
               Children

Matilda	Mary
Thomas	John
William	

             George - r. Dearborn, Michigan
             Truman - r. Highgate, Ontario

```
        dau - m. J.H. McLean
            r. Ord City, Nebraska, United States
        Lizzie - m. Stritch of Detroit, Michigan
        Bertha - m. Joseph Lauzon of Woodslee
        Albert - r. Woodslee
            d. aft 1930
```

Samuel Burns may have emigrated from Carlow County,
Ireland. Carlow was a flat area drained by the Barrow and
Slaney Rivers bordering the Blackstairs Mountains, in
southeastern Ireland.

But that birthplace is doubtful. While later censuses
indicated an Irish origin, many researchers believe Samuel was
actually born at sea.

Or he may have been the Samuel Burns who landed in
America in 1805, or the one who landed in New York in 1811.
But if Samuel was born at sea as was noted in the 1861 census,
his name would not have appeared on any ship registry It
should have been listed under his father's name or not at all,
but definitely not as a separate entry.

The family in this genealogy may have even been related
to a Dutch family in Schenectady, New York (see Appendix).

Several researchers have suggested that after landing in
New England, Samuel went on to Brockville, Leeds County,
Ontario, before ending up in Clearville. And Truman Landon
suggested that for a time the Samuel Burns' family might have
resided in Lansdowne, Ontario; like his Clearville neighbors.
As evidence, Landon reported that a number of Burns were
buried in the Lansdowne Cemetery.

Wherever he came from, Samuel and his young wife Ann
became one of the first three families to settle in Clearville
after its 1816 founding as part of Col. Thomas Talbot's
development. Talbot surveyed and slashed trails through the
impassable forest. In 1816, Talbot Road was first constructed
as a trail. Most of Talbot's early settlers were Scotch or
Irish who came under sail before walking the last 150-250
miles. Others came up Lake Erie on board rough boats.

Orford was in what was originally known as the "Western
Division"; then Suffolk County; and, finally, Kent County,
Ontario.

According to Landon, the family settled in Clearville
across the road from Baldwin's Inn on lot 58 NTR (north side
of Talbot Road) sometime in 1816 or 1817. Years later the
Samuel Burns home also served as an inn. But in those early
years Samuel was a farmer.

Later, when Robert, William, and James Ruddle established
the village of Antrim in Howard Township on Lake Erie in 1837.
Samuel Burns was one of the first purchases of land at Antrim.
Morpeth was 10 miles west of Clearville on Talbot road and
Antrim was 3 miles southwest of Morpeth. But few other parcels
of land were sold and in 1846 the Ruddle partnership was
dissolved. After the harbour filled in with sand and the
railroad made Ridgetown the commercial center of Howard

Township; Antrim disappeared altogether. Although Samuel owned the land at Antrim, records seem to indicate he never lived there.

Francis Phillips suggested that Samuel's wife might have been Ann Sawyer. Granted, the Sawyer name continued through the family after that. But there was no record kept of Ann's maiden name. Since Caroline was born in 1818 and Samuel arrived in Clearville in 1816/1817, most likely Samuel and Ann were married prior to their arrival in the area. If they were married after Samuel's arrival in Clearville, their marriage was probably performed by one of the circuit riders who came to the area every three or four weeks. Many such marriages were not recorded.

And birth certificates for Ontario only went back to 1869. Some churches kept baptismal records. But the earliest church in the Clearville area was not established until 1844. In early census records Sam and Ann were listed as members of the "Free Church". But later Samuel's children were listed as Wesleyan Methodist.

On May 12, 1827, Samuel purchased one share in the new school. He paid "3 shilling 7 pense in Merchantable produce" and agreed to pay an additional $30 annually in produce for the teacher's salary. The first teacher was George Biggs and school was held irregularly in winter. Samuel's children attended that school.

In the 1861 census Samuel was living with his widowed daughter Nancy Ward and was listed as a 75-year-old widower. However, 10 years earlier, in 1851, Samuel had been listed as 70, only 5 years younger. By 1871 Samuel no longer appeared in the censuses. Frances Phillips reported she thought she read somewhere that Samuel had died of consumption.

In the 1861 census, his son Samuel II was listed as an innkeeper. Samuel II's wife Catherine and he were buried in the Trinity Anglican Church Cemetery in Howard Township.

Samuel I's daughter Caroline was born July 29, 1818 as the first white female born in Orford township. She married Truman Landon. He has been called the first teacher in Highgate. However, the school he taught in was in Orford township. They lived in the area until 1851 when Caroline and Truman removed to Orangeville. Truman died there in 1856 and Caroline and her small family returned to her family home in Orford.

In the 1861 census, Caroline was listed as an innkeeper, probably keeping Burns Inn with her brother Samuel II. Although the inn has survived to modern times, it was moved about 100 yards north of the original site in the early 1900's. In 1851 and 1871 she was listed as a Wesleyan Methodist. Then, in 1869, a C. Landon was listed as a cabinetmaker in Clearville in Lovell's Directory.

Caroline outlived her husband, her sisters, her brother, and her son Joseph. In her advanced years she lived with her daughter-in-law, Joseph's widow. According to an old clipping from the <u>Highgate Monitor</u> (see Appendix), Caroline had 25 grandchildren and 18 great grandchildren in 1896. She was living with Joseph's wife Harriet Ann in the police village of Highgate, Ontario, when she died on June 2, 1906 at age 87. Her occupation was listed as "old lady". She was buried in the Gosnell Cemetery, Highgate, Ontario.

Burns Family II

Nicholas Burns Family

Nicholas Burns
- m. Janet Maude? on board ship to Canada
- r. Erin Township, Ontario
- Children
  - Melinda (adopted) - b. November 19, 1862; Westminster Township, Ontario
    - m. Alex Anderson
    - d. February 13, 1888
    - Children
      - dau - b/d December 21, 1862
  - William - d. young, Westminster Township, Ontario
  - James L. - b. March 14, 1865; Westminster Township, Ontario
    - d. May 20, 1865
  - Jane Maude - b. May 3, 1868; London, Ontario
    - d. 1881
  - Ida "Maercy" Louise - b. December 17, 1869; London, Ontario
    - d. 1881
  - Florence Mary - b. September 13, 1874; London, Ontario
    - m. Dr. Anson Jones; December 16, 1896
  - Sarah Ethel - b. November 25, 1879; London, Ontario
    - m. Dr. Frank Plewes; November 25, 1903

James Burns, son of Nicholas and Janet, was a schoolteacher and accountant in London, Ontario, Canada. As a Wesleyan Methodist, his family resided first on the southern part of concession 1, Lot 7, and then art 26 Craig Street in Westminster Township, London, Ontario, Canada.

Two of James' daughters, Ida and Jane, died in a ship disaster on the Thames River on Victoria Day, 1881.

Campau/Campeau/Campault Family

Leonard Campau
   b. France
   m. Frances Mauger
   Children
      Etienne (see below)

Etienne Campau
   b. 1638; prob La Rochelle, France
   m. Catherine Pauls (b. 1646; St. Nicholas, La Rochelle,
   France bur. April 16, 1721; Montreal, Quebec), dau of
   Pierre Pauls and Rene Cordelette; November 26, 1663;
   Montreal, Quebec
   d. by 1721, Canada
   Children
      Jacques (see below)
      Etienne - b. September 2, 1664
         m. Jane Foucher (b. 1669 bur October 9, 1745;
         Montreal Quebec), dau of Louis Foucher and
         Helena Damours
         bur. September 8, 1723
      Marie - b. November 24, 1665
         m1. Nicholas Le Pileur (b. 1656; St. Laurent,
         Paris, France), son of Nicholas Le Pileur and
         Guilemette Gouin; December 2, 1684
         m2. Stephen Debien (b. 1691 bur. October 19,
         1708; Montreal, Quebec), son of Denis Debien
         and Susanne ____; January 12, 1710
         m3. Julian Perusie dit Baquette (b. St.
         Pierre, Tulles, Limousin, France), son of Jean
         Perusie and Antoinette Percale; July 12, 1710;
         Montreal, Quebec
      Michael - b. June 14, 1667; Montreal, Quebec
         m. Jeanne Mace/Masse (b. April 25, 1677 bur.
         September 5, 1764; Detroit, Michigan), dau of
         Martin Masse and Jane Decours; January 7,
         1696; Montreal, Quebec
         Children
            Infant - b. March 26, 1697; Montreal,
            Quebec
               bur. March 26, 1697; Montreal,
               Quebec
            Jane - b. February 6, 1698
               m. Andrew Marsil (b. 1683 bur. April
               13, 1740; Longueuil), son of Andrew
               Marsil dit L'Espagnol and Mary
               Margaret Lefebvre; February 3, 1718
            Michael - b. February 25, 1700; Montreal,
            Quebec
               bur. February 28, 1700; Montreal,
               Quebec
            Anthony - b. January 1, 1702
            Margaret - b. November 2, 1703; Montreal,
            Quebec
               bur. November 4, 1703; Montreal,
               Quebec
            Mary Ann - b. November 1, 1704; Montreal,
            Quebec
               bur. November 3, 1704; Montreal,
               Quebec

Lt. Michael II - b. January 22, 1706;
Montreal, Quebec
m. Marie Josephine Batear/Buteau (b. June
24, 1722; Detroit, Michigan), dau of
Pierre Batear and Magdelene Chavaudier;
February 7, 1740; Detroit, Michigan
bur. September 26, 1764
Children
Jane - b. July 28, 1741
d. young
Michael III - b. February 23, 1743
Mary Joseph - b. February 10, 1745;
Detroit, Michigan
Peter - b. March 4, 1747
Charles - b. July 16, 1749; Detroit,
Michigan
bur. March 11, 1826; Detroit,
Michigan
Anthony James - m. January 28, 1788
Teresa - b. July 3/31, 1754; south
coast of Detroit River
Frances Rene - b. July 16,   1761
Mary Jane - b. June 25, 1764
Margaret - b. March 2, 1708; Detroit, Michigan
Paul Alexander - b. September 14, 1709
Mary Ann - b. December 26, 1712
m. Peter Belleperche (b. September 15,
1699; Quebec bur. January 13, 1767;
Detroit, Michigan), wid of Angelica
Esteve dit La Jeunesse, son of Denis
Belleperche and Gertrude Guyon de
Buisson; March 20, 1734; Detroit,
Michigan
bur. November 20, 1796; Assumption
Church, Sandwich, Ontario
Charles - b. October 20, 1715
m1. Mary Catherine St. Aubin; October 1,
1751
m2. Mary Charlotte Juillet dit Montreuil/
Montrey; January 8, 1754; Detroit,
Michigan
Children

Mary Louisa	Mary Jane
Bridget	Charles
Mary	Catherine Francis
Josette	Infant
Charlotte	Margaret
Teresa	Rosalie
Mary Ann	

John - b. December, 1668
bur. December 4, 1668
Catherine - b. November 27, 1669
m. Francis Blau (b. 1641; La Trinite, Falaise,
Seez, France bur December 22, 1718; Montreal,
Quebec), wid of Elisabeth Benoit, son of
Francis Blau and Ann Sautin; December 1, 1685
Francis - b. October 18, 1671
m. Magdelene Brossard; January 28, 1698
bur. June 2, 1741
Children
Francis - b. May 30, 1699

Catherine - b. January 14, 1674
m. Peter Hay (b. 1661; Auxerres, Bourgogne, France bur. December 3, 1708; Montreal, Quebec), wid of Geneveva Benoit, son of Gabriel Hay and Catherine Baudoin.
Louisa - b. October 6, 1675
bur. December 20, 1730
Jane - b. June 1, 1679
m. Stephen Benoit dit Livernois (1662-1746), son of Paul Benoit dit Livernois and Elizabeth Gobinet; February 3, 1699; Montreal, Quebec
John Baptiste - b. March 16, 1681
m. Elizabeth Bernier (b. October 3, 1671 bur. February 2, 1747), wid of James Bietry, dau of Mathurin Bernier dit Marzelle and Jane Villain; October 25, 1705
Mary Elizabeth - b. June 20, 1683
m. Peter Valiquet, son of John Valiquet dit Laverdure and Renee Loppe
Agatha Barbara - b. February 27, 1685
m. Paul Chevalier (b. June 22, 1679; Pointe aux Trembles, Montreal, Quebec), son of James Chevalier and Jane Villain; June 1, 1705
Francois - b. November 12, 1686
m. Mary Ann Protot, 1704
Charles - b. December 27, 1688
bur. December 30, 1688

Jacques Campau I
b. May 31, 1677; Montreal, Quebec
m1. Jeanne Cecile/Cecilia Catin (b. August 26, 1681), sis of Nicholas Catin and dau of Henry Catin and Jane Brossard; December 1, 1699; Montreal, Quebec
bur. May 14, 1751; Detroit, Michigan
Children
Jean Louis (see below)
Henri - b. December, 1704; Montreal, Quebec
m. Margaret L'Huillier (b. March 1, 1709), dau of Charles Michall L'Huillier dit Chevalier and Margaret Renee Key; February 5, 1731; Montreal, Quebec
Children
William - b. January 9, 1734; Montreal, Quebec
Charlotte Joseph - b. November 13, 1747
m. Louis Amable Perthuis (b. December 27, 1729), wid of Catherine Joly and of Mary Catherine Giasson, son of Nicholas Perthuis and Louisa Chauvin; November 11, 1769
Mary Anne Cecilia - b. June 21, 1707; Montreal, Quebec
m. Joseph Douaire de Bondy (b. February 27, 1700; Montreal), son of James Douaire de Bondy and Magdelene Duplassis dit Gatineau; July 28, 1732; Detroit, Michigan
Mary Angelica - b. December 6, 1708; Detroit, Michigan
bur. July 1, 1720; Montreal, Quebec
Nicholas Campau dit Niagara - b. July, 1710; portage at Niagara, Ontario

bpt. by "voyageur"; August 4, 1710; Montreal,
Quebec
m. Agathe Casse dit St. Aubin (b. October 6,
1716; bur May 12, 1808; Detroit, Michigan),
dau of John Casse dit St. Aubin and Mary
Louisa Gaultier; September 4, 1737; Detroit,
Michigan
bur. December 16, 1756; Detroit, Michigan
Children
   Nicholas - b. November 13, 1737
      bur. November 17, 1737
   Mary Agatha - b. January 27, 1736
      m. Alexis Sequin dit Laderoute (b.
      1733), son of Joseph Sequin dit
      Laderoute and Frances Sauvage
   Nicholas - b. 1741
      d. 1743
   Angelica - b. September 16, 1742
      m. Anthony Louis Descomps dit
      Labadie (1730-1807); February 26,
      1759; Detroit, Michigan
      bur. December 11, 1767
      Children
         Mary Angelica - m. Pierre
         Drouillard; November 20,
         1776; Detroit, Michigan
   Catherine - b. January 4, 1744
      m. Rene Godet dit Marentette; March
      31, 1761
   Mary Ann - b. October 7, 1745; Detroit,
   Michigan
      m. Alexis Bienvenu dit Delisle
      (1740-1787); May 26, 1763
   Cecilia - b. December 17, 1747
      m1. Claude Leblond dit Dupont (b.
      1739); January 30, 1766
      m2. Pierre Chene (b. June 20, 1758;
      Northwest Coast of the Detroit
      River); February 23, 1784; Detroit,
      Michigan
   Nicholas Joseph - b. November 29, 1749;
   Detroit, Michigan
      bur. August 12, 1764
   Bernard - b. October 20, 1752; Detroit,
   Michigan
      m. Veronica Douaire de Bondy (1766-
      1819), dau of Joseph Douaire de
      Bondy and Marie Josephene Gamelin;
      February 23, 1784; Sandwich,
      Ontario, Canada
      Children
         Claude   Archange
         Monica   Henry
         Teresa   Nicholas
         Bernard
   Mary Jane - b. October 7, 1754; Detroit,
   Michigan
      bur. August 10, 1755; Detroit,
      Michigan
   Louis - d. young

Jean Baptiste - b. August 12, 1711; Montreal, Quebec
m. Catherine Perthuis (1718-1763), dau of Pierre Perthuis and Catherine Mallet; January 27, 1737; Detroit, Michigan
bur. June 12, 1783
Children
    Jean Baptiste - b. October 18, 1737
    Julia Catherine - b. February 22, 1739
        m. Jean "Chrysostom" Theriot dit Capucin (b. 1732)
    Hippolyte - b. May 13, 1741
        m. Mary Ann Louisa Pepin dit Descardonnets, wid of Peter Boyer, dau of Joseph Pepin dit Descardonnets and Angelica Robert; April 11, 1768
    Catherine - b. December 24, 1742; Detroit, Michigan
    bur. December 27, 1742
    Francis Basil - b. December 2, 1743; Detroit,Michigan
        m. Susanne Moran (bur. April 4, 1796), dau of Claude Charles Moran and Mary Ann Belleperche; February 7, 1785
    bur. October 16, 1795
    Mary Louisa - b. May 26, 1746; Detroit, Michigan
    bur. April 9, 1749
    Joseph Mary - b. March 29, 1749; Detroit, Michigan
    bur. - September 19, 1771; Detroit, Michigan
    Mary Ann - b. March 12, 1751; Detroit, Michigan
    bur. March 13, 1751; Detroit, Michigan
    James Philip - b. May 1, 1752; Detroit, Michigan
    bur. May 8, 1752; Detroit, Michigan
    Jane Mary - b. June 23, 1753; Detroit, Michigan
    Julian - b. September 10, 1755; Detroit, Michigan
    Mary Catherine - b. February 26, 1757; Detroit, Michigan
    bur. July 31, 1757
    Louis - b. March 6, 1758; Detroit, Michigan
    Mary Louisa - b. September 3, 176?, Northeast Coast of Detroit River
        m. Bernard Robert (b. August 9, 1756; Detroit, Michigan), son of Anthony Robert and Mary Louisa Becquemont; February, 8, 1796; Assumption, Ontario
        d. August 3, 1832 of Cholera
Teresa Cecilia - b. June 16, 1714; Detroit, Michigan

m. Frances Marsac (b. October 22, 1706 bur.
November 17, 1777; Detroit, Michigan), son of
Jacob Marsac de L'Omtrou/L'Obtrou and Teresa
David; May 19, 1734
bur. November 22, 1746; Detroit, Michigan
Children
        Paul - m. Marie Chene; December 20, 1779
Claude - b. August 25, 1715; Montreal, Quebec
    m. Catherine Casse dit St. Aubin (b. December
    25, 1720 bur. March 7, 1805), dau of John
    Casse dit St. Aubin and Mary Louisa Gaultier;
    January 22, 1742; Detroit, Michigan
    bur. May 31, 1787; Detroit, Michigan

Jean Louis (Louisan) Campau
    b. August 26, 1702; Montreal, Quebec
    m. Mary Louisa Robert (b. December 15, 1698; Lachine,
    Ontario bur. April 2, 1776; Detroit, Michigan), wid of
    John Francis Peltier, dau of Pierre Robert and Angelica
    Ptolome(e); January 7, 1724; Detroit, Michigan
    Children
        Jacques II (see below)
        Mary Louisa - b. November 28, 1725; Detroit,
        Michigan
            bur. December 1, 1725; Detroit, Michigan
        Cecilia - b. January 27, 1727; Detroit, Michigan
            bur. March 28, 1730; Detroit, Michigan
        Mary Teresa - b. February 7, 1729; Detroit, Michigan
            m. Charles Andrew Barthe (b. February 22,
            1722; Montreal, Quebec bur. March 16, 1786;
            Detroit, Michigan), son of Theophile Barthe
            and Charlotte Alavoine; April 24, 1747;
            Detroit, Michigan
            bur. June 13, 1765; Detroit, Michigan
            Children
                (see Barthe)
        Louis - b. October 13, 1731; Detroit, Michigan
            bur. September 9, 1747
        Francis - b. April 19, 1734
            m. Veronica Bourdeau (b. December 12, 1744;
            Laprairie), dau of Joseph Bourdeau and
            Margaret Guerin dit LaFontaune
            bur. March 29, 1803
            Children
                Infant - b./d. August 16, 1763; Detroit,
                Michigan
                Mary Veronica - b. August 23, 1764
                    bur. May 21, 1784; Detroit, Michigan
                Mary Archange - b. December 17, 1766
                    m. John Robert McDougall (b. June
                    30, 1764; January 26, 1786; Detroit,
                    Michigan
                    bur. December, 1821; Detroit,
                    Michigan
                Simon Charles - b. August 21, 1769
                    Children
                        Simon   Veronica   Teresa
                Mary Geneveva - b. August 18, 1771
                    m. Lambert Cuillerier dit Beaubien
                    (b. April 7, 1767 bur. September 25,
                    1819; Detroit, Michigan), son of

Jean Baptiste Cuillerier dit
Beaubien and Mary Ann Lootman dit
Barrois: August 25, 1788; Detroit,
Michigan
Henry - b. October, 1773; Northeast Coast
of the Detroit River
Children

Geneveva	Monica
Josette	Felicity
Teresa	Henry
Elizabeth	Archange
Anthony	Simon
Toussaint	

Charles - b. May 21, 1775; Northeast
Coast of the Detroit River
m. Jane Godet dit Marentette
Children

Jane	Charles
Veronica	Eugenia
Robert	Charles
Simon	Geneveva
Ann	Jean Baptiste
Lucy	

Mary Magdelene - b. August 17, 177?;
Northeast Coast of the Detroit River
m. Hippolyte Bernard (b. August 4,
1769), son of William Bernard;
January 28, 1799; Detroit, Michigan
bur. May 26, 1802
Claude b. February, 1778; Northeast Coast
of the Detroit River
Angelica - b. September 26, 1780;
Detroit, Michigan
m. Anselm Petite, son of Nicholas
Petite and Magdelene Lamothe;
October 23, 1804; Detroit, Michigan
Mary Felicity - b. 1782; Detroit,
Michigan
m. Charles Poupard dit Lafleur (b.
September 22, 1755; Detroit,
Michigan
bur. April 17, 1804; Detroit,
Michigan
Louis - b. October 8, 1783
bur. November 4, 1783; Detroit,
Michigan
Anthony - b. December 31, 1784
bur. October 19, 1808; Detroit,
Michigan
Veronica - b. August 6, 1786; Detroit,
Michigan
bur. December 24, 1786; Detroit,
Michigan
Jean Baptiste - b. June 14, 1743; Detroit, Michigan
m. Geneveva Godet dit Marentette (b. April 26,
1751; Detroit, Michigan), dau of James Godet
dit Marentette and Mary Louisa Baudry dit St.
Martin Desbuttes

Jacques (James) Campau II
b. March 30, 1735; Detroit, Michigan

77

m1. Catherine Menard (November 26, 1739 -1781/2), dau of
James Menard and Susanne Prenjean dit Prudhomme; August
17, 1761
m2. Mary Frances Navarre (b. January 9, 1735; Detroit,
Michigan), wid of George McDougall, dau of Robert Navarre
and Mary Lootman dit Barrois; January 5, 1784; Detroit,
Michigan
bur. February 17, 1789; Detroit, Michigan
Children
    Joseph (see below)
    Louis - b. July 26, 1767
        m. Therese Moran
        bur. May 13, 1834; Clinton River, Michigan
        Children
            Louis - b. August 11, 1791; Detroit,
            Michigan
                m1. Ann Knaggs (September 23, 1800 -
                April, 1824), dau of George Knaggs
                and Elizabeth Chene; 1818
                m2. Sophie Marsac; April 9, 1825;
                Detroit, Michigan
            Toussaint
            Antoine
            George
    Infant - b. October 18, 1763
        bur. October 19, 1763
    Mary Cecilia - b. September 11, 1764; Northeast
    Coast of the Detroit River
        m1. Thomas Williams (b. Albany, New York d.c.
        1785/86); May 7, 1781; Detroit, Michigan
        m2. James Lauson (b. December 3, 1760), son of
        Anthony Nicholas Lauson and Angelica
        Chevalier; May 1, 1790; Assumption, Sandwich,
        Ontario
        Children by Thomas Williams
            John R. Williams (Mayor of Detroit) - b.
            May 4, 1782
                m. Mary Mott of Albany, New York;
                1805
                d. October 20, 1854
    Jacques (James) III - b. February 7, 1766
        m. Susanna Cuillerier dit Beaubien (b. May 30,
        1769), dau of Jean Baptiste Cuillerier dit
        Beaubien and Mary Ann Lootman dit Barrois;
        November 26, 1789; Detroit, Michigan
        bur. October 5, 1838; Detroit, Michigan
        Children
            James - b. August 24, 1793; Detroit,
            Michigan
            Thomas - b. October 23, 1804; Detroit,
            Michigan
            Sophia - b. November 12, 1807; Detroit,
            Michigan
    Louis (Capt.) - b. July 28, 1767
        r. Grand Rapid, Michigan; 1820
        m. Teresa Moran (1770-1864), dau of Claude
        Charles Moran and Mary Ann Belleperche;
        October 26, 1789; Detroit, Michigan
        bur. May 13, 1834; "Cottrelluille", Michigan
        Children

                Theotiste - b. July 26, 1790; Detroit,
                    Michigan
                Louis - b. August 11, 1791; Detroit,
                    Michigan
                Mary Ann - b. February 20, 1794; Detroit,
                    Michigan
                Anthony - b. June 13, 1797; Detroit,
                    Michigan
                James - b. May 26, 1799; Detroit,
                    Michigan
                    m. Eulalie Rivard
                Appolonia - b. May 16, 1801; Detroit,
                    Michigan
                George - b. 1802
                Toussaint - b. October 11, 1811
        Nicholas - b. September 28, 1770
            d. young
        Toussaint - b. October 28, 1771
            bur. March 3, 1810; unmarried
        Nicholas - b. October 20, 1773
            bur. September 23, 1811
        Barnaby/Barnabas - b. June 12, 1775
            m1. Teresa Cicot, 1808
            m2. Archange McDougall
            d. October 8, 1845; Detroit, Michigan
        Catherine - b. June 13, 1779
            m. Louis Vessiere dit Laferte (b. June 30,
            1772); June 16, 1800; Detroit, Michigan
            bur. October, 17, 1854
        Denis - b. October 10, 1781; Detroit, Michigan
            m. Felicity de Jocaire dit Chabut; May 8,
            1812; Assumption, Sandwich, Ontario
            bur. December 19, 1818; Detroit, Michigan

Joseph Campau
    b. February 25, 1769; Northeast Coast of Detroit River
    m. Adelaide Dagneau Dequindre (b. August 21, 1788 bur.
    June 2, 1862), dau of Anthony Dagneau DeQuindre and
    Catherine Desrivieres de la Mordiere; May 18, 1808;
    Detroit, Michigan
    d. July 23, 1863; Detroit, Michigan
    bur. Elmwood Cemetery, Detroit, Michigan
    Children
        Child - b. April 27, 1809; Detroit, Michigan
            d. May 17, 1809; Detroit, Michigan
        Joseph - b. April 8, 1810; Detroit, Michigan
            d. btwn 1850-60, unmarried
        Adelaide - b. November 23, 1811; Detroit, Michigan
            bpt. January 27, 1812; Detroit, Michigan
            m. John Johnson; March 20, 1832; Assumption,
            Sandwich, Ontario
            d. February 14, 1864; Detroit, Michigan
        Daniel Joseph - b. November 18, 1813; Detroit,
            Michigan
            m. Mary Palms
        son - b. August 30, 1815; Detroit, Michigan
            bur. August 31, 1815; Detroit, Michigan
        Catherine - b. October 15, 1816; Detroit, Michigan
            m. Frances Palms (b. December 13, 1809;
            Antwerp, Belgium bur. November 27, 1886), wid
            of Martha Burnett, son of Ange Palms and

            Jeannette Catherine Peeters; November 26,
            1842; Detroit, Michigan
            d. 1880
    Denis Joseph - b. March 18, 1819; Detroit, Michigan
            bpt. October 5, 1819
            d. unmarried
            bur. August 18, 1878; Detroit, Michigan
    Jacques Joseph/James Edward - b. February 21, 1821;
            Detroit, Michigan
    Emilie - b. February 13, 1823
            m. George W. Lewis
            bur. February 15, 1864; Detroit, Michigan
    Theodore - b. April 26, 1825; Detroit, Michigan
            bpt. June 10, 1827; Detroit, Michigan
            m. Eleonora Lewis/Messels; March 24, 1852;
            Detroit, Michigan
    Matilda - b. June 8, 1827
            m. Eustache Chapoton (b. August 29, 1823;
            Detroit, Michigan bur. February 4, 1874;
            Detroit, Michigan), son of Eustache Chapoton
            and Judith Adelaide Serat dit Coquillard
            bur. September 6, 1871
    Timothy Alexander - b. September 10 or 17, 1829;
            Detroit, Michigan
            m. Millie Haworth

    Despite the various spellings (Campau/Campeau/Campault),
Campau will be used throughout this genealogy, except when
used in direct quotes.

    The family may have originated in LaRochelle, France.
However, William Etten claimed Etienne (Stephen) Campau, a
mason, arrived in Montreal, Canada, from Picardy in the
seventeenth century. Etienne was definitely in Canada by his
1663 marriage to Catherine Paulo of LaRochelle, France.
Etienne and Catherine resided at Ville Marie, Montreal, and
had fifteen children.

    Two of Etienne and Catherine's sons, Michael and Jacques,
took their families to Detroit. Michael was supposedly in
Detroit in 1703 when he got into trouble because he accused
another resident of setting the fort on fire. But <u>History of
Wayne County and the City of Detroit</u> related that in 1706
Jacques I, not Michael, accused Pierre Roquant dit La Ville of
having set the 1703 fire. Roquant was arrested and tried in
Quebec with Campau testifying. Roquant was found innocent and
Campau was fined 500 livres for bringing "groundless charges."

    Although that incident has been reported for both Michael
and Jacques I, it was definitely Jacques who was the toolsmith
who, in 1734, received a French land grant for Private Claim
18, or the Meldrum Farm. And Jacques became a farmer.

    According to <u>The Windsor Border Region</u>, Etienne's
grandson "Charles Campault" by his son Michael was granted 3
arpents by 40 arpents land in Detroit in 1749. And "in
consideration of work he has done on a farm and his marriage"
to Prudhomme's daughter, Charles received a ration from
September 14, 1752 to March 14, 1754. However, according to
most sources, on October 1, 1751, Charles married Mary
Catherine St. Aubin.

Jacques I and his wife Catherine had ten sons and two daughters. Quaife presented a translated version of a June, 1750 document in which Jacques Campau I was described as
"Jacques Campau, senior, habitant, living at Detroit, in the house of Desmouchelle, on Ste. Anne Street which house he names as his dwelling..."
The document reported that when Jacques became severely ill in the late 1740's, his eldest son Jean Louis helped pay expenses. For that help, Jacques I deeded the lot on Ste. Anne's Street in the fort to him. Jean Louis was already living in the house. Jacques died in 1751.

The History of Wayne County... described Jacques I's children "respectable citizens, honest and industrious people who left good names behind them when they died."

His son Nicholas was born to Jacques and Cecilia, at the Niagara portage in July, 1710. He became known as Nicholas Campau dit Niagara, with the sobriquet being derived from the circumstances of his birth at Niagara.

Niagara frequently did business with the Jesuit Mission. In fact, mission records from 1743 showed that Niagara delivered a total of 560 boards and planks from Meloche's mill. In December, 1747, de la Richardie noted that the next spring he would owe Niagara and "Charlot St. Aubin" 700 livres for a "frame barn, with roof and casing of sawn planks, and a threshing-floor," and for fencing de la Richardie's yard and garden.

On September 1, 1748 Niagara took charge of the mission's farm, agreeing to share all produce with the mission fathers. In exchange, the mission furnished the seed, livestock and 150 livres to build a house and a stable. Financial dealings concerning the farm continued even when Father Potier headed the mission for a short term.

On July 11, 1751, Father de la Richardie wrote that on that day
"Niagara, the farmer of The Huron mission at La point du Montreal has agreed to make, for the benefit of this mission, for The use of the animals belonging to it, 2 collars for The horses, with Their bridles; and a saddle, with the traces and other straps necessary for harnessing them to the cart the seed, or the plow. Also 2 yokes for 2 pairs of oxen, with The necessary straps for harnessing Them; and, finally 2 carts, one for wheat and The other for general purpose. All to be Delivered to the said Niagara's successor on The said farm, on The 1st of September next -on condition that Father de la richardie, the superior of the said mission, gives to Niagara his share of 2 bulls 2 years old, as well as of a heifer 15 months old; in consideration whereof Niagara will Deliver, at the aforesaid time, all The above mentioned, in good and due condition."
Later, de la Richardie added that
"Nicholas Campeau, otherwise called Niagara, shall at The end of his lease return The seed which Father de la Richardie and he have agreed upon, consisting of 15 minots of wheat, 6 of oats and 5 of pease, less a quarter

of a livre. The whole is to be taken from The share of the said Niagara."

A Mr. James took over the farm in September, 1751.

The mission farm was not the only land Niagara had. On May 28, 1759, Nicholas' widow Agathe, as her children's guardian, sought permission to sell land from Nicholas' estate.

His daughter Angelica Campau married Anthony Louis Decomps dit Labadie. After her death, Anthony took a Chippewa consort and, then, married Charlotte Barthe Reaume. From those thee relationships, Anthony fathered 23 children.

<u>Canadian Passports 1681-1752</u> reported that on May 22, 1729, a passport was requested by Jacques I's son "Henry Campault" of Detroit "de partir avec un canet equipe de 4 hommes" (to depart with a canoe equipped with 4 men).

Jesuit mission records dated 1743 listed "Claude de Campeau", another of Jacques I's sons, as earning 82 livres for "carting a boat-load of stone."

In 1749, Jacques I's son Jean Baptiste Campau purchased land east of the fort which he sold in 1750. It was known as Private Claim 15, or the Leib Farm. The entire farm eventually became Detroit's Mount Elliot Cemetery. Several times in 1750 he sold beef, probably from that farm, to the mission. He was listed simply as "Baptiste" in the 1762 census and was living "northeast of the River" between the Fort and Grosse Pointe on Lake St. Clair. Baptiste was 51 years old and had 11 people living in his home.

Jacques I's son Jean Louis Campau was also listed as living in the same area with seven people in his family. In addition, he had three acres south of the Detroit River between "the Ottawas Village and River Canard." But no one lived on that piece of land.

On July 5, 1734, Jean Louis had received Private Claim 733, or the Chene Farm, as a land grant. Then Jean Louis' son Jacques II purchased Private Claim 91, a farm originally belonging to Pierre Esteve. During the Battle of Bloody Run in 1763, Major Rogers and his troops took refuge in Jacques Campau II's house, described in <u>The History of Wayne County...</u> as "a well-built dwelling from which a stout defence could be maintained." Although Burton claimed the battle took place at the home of Jacques I, the father of Jean Louis, rather than son, the elder Jacques died in 1751 and the battle occurred in 1763.

On September 8, 1766, Jacques Campau II sold to Pierre Javerais dit Laderoute 3 by 40 arpents opposite Turkey Island between the Suzor and Bonaventure Reaume properties in exchange for land on the other side of the river. Father Louis had given Jacques II the land, although Prudhomme had been the original grantee.

At age 28, Jacques Campau II was an officer in the militia for Detroit's northeast coast. In Detroit Notarial

Records, liber A, page 187, dated August 27, 1764, there appeared Jacques II's appointment to captain which read "Having special confidence in your attachment to his Majesty George the third and the interest of the English. I do hereby constitute and appoint you Capt. of Militia to be raised in the District of Detroit." Then in 1770 Jacques II was Marguill er compatable (treasurer) of Ste. Anne's Church in Detroit.

In the 1779 census, Jacques Campau II and his wife had one young woman, and six boys in their family. In addition, they owned one male and one female slave.

When his daughter Marie Cecilia married Thomas Williams of Albany, New York; they were married by the military commandant, not a priest, because Thomas Williams was not Catholic. Eventually, Thomas became a merchant, trader, court justice, public records keeper and notary, and one of Detroit's most prominent citizens.

Thomas and Marie Cecilia Campau Williams had a son, John R. Williams. In 1802, John R. became an employee of his uncle Joseph Campau and by July 20th of that year became his business partner. At Fort Erie, while returning from a business trip to Montreal on October 1, 1802, John R. shot Jacques Lacelle, another young Detroit merchant. According to Quaife, Lacelle recovered but sued Williams for $3000. Although that jury ruled in Williams favor, criminal court found John R. guilty and sentenced him to one year in an Upper Canada prison beginning in 1804. Later he served as trustee for Detroit, in 1807 as justice of the peace, and in 1817 as adjutant general of the militia.

When John R. Williams ran for congress in 1823, Father Gabriel Richard ran against him. Williams fumed and wrote a broadside which read "calling upon the priest to attend to his clerical duties and to leave political offices alone..." Richard was elected to congress and Williams left the church.

Although the incident had a negative effect on his religious beliefs, it did not hinder his political ambitions. He became Detroit's first mayor in 1824.

Jacques II's son Barnabas Campau purchased Belle Isle (Hog Island) from David Macomb on March 3, 1817, for $5000. And another son, Louis married Therese Moran and settled on the Clinton River. It appeared that Louis spent few months in school. But then, according to A Citizen's History of Grand Rapids, Michigan, his uncle Joseph took Louis at age eight as a sort of under servant or apprentice.

At age 21, Louis Campau joined the French-American military and fought in the War of 1812 against the British eventually attaining the rank of captain. But before that, he served in General William Hull's army under Captain Rene de Marsac. Hull was the general who surrendered Detroit to the British.

After the war, Louis worked again for his uncle selling goods to and buying fur from the Indians of the Saginaw

Valley. In 1819 Louis was put in charge of negotiations between the Indians and territorial governor Lewis Cass.

After his second marriage Louis Campau sold his business to his brother Antoine and moved south to the Shiawassee River and set up a trading post near present-day Owosso.

Then in 1826 Louis moved west from the Shiawassee, arriving at the "grand rapids" of the Grand River where he had been licensed to set a trading post. In Spring, 1827, he erected the trading post and a house. That was the beginning of the city of Grand Rapids, Michigan. Through the years, Louis became quite wealthy.

Louis' uncle Joseph who helped start him on his way to success, was the Joseph Campau who became a major force in Detroit. He had been educated in Montreal and was fluent in both English and French. In his biography of Joseph, Robert Ross described him in his later years as a "six-footer, spare, wrinkled, clean shaven, white haired and dark complexioned."

In The History of Wayne County... Joseph was described as "frugal, honest, diligent and foresighted. He was able to invest in large parcels of land," which led to a successful trading business.

After Campau's house was destroyed by fire in 1805, he rebuilt on the same lot. In fact, after the fire Joseph purchased a number of lots in the area of his home. That was the beginning of his eventual vast real estate holdings including a lot he purchased for 600 pounds ($1500) on July 19, 1811 at the eastern boundary of the old village plat.

In addition to his real estate holdings Campau engaged in trade, owning a main store in Detroit and several others in outlying areas. In 1831, he began the Democratic Free Press and Michigan Intelligencer Newspaper, the predecessor of The Detroit Free Press. He retired from active work in 1837 to spend time improving his investments.

Through the years Joseph Campau served as Detroit's trustee, assessor, overseer of the poor, inspector of water barrels and city treasurer. On January 1, 1831, he was one of several Detroit residents who presented a petition concerning previous city plans. In addition, Joseph Campau served as captain and then major of the militia.

Joseph Campau was outspoken in his political and religious beliefs and was often offended by the priests at Ste. Anne's Church. He often called them "rascals". In 1800 he left the church and, on August 1st joined the Masonic Order. But he still continued to rent his seat at the Catholic church.

After the 1805 fire, the governor requested Ste. Anne's Catholic Church be moved so more plots of land could be laid out. Supposedly concerned about those buried in the burned church's cemetery, Joseph Campau, along with Charles Moran and Jonathan Williams, led a group objecting to the move. In the compromise, the cemetery part of the church land was saved.

However, it has also been suspected that Campau's fight for the church to remain in the same location had more to do with financial reasons and that his hoped for reconstruction of the old church would increase the value of the many lots owned by him in the area.

The History of Wayne County... related that Joseph was so desperate to keep the church in his neighborhood that he laid a foundation for one and blessed the cornerstone himself. This infuriated the church and the Bishop replied

"As regards Mons. Joseph Campeau who has turned into ridicule the august ceremonies of our Holy Church and who has himself made impious and sacreligious ceremonies upon the foundation stone of the Church of Sainte Anne of Detroit, we declare that if he does not humbly ask pardon for his sin, either at parish mass or at a general assembly of the parish, after having been personally requested so to do, we will proclaim against him the sentence of excommunication."

Since he had not been an active church member, excommunication did not really bother Joseph. In fact, he ended up building a Masonic Temple on the site on which he had wanted the church rebuilt.

But that was not the end of his problems with the Catholic Church. In 1824 Joseph began sabotaging the church's ownership of a "public" farm. It came to a head in 1834 when Joseph along with several others sued to have the farm divided, or sold and the proceeds divided.

Even though Joseph had not won his battle to keep the church in his neighborhood, when he died, Joseph Campau was the richest man in Michigan.

Cassidy / Casety / Cassedy Family

James Casety
    m. pos Marguerite
    d. 1824, New York
    Children
        John (see below)
        1 son
        2 daughters

John Casety
    m. Therese Baby (c. 1767-1847; Quebec, Quebec), dau of
    Jacques Duperon Baby
    d. 1787
    Children
        Thomas

The name Casety / Cassidy / Cassedy was probably derived for the Irish "Cashen" or "Cassidy" which meant curly hair. One such ancient Celtic family was the Ua Caiside / O'Cassidy family of Ballycassidy from the county of Fermanagh in Ireland.

In most sources, family members of this genealogy were referred to with the "Casety" spelling. James Casety resided in Detroit as early as 1769 when he purchased a lot on St. Peter Street. He proceeded to accumulate a great deal of property, including a farm on Hog Island (Belle Isle) which he leased to John Laughton, commander of royal vessels on Lake Erie, in 1776. The next year James Casety purchased a farm at Windmill or Grosse Pointe from James Sterling.

James Casety and his wife appeared in the 1779 census where they were listed as having one man, one woman, two lodgers or young men, two girls, and two male slaves in their household. In the 1782 census a "Mrs. Casety" was living on the North Shore or Detroit side of the river. Living with her were one young or hired man, two male slaves, and one female slave.

In land abstracts for May 18, 1780, a Marguerite Casety sold to Julien Parent "3 x 80 Arpents" west southwest of Martin Levrit and east northeast of George McDougal for 3,500 livres. Marguerite was most probably James' wife.

Although James did not die until 1824, his wife was found living separate from him probably because during the American Revolution both James Casety and James Sterling were accused of being American sympathizers and were taken to Quebec in chains. Casety spent three years in prison before he eventually escaped and fled to the United States. He died in New York before 1824.

Although James and his wife fled the Detroit area, his son John remained. After the war John Casety became the clerk of Thomas Williams, witnessing during that time deeds for farms from 150 to 2000 acres. Then in 1786, John Casety was listed as having paid six pounds eight shillings to help defray the salary of Rev. George Mitchell.

John eventually became Williams' partner, but after Williams' death, the business failed. According to Quaiffe, the Williams family version blamed the company's collapse on the "incompetence or rascality of Casety."

Whether it was true or not, John Casety died just two years later leaving a widow only 20 years old; a young son named Thomas; and an estate in shambles. Although John's widow Therese maintained she would never marry again, in 1795 she did marry Capt. Thomas Allison.

James Fraser, a rather dubious attorney from Detroit got himself appointed "curator of the estate of John Casety", according to Alexander Hamilton, in order "to defraud the creditors."

Other descendants of this Casety family may have been Eliza Cassidy who married William Askin [see Askin genealogy] or Daniel Cassidy who was a Loyalist soldier.

Chapoton Family

Andre Chapoton I
    m. Ann Lassaigne
    Children
        Jean Baptiste (see below)

Jean Baptiste Chapoton (Dr.)
    b. 1684; St. Jean Baptiste, Uzes, Bagnoles, Languedoc,
    France
    m. Mary Magdelene Esteve / Estene (1704-1753), dau of
    Peter Esteve / Estene dit Lajeunesse and Mary Magdelene
    Frappier; July 16, 1720; Detroit, Michigan
    bur. November 12, 1760; Detroit, Michigan
    Children
        Jean Baptiste (see below)
        Pierre - b. October 7, 1722; Detroit, Michigan
            bur. August 3, 1726; Detroit, Michigan
        Anthony - b. March 16, 1724; Detroit, Michigan
        Clemence - b. September 20, 1725; Detroit, Michigan
            bur. September 23, 1725; Detroit, Michigan
        Mary Clemence - b. September 13, 1726; Detroit
            m1 James/Jacques Marsac de L'Omtrou/L'Obtrou
            (b. November 7, 1707; Detroit, Michigan bur.
            1745; Detroit, Michigan), son of Jacob Marsac
            de l'Omtrou and Teresa David; January 25,
            1745; Detroit, Michigan
            m2 Pierre Chene (b. September 22, 1724 bur.
            September 27, 1804; Assumption, Sandwich,
            Ontario), son of Charles Chene and Catherine
            Sauvage; May 7, 1747; Detroit, Michigan
            bur. November 20, 1753; Detroit, Michigan
        Andrew - b. May 29, 1728; Detroit, Michigan
            bur. April 24, 1753; Detroit, Michigan
        Charles - b. December 1, 1729; Detroit, Michigan
            bur. April 24, 1753; Detroit, Michigan
        Louis - b. March 29, 1731; Detroit, Michigan
            bur. April 3, 1731; Detroit, Michigan
        Geneveva Charlotte - b. May 6, 1732; Detroit,
        Michigan
            bur. May 9, 1732; Detroit, Michigan
        Agatha - b. December 29, 1733; Detroit, Michigan
            bur. January 1, 1734; Detroit, Michigan
        Jane - b. December 29, 1734; Detroit, Michigan
            m. Paul Dumouchel (b. June 11, 1717; Montreal,
            Quebec bur. September 25, 1780; Montreal,
            Quebec), son of Paul Dumouchel and Mary Louisa
            Tessier, grandson of Bernard Dumouchel dit La
            Roche of Rouen, France, and Jeanne Juin
            bur. July 23, 1750; Detroit, Michigan
        Joseph - b. May 25, 1736; Detroit, Michigan
            bur. April 27, 1761
        Mary Charlotte - b. November 21, 1737; Detroit
            m. Pierre Barthe, son of Theophile Barthe and
            Margaret Charlotte Alavoine; March 3, 1760;
            Detroit, Michigan
            Children
                Charlotte - m1 Louis Reaume
                      m2 Anthony Louis Descomps dit
                      Labadie; October, 1784
        Mary Magdelene - b. May 17, 1739; Detroit, Michigan

m. Gabriel Christopher Legrand (b. LeRoche,
Avranches, Normandy, France), son of Gabriel
Louis Legrand, Sieur de Sinfre and Vicomte de
Mortain and Ann Henrietta Catherine de Crenay;
April 1 or 17, 1758; Detroit, Michigan
bur. January 7, 1763; Detroit, Michigan
Louisa Clotilda / Clothilde - b. April 10, 1741;
Detroit, Michigan
m. James (Jacques) Godfroy (b. January 6,
1722; Detroit, Michigan bur. June 29, 1795;
Detroit, Michigan), son of James Godfroy and
Mary St. Onge dit Chene; January 23, 1758;
Detroit, Michigan
bur. September 18, 1762; Ste. Anne, Detroit,
Michigan
Children
    Gabriel Jacques - b. November 10, 1758
      m1 Mary Catherine Couture; January
      8, 1781
      m2 Mary Therese Bondy; February 14,
      1795
      m3 Monica Campau; January 14, 1817
      Children (15)
        Gabriel - b. July 3, 1783
          m. Terese Bondy and/or
          Elizabeth Ann May
          d. 1848
Charlotte - b. October 22, 1742
Anthony Alexis - b. June 13, 1744
Mary Joseph - b. February 5, 1746; Detroit,
Michigan
m. Augustine Chaboille (b. July 16, 1739;
Mackinac, Michigan), son of Charles Chaboille
and Mary Ann Chavalier; February 2, 1765;
Detroit, Michigan
d. by January, 1770
Elizabeth - b. October 4, 1747; Detroit, Michigan
bur. October 8, 1747; Detroit, Michigan
Louis - b. September 7, 1750; Detroit, Michigan
bur. September 18, 1750; Detroit, Michigan

Jean Baptiste Chapoton (Capt.)
b. June 17, 1721; Detroit, Michigan
m1 Elizabeth Godfroy (b. September 30, 1728; Detroit,
Michigan bur. July 25, 1750), dau of Jacques (James)
Godfroy de Mauboeuf and Mary Chene; September 10, 1749;
Detroit, Michigan
m2 Felicity Cesire (b. December 20, 1737 bur. June 7,
1809), dau of John Cesire and Mary Charlotte Girard;
September 22, 1755; Detroit, Michigan
bur. January 22, 1803; Detroit, Michigan
Children
Charles Jean Baptiste (see below)
Jean Baptiste Bonaventure - b. August 25, 1756;
Detroit, Michigan
bur. September 5, 1756; Detroit, Michigan
Benedict Joseph - b. December 1, 1756; Detroit,
Michigan
m. Teresa Meloche (b. March 10, 1769; Bloody
Run, Michigan), dau of Jean Baptiste Meloche

and Mary Louisa Robert; January 8, 1788;
Detroit, Michigan
d. January 2, 1830; Detroit, Michigan
Children
    Teresa - b. December 1, 1788; Detroit,
        Michigan
    Joseph Benedict - b. August 20, 1790;
        Detroit,Michigan
    Jean Baptiste - b. September 12, 1792;
        Detroit, Michigan
    Mary Louisa - b. January 7, 1797;
        Detroit, Michigan
    Felicity - b. February 9, 1797; Detroit,
        Michigan
    Mary Josephene - b. May 14, 1799;
        Detroit, Michigan
    Louis - b. September 10, 1801; Detroit,
        Michigan
    Felicity 2 - b. November 11, 1803;
        Detroit, Michigan
    Nicholas - b. October 11, 1806; Detroit,
        Michigan
    Sophia - b. March 21, 1810; Detroit,
        Michigan
Louis Alexis - b. June 20, 1764; Detroit, Michigan
    m. Mary Catherine Meloche (b. February 8,
    1765; northeast coast of Detroit River at
    Bloody Run bur. August 27, 1835; Detroit,
    Michigan), dau of Jean Baptiste Meloche and
    Mary Louisa Robert; February 26, 1783;
    Detroit, Michigan
    bur. August 5, 1837; Detroit, Michigan
    Children
        Mary Felicity - b. April 18, 1784;
            Detroit, Michigan
        Cecilia - b. August 16, 1786; Assumption,
            Sandwich, Ontario
        Mary Catherine - b. December 8, 1788;
            Detroit, Michigan
            m. Maj. Antoine Dequindre Jr. (June
            18, 1781-February 24, 1843), son of
            Antoine Dagneau Dequindre and
            Catherine Desrivieres de la
            Morandiere; September 9, 1809
            Children (9)
        Louis - b. January 24, 1791; Detroit,
            Michigan
        Mary Angelica - b. June 13, 1792;
            Detroit, Michigan
        Elizabeth - b. October 2, 1794; Detroit,
            Michigan
        Margaret - b. April 9, 1797; Detroit,
            Michigan
        Alexis - b. July 9, 1798; Detroit,
            Michigan
        Ann / Nancy - b. December 28, 1800;
            Detroit, Michigan
        Margaret Adelaide - b. August 17, 1805;
            Detroit, Michigan

Mary Ann (adopted)
Henry Martin - b. February 13, 1766; Detroit,
    Michigan
    bur. March 5, 1766; Detroit, Michigan
Mary Felicity - b. June 24, 1767; Detroit, Michigan
    bur. May 1, 1774
Mary Catherine Angelica - b. June 1, 1769; Detroit,
    Michigan
    m. George Meldrum (b.c. 1737, Scotland d.c.
    1810); 1782; Detroit, Michigan
    bur. March 4, 1815; northeast coast of Detroit
    River, Michigan
    Children
            Mary Ann - b. September 2, 1786;
            Sandwich, Ontario
            m1 William McDowell Scott (d.c.
            1815)
            m2 Melvin Dorr
            bur. August 1, 1825; Ste. Anne's
            Church, Detroit, Michigan
        Sons
Mary Isabella - b. March 5, 1791; northeast coast
    of Detroit River
    m. Frances Rivard (b. November 10, 1773;
    Grosse Pointe, Michigan bur. December 22,
    1841; Ste. Anne, Detroit, Michigan), son of
    Jean Baptiste Rivard and Mary Catherine Yax);
    August 20, 1800
Mary Joseph(ine) - b. April 23, 1773; northeast
    coast of Detroit River
    m. Michael Tremblay (b. March 22, 1768; Fox
    Creek, Grosse Pointe, Michigan) wid of Mary
    Joseph Lauson, son of Louis Tremblay and
    Cecilia Yax); November 7, 1795; Ste. Anne's
    Church, Detroit, Michigan
Nicholas - b. August 8, 1776; northeast coast of
    Detroit River
    r. Baton Rouge, Louisiana

Charles Jean Baptiste Chapoton
    b. May 22, 1758; Detroit, Michigan
    m. Teresa Pelier (b. March 8, 1759 bur. Jul 17,
    1795), dau of Jean Baptiste Peltier and Mary Joseph
    Cornet; February 1, 1780; Detroit, Michigan
    bur. October 23, 1837; Detroit, Michigan
    Children
            Louis - b. December 9, 1782; Assumption,
            Sandwich, Ontario
            m1 Susanne Tucker (b. Clinton River,
            Macomb County, Michigan), dau of Henry
            Tucker and Nancy Edwards; 1818
            m2 Sophie Robitaille (b. 1817; Mt.
            Clemens, Michigan), dau of Joseph
            Robitaille and Archange Dubay
            bur. May 3, 1851; Mt. Clemens, Michigan
            Children
                Jean Baptiste Henry   William
                Henrietta   Thomas   David
                Louis   Nancy   Emily

Anthony - b. July 2, 1786; Assumption,
Sandwich, Ontario
m. Angelica Moore (b. April 13, 1790;
Detroit, Michigan bur. November 9, 1896;
Ste. Anne's Church, Detroit, Michigan),
dau of Louis Moore and Mary Moreau; July
30, 1810; Detroit, Michigan
bur. July 30, 1847; Detroit, Michigan
Children

Augustin	Henry	Victoria
Catherine	Lucille	twins
Eleonora	Peter	Mary Ann
Louis Charles		

Mary Joseph - b. March 19, 1788; Assumption,
Sandwich, Ontario
m. John Tucker, son of Henry Tucker and
Nancy Edwards
Henry - b. June 5, 1790; Assumption, Sandwich,
Ontario
m1 Magdelene Drouillard; February 18,
1817; River Raisin, Michigan
m2 Angelica Lafoy (February 13, 1797 -
November, 1832), dau of Augustin Lafoy
and Catherine Bourdeau; January 7, 1829;
Detroit, Michigan
m3 Victoria Petit (b. May, 1803), dau of
Louis Petit and Mary Frances Meny; May
24, 1834
bur. September 5, 1859; Mt. Clemens,
Michigan
Children

Dominic	Monica	Daniel
Charles	Oliver	Robert

Eustache - b. February 20, 1792; Assumption,
Sandwich, Ontario
m. Judith Adelaide Serat dit Coquillard
(February 20, 1794; Detroit, Michigan -
June 17, 1885), dau of Alexis Serat dit
Coquillard and Cecilia Tremblay
d. January 13, 1871; Detroit, Michigan
bur. January 17, 1871; Mt. Elliot
Cemetery
Children

Benedict	Alexis	Infant
Eustache	August	William
Adelaide	Teresa	Julia
Felicity	Stephen	Theodore

Mary Louisa - b. March 20, 1794; Assumption,
Sandwich, Ontario
Isidore - b. July 10, 1795; Detroit, Michigan
bur. July 21, 1795; Detroit, Michigan

Jean Baptiste Chapoton I was born between 1684 and 1690
to Andre Chapoton and his wife Anne Lassaigne in St. Jean
Baptiste Parish, Bagnols (Bagnols-sur-Ceze, Department Gord)
on the Rhone River in France. After studying surgery in
France, Jean Baptiste became a surgeon in the French army.

He was sent to Detroit's Ft. Pontchartrain as garrison
surgeon-major as late as 1719. Although he involved himself in
many other interests, for quite a while Jean Baptiste Chapoton

I was the only physician for both the garrison and the surrounding area. A 1758 parish register referred to him as the "master surgeon of this town."

In addition, Chapoton became quite a tradesman, dealing at various times with medicine, grain, and building materials. And he appeared in records as groomsman at the wedding of Jean Baptiste Gouyou dit la Garde and Mary Rose.

According to Thwaites, when Chapoton married Marie Madeleine Estene / Esteve in July of 1720, his bride was only thirteen years old. But other records gave her birth year as 1704, making Marie approximately sixteen years old at the time of her marriage.

In 1734 Jean Baptiste Chapoton I was recommended for a grant of land by Commandant Jacques-Hugues-Penn and former Commandant Henri-Louis Deschamp de Boishebert. On June 18, 1734, he was given private claim #5, which was twenty arpents by forty arpents in size. But he sold that land nine year later because it was too far from the "sick". So he was granted a new piece of land four by forty arpents located closer to his patients.

In addition, Dr. Chapoton maintained a home inside the fort and appeared in Father Pierre Potier's census of French living in Detroit in 1743. In the 1750 his family included 1 woman, 3 boys 15 years of age or older, 1 girl 15 or older, 1 boy under 15, 2 girls under 15. He had 1200 sheaves of wheat, 303 sheaves of oats, 3 horses, 4 oxen, 13 cows, 2 hogs, and 30 poultry and he had 50 arpents of land under cultivation. Then in 1751, his land grant was doubled.

Jean Baptiste Chapoton I had twenty children. He retired circa 1752, leaving his surgeon's post at the fort to his son-in-law, Gabriel Legrand de Sentre, husband of his daughter Mary Magdelene. Legrand was appointed judge in 1763. Burton wrote that as a notary, Legrand
"seems to have been incompetent ... Not finding sufficient employment in Detroit, he wandered off to Kaskaskia [on the Mississippi River] to reside, and there succeeded in getting the land titles so badly mixed up that the land commissioners made loud complaint of his inefficiency."

Chapoton's daughter Marie Joseph did not reach old age. Records indicated that she married in 1765, and that her husband Augustin Chaboillez married for the second time on January 16, 1775. Augustin probably took part in the fur trade.

Mary Clemence, another of Jean Baptiste's daughters married twice. She had four children by her second husband Pierre Chene. But all of the children died young. In fact, according to Quaiffe, two of the children burned to death in their father's home in December, 1752.

Chapoton's daughter Jane married Paul Dumouchel, whose father, also named Paul, was a shoemaker. The Dumouchel / Demouchell / Desmouchelle family of Sandwich, Ontario originated in North America with Paul II's grandfather Bernard Dumouchel dit Laroche, a native of Rouen, France.

Jean Baptiste Chapoton II was a captain in the militia who appeared in the 1762 census as living at the fort and having two lots, one 40-foot wide and another one 80-foot wide. In the 1779 census his family was listed as consisting of 1 man, 1 woman, 4 young men, 1 young woman, 1 boy, 1 girl, 2 male slaves, 2 female slave. In 1782 the family had 1 man, 1 woman, 6 young men, 1 boy, 3 girls, 2 male slaves, and 2 female slaves.

On September 18, 1765, Jean Baptiste Chapoton II witnessed Pontiac's gift of land to Alexis Masonville on the south side of the Detroit River. According to land records, on October 2, 1780, Jean Baptiste II received his own grant of land from the Ottawas. The land he received was described as the area "from land of Pierre Pare to Riviere aux Puces" which was given "out of sincere friendship."

His first wife died in 1750 which is probably why, according to the History of Wayne County and the City of Detroit, Michigan, Father de la Richardie said 18 masses for "baptiste Chapoton" that year.

Jean Baptiste Chapoton II and his wives Elizabeth Godfroy and Felicity Cesire had ten children. Daughter Mary Isabella married Francis Rivard, a trustee of the church on the northeast coast.

Daughter Mary Catherine Angelica Chapoton married George Meldrum, a prominent landowner and merchant in Detroit from 1768 until his death. However, his dealings were not all successful. First in 1774, Meldrum was forced to apologize to Justice Dejean for some undisclosed insult to Dejean's dignity. Then in March, 1814, Meldrum wrote from Detroit to John Askin in Sandwich that he and his wife were starving. He begged for salt and explained
"The Indians whilst I was on my back killed all my pigs to the number of thirty four oxen ten sheep all (our) Fowls and burned our hen house and like to have set the house in fire and I could not let my sons interfere as the Indians knew and reproached them being Yankies and was not able to go out myself. We now eat Rye bread for want of better and our Porke which I chansd of Getting last fall is most out and worst of all no money to gett more."

Mary Catherine Angelica Chapoton and George Meldrum had Mary Anne Meldrum who married William McDowell Scott. According to Quaiffe, Scott who emigrated to the United States from Britain in 1796, served at various times as trustee of Detroit, U.S. Marshall, justice of the peace, attorney, and captain of the riflemen of the Legionary Corps.

In 1813 Col. Proctor ordered Scott to leave the territory. On his way to New York British troops captured him and held him in prison in Quebec charged with treason. He returned to Detroit in 1814 as the garrison's surgeon-mate. He died shortly after his return and Mary Ann took Melvin Dorr as her second husband.

Donovan Family

Matthew Donovan
  m. Mary
  d. by July 31, 1809; Amherstburg, Ontario
  Children
    Sarah - m. Matthew Elliott
      Children
        See Elliott genealogy
    Catherine - m. Welsh
      d. Ireland
    Elizabeth - m. Capt. Jonathan Nelson
    Margaret - m. Robert Innes
    Mary Fullerton - d. unmarried
    son - d. c. 1805

The O'Donovan name belonged to one of the most ancient families of Ireland dating back to Callaghan whose son Donovan ruled as King of Munster in 977 A.D. In *Irish Family Names*, Grehan related that they were chiefs of Carberry who fled to southwest Cork in the wake of the Norman Invasion in the 1170's. The O'Donovan crest depicted a hand holding a sword with a serpent coiled around its shaft.

A Donel Oge Na Cartan O'Donovan of Cloghatradbally Castle, Co. Cork was forced to surrender his estates to the King in 1615. He was the progenitor of the Donovan family of Ballymore.

But more likely, the Donovan / Donavan / Donevan name of this genealogy derived from Donndubhan with "donn" meaning "brown" and " Dubhan" meaning "black" in Irish.

Several Donovans appeared in the early records of the region. A Richard Donovan, age 16-50, appeared in the 1792 Petite Cote (South Shore) census. But he had died intestate by December, 1805.

Matthew Donovan of this genealogy first appeared in area records as a schoolmaster in Kingston, Ontario, between 1788 and 1792. At the time, Rev. John Stuart described Donovan as "an Irishman, an excellent Latin Scholar, and long experience in his profession."

Donovan arrived in Detroit circa 1794 and showed up in the 1796 census of the northeast and southwest suburbs of Detroit. He ran a private school for which he received thirty pounds per year tuition from a number of prominent Detroiters. However, on November 26, 1798, John Askin, Sr. wrote a scathing letter accusing Donovan of overcharging. Askin requested a new billing be made out for him, using the old rates.

And that was not the end of Donovan's problems with Askin. In November, 1799, Donovan wrote Askin that he had heard that Askin was intending to open a competitive school in Detroit. Donovan admitted that his "conduct of the 29th of october was irregular" and that he had committed his crime "owing to the want of wood & to the Inclemency of the weather." He added that he "made an absolute promise never to taste any Spiritious liquors as long as (he kept) School in

Detroit." What the exact crime was that he had committed under the influence of liquor was not specified, but it seemed likely to be theft.

Eventually Askin place his son Alexander (Alick) David Askin at Rev. Bacon's school. But then sometime in 1804, Alick Askin returned to Donovan's tutorlege.

But Donovan's problems with the law were not over. On June 4, 1804; according to Quaiffe; a complaint was lodged against a Matthew Donovan for not sweeping the street in front of his school.

After Detroit's fire of 1805, Matthew Donovan was granted a lot under an act of Congress for the new town. However, in 1806 he removed to Amherstburg where Donovan and his wife Mary raised at least five daughters and one son. But the son may have died young, because in 1805, Alexander Askin wrote that he was sorry to hear about the death of "Young man poor Donovan". And Askin referred to young Donovan's father and mother as a "poor distressed couple."

Matthew Donovan's daughter Margaret married Robert Innes. Innes arrived in Detroit in June, 1793. But when the time came, he chose to remain a British subject and moved across the river. There Innes was in partnership with Robert Grant. Later, along with McGregor, he owned an eighty ton ship.

In the War of 1812, Innes served as Quarter Master under his brother-in-law Matthew Elliott, who had married Sarah Donovan sometime after 1809.

Jonathan Nelson married Matthew Donovan's daughter Elizabeth. Nelson served in the War of 1812 on the British side in the marine service.

Elliott Family

Matthew Elliott (Col.)
    b. prior to 1761; Ireland
    m1 Indian woman
    m2 Sarah Donovan, dau of Matthew and Mary Donovan, aft
    July, 1809
    d. May 7, 1814; Burlington, Vermont
    Children by Indian wife
        Alexander - b. Sandwich, Ontario
            d. 1812
        Matthew, Jr.
    Children by Sarah Donovan
        Rev. Francis Gore - b. January, 1812
            d. 1880
        Robert Herriot Barclay - b. December, 1813
            d. 1858

According to Sim's *Origin and Signification of Scottish Surnames*, the Elliott family sprang from Sir William de Aliot who arrived in England with William the Conqueror. De Aliot's descendants settled in an area later known as Elliot, Forfarshire, Scotland and then in Liddesdale.

Among the more well-known with the name was Hugh Eliot / Elliott / Elyot / Ellyot / Eliott, a Bristol, England merchant. It has been claimed that Robert Thorne, Sr. and he were the English discoverers of America. They traded with both France and Spain from 1492 on and may have accompanied John Cabot in 1497. In 1502, Eliot, along with Robert and William Thorne owned the ship *The Gabriel*.

Matthew Elliott of this genealogy arrived in America from Ireland in 1761. In 1763, he served with Bouquet's expedition to relieve Ft. Pitt. Afterwards, Elliott was headquartered in the Indian trade at Pittsburgh and became quite influential with the Indians of the Ohio Valley.

When the American Revolution arrived, Matthew Elliot left Pittsburgh bound for Detroit with a large caravan of goods. However, along the way Indians captured his goods. When Elliott finally arrived in Detroit empty handed, he was regarded with suspicion and Gov. Hamilton sent him to Quebec for questioning.

Upon his return to Pittsburgh, Elliott declared himself a Loyalist. Joined by Alexander McKee and Simon Girty, Elliott again left for Detroit. From that time on, McKee was frequently linked with Elliott.

Back in Detroit, Matthew Elliott was employed by the Indian Department. As the American Revolution continued, Elliott led 300 Indians to defeat Col. Crawford's expedition, he helped slaughter Kentuckians at Blue Lick, and he served during the Vincennes Campaign.

Before the Americans finally took Detroit, Elliott removed to Amherstburg where he farmed, accumulated land, and served again with the Indian Department. On March 25, 1785, Deputy Surveyor Philip Fry was told to reserve a six acre lot for "Mr. Elliott" near the mouth of the Thames River. Then on May 2, 1786, Matthew Elliott and William Caldwell purchased John Peck's farm on the south or Canadian side of the Detroit River, all the stock in Peck's store, and his furniture. In 1794 both Matthew Elliott and Chatham Elliot were listed as owners of lots in Malden township. Then on August 14, 1797, Matthew was awarded lot #13 on the east side of Bedford Street in Sandwich, Ontario. And finally, by 1798, Elliott owned a lot in Raleigh, where he was listed as an Irish Loyalist from Pennsylvania.

Meanwhile, Matthew Elliott was making himself useful in a number of public endeavors. In 1788, he was appointed Justice of the Peace while still serving with the Indian Department. Between 1790 and 1794, Elliott supposedly served with the Indian Department in Western Ohio. But Russell reported that in the summer of 1793, when Col. England refused to let American commissioners go to Detroit to confer with Indians, they went to Capt. Elliott's home on the Canadian side of the river. Then in July, 1796, he became Superintendent of Indian Affairs.

But after being appointed to that last position, Matthew began having serious problems. In November, 1797, Hector McLean complained to General Prescott that Matthew Elliott had been "giving in a false return of the indians at Chenail Ecarte Settlement". Elliott had supposedly requested provisions for 543 Indians, while in reality, only approximately 180 lived at the settlement. No explanation was given as to what Elliott had intended to do with the additional supplies. Prescott answered that Matthew's conduct had "been such as to have considerably shaken confidence" for some time. As his superior, Prescott removed Elliott from the office and directed "Mr. McKee" to replace Elliott at Amherstburg. However Quaiffe reported that Elliott was dismissed because of "garrison intrigue." Whatever the cause, Elliott remained unemployed for 1 1/2 years.

Quaiffe claimed it was not until 1812 that Elliott was actually vindicated. At that time it was discovered no one but Elliott could control western Indians. So because they needed him, Elliott was exonerated of the crime and reappointed Superintendent of Indians.

In that role, he promised the Moravian Indians that if they fought for their "Grandfather the king," they would receive a double claim to the land on which their town of Fairfield, Upper Canada stood.

Also during the War of 1812, Elliott led the Indian contingency when Brock captured Detroit. Then when Proctor fled Detroit in 1813, Elliott left with him. Then in December, 1813, he led the Indians on an assault on Ft. Niagara. Matthew Elliott died in Burlington, Vermont in 1814.

During the War of 1812, Matthew Elliot lost much of his far-reaching landholdings in the Amherstburg area. Although Sarah Donovan Elliott, Matthew's second wife and widow, was willed 500 pounds at his death and her spinster sister Mary inherited 300 pounds, their inheritance would not support them for long. Sarah was still a young woman and at her husband's death she went to Lower Canada to try and get some financial relief. After the war she returned to Amherstburg where she remained as a widow for another fifty years.

Sarah's son Francis Gore Elliott became a clergyman for the Church of England. Her other son, Robert Herriot Barclay Elliott was named for the British Naval Commander on Lake Erie, and grew to become a gentleman farmer.

Alexander, one of Matthew Elliott's sons by his Indian wife, was admitted to the bar in Montreal in February, 1812. In 1808, Alexander Askin was bound to "Mr. Elliott" to learn the law. In a letter to his brother Charles Askin, Alexander wrote

"The terms of the Agreement are; that Mr. Elliott is to board, Lodge, and wash me, and my Father is to clothe me. (Elliott) is a good man, and i'm sure will Do, what he can for me."

The "Mr. Elliott" was not specified. And although Alexander Elliott was the son who became a lawyer, he was not admitted to the bar in Montreal until 1812. However, perhaps he practiced somewhere else before going to Montreal.

Elliott's professional life ended early with the War of 1812, when Alexander, part Indian himself, was ambushed by Indian prisoners headed by a Shawnee chief. A variety of death dates have been given for Alexander Elliott. Depending upon the source, Alexander was killed either on November 22, 1812, or early in December, 1812. And he was buried either on December 17, 1812 or February 17, 1813.

A number of Elliotts listed under a variety of spellings appeared in the Michigan / Canadian border area who may have been related to Matthew. David, Jacob and Thomas Elliot all settled in Elizabethtown, Ontario. Capt. G.A. Elliott was Quarter Master of 103rd Regiment in 1814. Then in early 1838, Col. William Elliott was in command of the 2nd Regiment of Essex Militia. An Isaac Elliot was ordained as a Baptist minister in 1831 in Chatham Township. Joseph Landon [see Landon Genealogy] married a Rebecca Elliott (1796-1891) in 1819.

A Charles Elliott of Sandwich, Ontario became well-known for his outspokenness and public stands. In 1833 he complained to the lieutenant-governor's secretary that Sheriff William Hands of Howard (Morpeth) was senile and an imbecile.

When a rebellion led by William Mackenzie broke out in December, 1837, the same Charles Elliott became concerned. On January 2, 1838 he wrote about his concerns that French Canadians in the Amherstburg area were hostile towards the government. He wrote

"Living in the midst of the French, I had always a good opinion of their loyalty, and it is with unwillingness that I am driven now to suspect them. So anxious do I feel on the subject, that if the roads will admit of it, I intend to send Mrs. Eliot (Jane, daughter of John McGregor) and our little ones to Chatham."

But the Elliott name probably received its most notoriety in Canada when Pierre-Elliott Trudeau, ninth generation descendant of Charles-Emile Trudeau and Grace Elliot, became Canada's Prime Minister.

Fields Family

George Fields
 b. 1721, pos Pennsylvania
 m. Rebecca Hanes (b. 1725; pos Staten Island, New York d.
 January 2, 1798 bur. St. Marks Anglican Cemetery,
 Niagara, Ontario) wid of Jeremiah Johnson; aft 1749
 d. 1784 or 1787; Lincoln County, Ontario
 Children
   Daniel (see below)
   Mary - b. 1751
     m. Isaac Dolsen, Sr.
     Children
       Isaac Jr. - 1777
         m2 Elizabeth Armstrong
         d. March 2, 1855
         Children
           William - b. December 6, 1806
             m. Nancy Evans (b. May
             26, 1814; Pennsylvania
             d.c. 1883), dau of Israel
             Evans of Chatham, Ontario
             d. 1886
       Matthew - wll dtd. September 20, 1805
         est dvd. October 15, 1813
         Children
           John - b.c. 1776
             m. Elizabeth Ridley
             Children
               Matthew (tw) - b. 1800
               Hannah (tw) - b. 1800
               Uriah
               John
   Isaac - m. August 23, 1786
     d. September 10, 1861
   Hannah - b. 1753
     m. Matthew Dolsen, son of Isaac Dolsen
   Ann - b. 1756
     m. Allen McDonald
   Gilbert - b. 1765
     m. Eleanor Morden (b. September, 1770; Mount
     Bethel, Northampton, Pennsylvania d. April 21,
     1850 bur. Field Vrooman Brown Cemetery), dau
     of Ralph and Ann Durham; 1789
     d. December 18, 1815
     bur. Field Vrooman Brown Cemetery
     Children
       George - b. February 21, 1790
       Daniel - b. January 14, 1792; Niagara
         Township, Lincoln County, Ontario
         m. Catherine Durham (b. 1796), dau
         of James and Mary Durham
         d. October 31, 1873
         bur. Field Vrooman Brown Cemetery
         Children
           Eliza - b. 1817
             m. Nelson Clement
           James b. 1819
             m. Mariah Clement

William Gilbert - b. September 8, 1821; Niagara Township, Lincoln County, Ontario
m. Sarah Clement (b. January 5, 1829), dau of Col. Joseph and Ann Coughill; March 30, 1848; Niagara-on-the-Lake, Ontario
r. Windham Township, Lt 6 Com 6 Norfolk County, Ontario
d. May 6, 1894
Children

Mary	Sarah
Joseph	Melissa
Charles	Gilbert
Daniel	Morden
Julia Ann	Rebecca
James	Emma Jane
William Henry	
Alonzo Murray	

Murray - b. 1824
  m. Nancy McCarthy
Eleanor - b. 1829
  m. William Robinson
Rebecca - b. 1831
  m. Solomon Johnson Brown
Daniel - m. 1832
  d. 1836
Catherine - b. 1834
  m. John Harris
Maria Melissa - b. 1839
John Morden - b. December 4, 1793
David McFall - October 13, 1795
Ralph - b. March 19, 1798
Rebecca - b. May 13, 1800
James - b. August 16, 1802
Nathan - b. March 16, 1805
Gilbert - b. August 9, 1807
Hiram - b. August 13, 1811
Thomas - b. 1769
Nathan - m. dau of James Stack
  Children (3)

Daniel Fields (Sgt.)
  b. 1749; pos Wyoming, Northumberland County, Pennsylvania
  r. Petite Cote, 1784
  Children (5)
    George - r. 1809; Chatham, Ontario

As might be expected, the name "Field" arose among people living near open land. According to Osgood Field, the name was actually spelt De la Feld, Del Feld, or Feld until the mid 1500's. After that the name might have been spelt FFyld, Fieald, Feild, Field, or Feld; or any of those spellings only with an "e" on the end. While some branches have clung to the old "Feild" or "Feilde" spellings, for the last three centuries the "Field" spelling has been the most accepted.

Others might have been descended from the French de la Felds family. As far back as the sixth century there were Counts de la Feld. But many French families dropped the "de la" from their names when they emigrated to an English language nation. Many de la Felds ended up in Lancaster, Herts, Gloucester and Hereford counties in England. Hubertus de la Feld went to England with William the Conqueror in 1066. Circa 1240, a Roger del Feld was born in Sowerby, England. A Field / Feyld family was residing in Algarkirke, Lincolnshire in England in the early 1600's.

Among early Fields emigrating to the New World were Barbary Feild, who at age 11 was apprenticed to Thomas Boile, a "chirurgion" in Jamaica in 1683; and Robert Feild of Yearling, a laborer who left Hampton, England, on board the *James* in 1635, bound for New England.

This genealogy begins with George Fields and his wife Rebecca who lived for three years on 300 acres of land purchased from Daniel Rees on the Susquehanna River in Northumberland County, Pennsylvania. George cleared forty of the acres, built a house, and planted an orchard. But when George was accused of treason, the land was confiscated.

In 1778 he fled to Niagara with his family where he joined Butler's Rangers. George Fields died at Niagara in either 1784 or 1787. His wife Rebecca and sons Nathan and Gilbert remained in Niagara after his death. Rebecca claimed a loss of 393 pounds sterling, but was reimbursed only 109 pounds sterling. George was listed as a Loyalist who had lived in Williamsburg before his death. As widow of a Loyalist, Rebecca was granted land in Ancaster Township, Canada.

Like his father, George's son Gilbert Fields was declared a traitor and fled to Canada where he also joined Butler's Rangers. He was also granted land in Ancaster Township. He resided at Field House Lt. 15. in Niagara Township after his marriage to Eleanor Morden.

In 1796 George's son Nathan also joined Butler's Rangers and was granted land on the Thames River. James Stack, his father-in-law had been imprisoned for his loyalty to the King.

Matthew Fields went on to Detroit where, in 1781, he was employed in a tavern. But later he removed to the Canadian side and, in 1789, Matthew, like his brother Nathan, was residing along the Thames River.

George's daughter, Mary Fields, married Isaac Dolsen, Sr. Their grandson William Dolsen, son of Isaac, Jr. eventually worked as a carpenter in Chatham, Ontario.

Daniel, George's eldest son, was born in Northumberland Co., Pennsylvania, probably in the town of Wyoming. Before the American Revolution, he owned 150 acres there; but, like his father, the land was confiscated. Daniel estimated his loss during the Revolution equaled 81 pounds in New York currency.

Like his father and several of his brothers, Daniel was accused of treason and joined Butler's Rangers. He served as a sergeant in Capt. Caldwell's company during the war.

After the American Revolution, Daniel Fields removed to the Detroit area. He purchased a farm at Petite Cote in 1784 and purchased more farm land on the south side of the Thames River circa 1787 from Farrit Tellor. However, in 1790, Daniel had yet to move to the river property. Although, it could have been that laborers were working the farm. In 1789 and 1792, he petitioned for more land and was granted lot 10 in the first and second concessions in Raleigh by the Land Board. In January, 1794, he requested permission to make major improvements to the land on the Thames River.

He later appeared on a list of disbanded troops and Loyalists who were settled in an area on the north side of Lake Erie between a creek four miles from the mouth of the Detroit River and a creek one and one-half miles beyond Cedar River. In the 1794 census Daniel Fields was listed as living on lot number 89, Colchester, probably the same piece of land as the one he had been granted earlier.

In June, 1795, Capt. "Donald" Fields was running a mill and "Daniel" was referred to as a miller in letters written by John Drake and James Freeman respectively. However, Daniel Fields had previously (1790 and 1792) served as a blacksmith, working for Alexander McKee.

According to The Valley of the Lower Thames, Daniel Fields arrived in the area with the Dolsen family. Both the Fields and Dolsens were from Wyoming, Pennsylvania. In fact, Daniel Fields sister Mary was married to Isaac Dolsen, Sr., and Daniel's niece Hannah, daughter of Matthew, married Isaac Dolsen's son Matthew. Like the Fields, the Dolsen's land was also confiscated when they remained loyal to the King. Isaac Dolsen, Sr. arrived in the Detroit area in 1784 and bought a farm next to Daniel at Petite Cote. Abstracts in Detroit Notarial Records for September 2, 1784, indicated Theophile Lemay sold to Isaac Dolsen 3 x 4 arpents at Petite Cote for 500 pounds.
"One of the stages of Simcoe's winter post was at Isaac Dolson's and another was at Captain Daniel Fields, both in Raleigh."
Then in 1795 Isaac Dolsen and Daniel Fields were given permission to build a mill on lot number 18, Harwich.

Throughout his life, Daniel Fields served his community. On May 15, 1786, he was a witness when the chiefs of the Ottawas and Chippewas ceded land at River Canard and Bois Blanc. Then on June 18, 1790, he served as spokesman for fellow former Rangers trying to get government compensation for their military service. While Daniel was a captain with the Essex County militia, John Askin reported to Alexander McKee on August 17, 1794 that he had written
"Capt. fields at river al la Tranche, to examine & see what arms & accoutrements may be wanted for to complete on this side of the river."
Then on September 28, 1796, John Askin wrote to Capt. Daniel or Donald Fields of "River Thames" requesting a list of men "subject to Serve as Militia Men on the South side of the River Thames." Daniel Fields was 47 years old at the time.

Jacob Family

George Jacob (Capt.)
   b.c. 1762-64; England
   m. Mary Archange Chene dit Labutte, c. 1788
   d. December 24, 1833
   bur. St. John's Churchyard, Sandwich, Ontario
   Children
      George (see below)
      Jane / Ann - b. August 27, 1791; Assumption,
         Sandwich, Ontario
         bur. April 4, 1815; Assumption, Sandwich,
         Ontario
      Elizabeth - b. March 8, 1793; Sandwich, Ontario
         bpt. June 1, 1793; Assumption, Sandwich,
         Ontario
         m. Solomon Thibault of Thames, Ontario; August
         3, 1824; Assumption, Sandwich, Ontario
         d.c. 1829; Thames, Ontario
         bur. March 16, 1829; Assumption, Sandwich,
         Ontario
      Archange - m. John Watson
      Mary - b. November 19, 1797
         bpt. February 20, 1798; Assumption, Sandwich,
         Ontario
         bur. August 7, 1821; Assumption, Sandwich,
         Ontario
      Monica / Monique - b.c. March, 1799
         bpt. June 13, 1799; Assumption, Sandwich,
         Ontario
         m. Charles Askin (1785, Detroit - June 1,
         1869)
      Felicity - b.c. December 1800
         bpt. February 6, 1801; River Thames, Ontario
         m. Alexander McKee, son of Thomas McKee and
         Theresa Askin
         Children (see McKee)

George Jacob, Jr.
   b. September 4, 1789
   bpt. Assumption, Sandwich, Ontario
   m1 Catherine Dolsen
   m2 Eleanor, dau of Commodore Alexander Grant; 1820
   Children by Catherine
      John Edmond - b. August 1, 1814
         bpt. March 6, 1815; Assumption, Sandwich,
         Ontario
      Ellen - b.c. 1817
         m. William Baby
         d. 1841
   Children by Eleanor
      George Alexander
      Mary Archange

In the late 1600's and early 1700's, an Etienne Jacob was
notary on Ile d'Orleans, Quebec. He was probably the
"Estienne" Jacob who circa 1680 held land in the Fief de
Lounville, L'Ange-Gardien, Ile d'Orleans, Quebec. George Jacob
of this genealogy may have been a relation of this Etienne.

But there was also an Indian family named Jacob which lived on the Fairfield side of the Thames River. They were descendants of Joseph Bull, a white member of the Moravian Church. Bull had married an Indian woman named Schebosch or "Running Water".

Although the Moravian settlement at Fairfield was destroyed during the American Revolution, the Jacob family obviously remained. A May 6, 1801 letter to John Askin, Sr. from "Gottfr. Seb. Oppelt" concerned "the Goods Mr. Barthe left with Jacob" at the Moravian Indian village. Then, according to The Valley of the Lower Thames, in 1860 the "chief" of the fifty families at New Fairfield was Phillip Jacobs "who lived on the site of the old town".

Another hint of George Jacob's ancestry came in The Valley of the Lower Thames which suggested George Jacob may have been related to three widows of French families - Gamelin, Gouin, and Sterling. But gave no reason for that supposition.

On a 1798 petition, George wrote that he had resided in the two Canada's (Upper and Lower) for approximately 21 years. So he arrived circa 1777, or at the age of 13 or 14 years old if he was born in 1764 as stated in a military report. But he would have been 15 or 16 years old if he was born in 1762, as was claimed at his December 24, 1833 death. Whichever was correct, he was young upon he first entering Canada.

After the American Revolution, George Jacob resided in Detroit, but remained a British subject serving as a captain of a dragoon company of the Kent County militia during the War of 1812. According to Charles Askin's journal, during the Detroit campaign, between July 24 and September 12, 1812; a Capt. Jacobs was listed as a member of the militia. During the war, American soldiers confiscated supplies along the Thames River while on a raiding expedition and they seized "a large amount of military stores at Captain George Jacob's."

In addition to his military service George Jacob was a successful businessman. Just after the American Revolution, about the time he married Mary Archange Chene dit Labutte, George was partners with Daniel McKillip. McKillip was a Loyalist who had served as a sergeant in Butler's Rangers.

Then, in April, 1791, George Jacob and an Alexis Labutte purchased a farm on the Thames River. Most likely Alexis was related to George's wife Mary Archange dit Labutte. The land they purchased together was on the south or Canadian bank of the river and had originally been part of the estate of "Caldwell and Elliott." That could have been the land originally purchased from Matthew Elliot and William Caldwell in 1786. However, The Valley of the Lower Thames listed George Jacob as an original patentee of the land.

He built up his land holdings on the river in the Raleigh area. In January, 1794, George Jacob requested permission to make a large improvement to his lot in Raleigh where he had a store there.

Circa 1801 Angus McIntosh of Sandwich became George's partner in the store. George collected wheat and corn in payments: McIntosh sold it as flour. In addition, they distilled and sold whiskey. As a successful merchant George Jacob acquired two more farm lots on the Thames River in the Raleigh area in 1808. His store in Raleigh remained successful until after the War of 1812.

George held a number of public offices after the May 28, 1806 letter from John Askin, Sr. to Alexander Grant in which Askin wrote
"Should a new commission [be] Issued I once before recommended Captain McKee Mr. Barsto and Mr. George Jacobs as fit people for Magistrates."
That same year, after Abraham Iredell died, George Jacob took his office. Then in 1813, George was a magistrate from the Thames region.

Even after leaving office, George continued to serve others. On May 10, 1824, George Jacob and James Gordon were given letters of administration for the estate of Sarah Ainse of Amherstburg, Ontario.

Like many of his contemporaries, Jacob did not find slavery abhorrent. According to The British Regime in Michigan and the Old Northwest 1760-1796, in the late 1700's; George Jacob purchased a panis (Indian slave) woman named Susannah and one of her children, a one-year-old daughter also named Susannah, from John Askin for 100 pounds.

Charles Askin, the son of John who later married George Jacob's daughter Monique / Monica, was a friend of George's and a frequent visitor to his home. Charles went on to develop a farm in Western Ontario and resided in Windsor, Ontario.

In the 1830's a George Jacob was operating a tavern in Raleigh. That could have been either George Sr. who died in 1833 and could have been as old as sixty-eight years old, or George Jr. who was born in 1789 and would have been forty-one years old. According to The Valley of the Lower Thames, in 1843 George Jr. was "operating a highly lucrative potashery run by horsepower... (which) burned to the ground" in Chatham, Ontario. But George Sr. had been associated with the sale of whiskey as early as 1801. So either father or son could have been operating the tavern.

George Jacob, Jr. was an avid horseman. In August, 1843, while he was living in Chatham, he challenged the winner of the Sandwich races against his horse Wawascash. Stating that he was unwilling "to contend against the common herd" at the Sandwich races, George suggested his race be run at the Thames River.

George Jacob, Jr. took Eleanor, the daughter of Commodore Alexander Grant, as his second wife. Their son George Alexander Jacob joined the First Michigan Cavalry and surprisingly, considering his grandfather's loyalties, he died fighting in the American Civil War.

Landon Family

All Landon genealogies that follow descended from James Landon, below, and his first wife Mary Vail.

James Landon I
   b. March 29, 1685; Bristol County, Massachusetts or Bristol, Rhode Island
   m1. Mary Vail (d. 1722), dau of John Vail and Grace Brockett; May, 1707; Southold, Long Island, New York
   m2. Mary Wilmont (d. 1753), dau of Francis Brown, wid of Alexander Wilmont of Southampton, Long Island, New York; June 12, 1723
   d. September 19, 1738; Litchfield, Connecticut
   Children
      James II (see below)
      Daniel (see below)
      Mary - b. November 26, 1707; Southold, Long Island
      Joseph - b. December 18, 1708
      Rachel - b. October 12, 1716
      David - b. July 5, 1718
         m1. Mary Osborn
         m2. Thankful Dickinson
         d. May 4, 1804
      John - b. July 21, 1720
      Lydia - b. 1722
      Nathan - b. April 15, 1727
      Anne

The Landon family may have originated with the noble Morin de Loudoun family of 1200-1500 Normandy, France. They became a united family when Geoffrey Morin, Seigneur du Tronchet au Maine married Alix de Loudoun, daughter of Richard Seigneur de Loudun in 1298. When life became difficult for the Protestants of France, at least one member of the Morin de Loudoun family fled to England in the 1500's and Anglicized the name.

Other genealogists have believed the Landon name may have derived from the Latin "Lande Sabulatum" or "ground covered with heath". Yet other sources have claimed its name originated with "lan" meaning "enclosure" and "dun" meaning "hill" or "town". Other researchers have believed those with the "Landon" spelling were originally French Huguenot while the "Langdon" spelling came from England. But during the English Reformation the name became associated with fortified areas known as Landons. All the spellings eventually became interchangeable. Other forms of the name were Landen, Landin, Lindon, Landoll, Langdon, Langton, Lanckton, and Lankton.

The first Landon in this genealogy was James Landon, who was probably the son of Daniel Landon of Bristol, Rhode Island or Taunton, Bristol County, Massachusetts. But from the age of 13, James I was raised by his uncle Nathan Landon of Southold, Long Island, New York.

In 1715, James I was a member of the Southold Military under Capt. Benjamin Youngs. He was a cordwainer (leather worker) or blacksmith throughout much of his life. His first

wife died and was buried in the Southold Cemetery. Her
gravestone read

Here Lyes ye
Body of Mrs
Mary Landon
Wife to Mr James Landon
Decd ___ August
Ye 28 1722
in ye
___ year of her age

James Landon I moved to Litchfield, Connecticut in 1735
and was made a freeman juror there in 1737. He died on
September 19, 1738.

Although he was buried in Litchfield, his will was filed
in Southold, Suffolk Co. 1738-1739 Book II, page 115. He
bequeathed his house and land in Litchfield to his son James
II and required James to pay son John 57 pounds when he
reached the age of 21. James I's son Joseph received the land
in Southold. In order to inherit, Joseph was required by his
father's will to give another son David his house and land.
Son Nathan received 15 pounds. Daniel was the only son not
mentioned in James I's will.

During the American Revolution, Landons, with their names
spelled in various ways, supported both sides. In 1778 Mark
Langden of Suffolk Co., New York was robbed by rebels of 1000
pounds in cash and goods. A Capt. John Langdon served aboard
a Continental frigate in Portsmouth, New Hampshire. The DAR
listed Daniel Langton; and James, Rufus and Ebenezer Landon as
Revolutionary War pensioners from Connecticut.

But several branches of James Landon I's tree ended up
going to Ontario. His son James II's produced Asa, a well
known Loyalist. According to Truman Landon's "The First
Settler" Oliver Landon of Lansdowne, another of James II's
sons, Samuel, was employed by the British Secret Service;
while son James III continued with the American militia.

Daniel, another of James I's sons, produced several
children, including Daniel, Jr. and Oliver who emigrated to
Canada. The genealogies for those who went to Canada follow.

Landon Family I

James Landon II Family

James Landon II
- b. August 5, 1711, Southold, Long Island, New York
- m1. Sarah Bishop (b. August 28, 1713), dau of Samuel Bishop and Abigail Wetmore; June 14, 1732; Guilford, Connecticut
- m2. wid of Jonathan Moore of Salisbury, Connecticut
- wll pr November 29, 1786
- Children
    - Asa (see below)
    - Sarah - b. November 12, 1732
        - m. John Catlin, son of John Catlin of Litchfield, Connecticut
    - James III - b. May 23, 1734
        - m. Mary Reed
    - Ezekiel - b. August 31, 1738
        - m1. Azubah Beebe, dau of John and Abigail Beebe
        - m2 Elizabeth; November 15, 1770
        - d.c. 1800
    - Thomas - b. September 10, 1740
        - m. Hannah Hubell, dau of Samuel Hubell
    - Rachel - b. October 11, 1742
    - Ambrose - b. September 9, 1744
        - m. Abigail
        - Children
            - John R.
            - Ambrose
    - Lois - b. July 11, 1746
        - d. young
    - Samuel - b.c. 1750; Salisbury, Connecticut
        - m1 pos Mary (b.c. 1749 d. November 12, 1771)
        - m2 Sarah Sprague, dau of Jonathan Sprague and Lydia Barrows; May 12, 1773; Connecticut
        - d. 1840; Brockville, Ontario
        - Children
            - ?Miles (tw) - b. November 12, 1771
            - ?Samuel (tw) - b. November 12, 1771
            - Electra - b. 1779
                - m. Daniel Burritt
            - Pamella - b. November 20, 1781
                - m. Stephen Collins
                - d. January 4, 1875
            - Reuben - b. January 11, 1776
                - m. Sarah Ann Phillips, dau of Ziba M. and Urania Burritt
                - bur. Read Cemetery, Augusta Twp. Ontario
                - Children
                    - James - b. 1808 or July 12, 1810
                        - m. Eliza Read
                        - d. September 22, 1857
                    - Ziba Marcus - b. 1809
                        - d. January 7, 1870
                    - Samuel - b. 1812
                    - Adelene - m. George Truesdale

110

```
            Sarah - b.c. 1795
                m. Abel Wright of Elmsley, Ontario,
                son of Ashel Wright and Eva Haynes
                d. 1879
            Rebecca - b. April 9, 1774
                m. Matthew Wing
                d. April, 1857
        Luther - b. September 16, 1752
        Nancy - b. January 18, 1755
            m. Oliver Everts; February 22, 1776
            d. 1785; Canada
        Nabby

Asa Landon, Sr.
    b. July 27, 1731 or 1736; Litchfield or Salisbury,
    Connecticut
    m. Jerusha Grifface (b. May 23, 1736); October 20 or 29,
    1757
    bur. Oakville Cemetery, Brockville, Ontario
    Children
        Asa, Jr. (see below)
        Louis - b. May 2, 1759
            m. James Sellech; January 17, 1783
        Sarah - b. October 1, 1761
        Hannah - b. January 6, 1764
            m. Caleb Clawson / Closson (c. 1758-1815)
            Children
                Ann/Nancy      Asa        Thirza/Thurza
                Sarah          Polly      Rebecca
        Heman - b. July 15, 1768; Salisbury, Connecticut
            m. Dorothy Brown (b. December 11, 1771 d.
            January 29, 1841 bur. 1841; Reed's Cemetery,
            Brockville, Ontario), dau of Jesse Brown, Jr.
            and Hannah Gray
            d. August 8, 1832
            Children
                Rebecca        Henry        Heman
                Guy            John         Alisha
                William        Minerva      Asa Duncan
                Thomas
        Electra - b. August 9, 1770
        Ezra - b. February 22, 1773
            d. September, 1776
        Nancy - b. September 26, 1775

Asa Landon, Jr.
    b. April 13, 1766; Salisbury, Connecticut
    m. Elizabeth Bissell, dau of David Bissell
    Children
        Solomon - b. 1796
            r. 1832; Elizabethtown, Ontario
            m. Catherine Fields
            d. 1848
        Elizabeth - m. George Canout
            d. November 30, 1830
        Wellington - m1. Melissa Burritt, dau of Adronion
            Burritt
            m2 Annie McCrea
            d. San Francisco, California
        Nelson - b. 1807
            m. Anne Dunham

                        111
```

d. 1865
Maria - m. Stephen Cooledge / Coolidge / Collidge
        of Elizabethtown, Ontario
Elisha - b. 1798
        m. Elizabeth Burell
        d. 1865
Harriet - m. Joseph Falconer / Falkner / Faulkner

James Landon II owned a large farm in Salisbury, Connecticut on what would eventually become appropriately known as Tory Hill. According to Data from Colonial New Haven Newspapers, in 1759, James Landon was listed as a representative from Salisbury to the lower house of the General Assembly of Connecticut. How things would change for the family in less than twenty years!

In 1761 James II's son Asa held a land patent on Otter Creek near the Castleton River of Vermont. But Asa did not move on to his patent land until much later. Instead, Asa became an ensign in the Salisbury, Connecticut Second Militia Company and became a lieutenant in 1773. Asa's uncle David Landon was a captain in the same militia and was even appointed by the Assembly to help raise volunteers for General Washington.

Asa was not feeling as rebellious against the British as some of his relatives. In 1775, as war became imminent, Asa and his future brother-in-law Oliver Everts, moved to Vermont and cleared a two hundred acre farm on the land patent Asa had received back in 1761. But he could no longer put off making a decision and in 1777, Asa Landon joined the British Army at "Skenesboro" as a foot soldier.

According to a later deposition signed by Asa Landon was assigned by General Burgoyne to Hessian General Baron von Riedesel. He carried intelligence and guided troops for "Redheazel", as Asa referred to von Riedesel. Actually, Coldham wrote that Asa was "dispatched as pilot to Germans with stores from Ticonderoga and brought information of provision secreted at Castleton by rebels."

But Burgoyne's army was a disaster. He allowed officers' wives and children to accompany the army. The general himself was a non-stop alcoholic who had an open affair with one of his officers' wives. Discipline was non-existent and Burgoyne's troops became disheartened.

On October 16, 1777, after his defeat at Saratoga, Burgoyne gathered Landon and his other American soldiers and urged them to leave before his surrender. Earlier, rebels had supposedly executed Loyalists with the British Army at the Battle of Bennington. And Burgoyne did not want a repeat. In fact Palmer and several other authors claimed Asa had actually been at Bennington, but had somehow managed to escape execution.

Although Landon did not lose his life while serving with Burgoyne, Asa did lose his Vermont farm and his personal belongings when they were confiscated by rebels. In a deposition, Asa claimed to have lost his two hundred acre farm in Vermont, a yoke of oxen, fourteen tons of mowed hay, tools, flax, wheat, farm, and furniture.

So Asa Landon returned to Connecticut where, according to Biographical Sketches of Loyalists of the American Revolution, he worked as a farmer and cooper. But Asa's family in Litchfield and Salisbury were having problems too. His brother James Landon III, who had been a part of the American militia, was mustered out because of "general neglect of his duty, and very great unfriendliness to the American cause..." In 1777 Asa Landon, Jr. supposedly joined the British Army and fought. However, Asa, Jr. would have been eleven years old at the time.

In October, 1777; Asa, along with his wife, 5 children, British spy / brother Samuel, and brother-in-law Oliver Everts; joined 20,000 other refuges in Halifax, Canada. Coldham, in his book concerning Loyalist claims, mistakenly recorded that Asa arrived from Castleton, New York. Coldham's confusion probably stemmed from the fact that Castleton, Vermont was very near the New York border.

Eventually Everts got a clerks job while Asa became a surveyor in Halifax. Asa spent six years in the Engineer's and Quartermaster General's Department. During that time, Asa joined in an operation into the colonies where he helped capture a rebel spy who was later sent to Quebec. Because of this, the Vermont Assembly added Asa's name officially to the list of traitors in their 1779 Act to Prevent Return in State of Certain Persons.

As Loyalists, Asa and Samuel Landon and Oliver Everts were granted land in Augusta Township near Brockville, Ontario along the St. Lawrence River. Asa and two sons arrived in Augusta before October 12, 1784, in order to enter the drawing to distribute parcels of land. At that time, approximately 600 people were crowded into the Brockville area hoping for land. And others followed, including Samuel Landon.

Under rules for land grants for Loyalist forces, field officers were eligible to receive 5000 acres, captains 3000 acres, staff and warrant officers 2000 acres, sergeants 500 acres, corporals 400 acres and privates 200 acres. Non-combattant Loyalists and their children could also receive 200 acres each.

In 1797 Asa Landon Sr. presented a 1782 Rutland Co., Vermont certificate proving his property in Castleton had been sold to Aruna Woodward and Reuben Moulton. Asa was granted 200 acres in the 18th concession and cattle.

His brother Samuel may have received 200 acres on the 4th concession in 1798. But according to Truman Landon's book, Samuel situated on the north end of lot 37 and the north end of the west 1/2 of lot 32 in the 2nd concession of Augusta Township.

Asa Landon; his children Hannah, Asa Jr. and Heman; and his brother Samuel were all recorded in the Ontario Archives United Empire Loyalist records. In his June 24, 1797 petition, Heman Landon claimed to have joined the British Army "before (the) treaty of separation". He petitioned for land, included a supporting petition for his wife Dorothy as the daughter of a United Empire Loyalist. In addition, he petitioned for his children's land, requesting 750 acres in all. Instead he was granted 400 acres.

Landon Family II

Daniel Landon Family

Daniel Landon I
- b. January 7, 1714; Southold, Long Island
- m1. pos _____ Fiske of Brooklyn, New York
- m2. Martha Youngs (d. September 20, 1800), dau of Christopher Youngs IV and Elizabeth Moore; May 22, 1736; Southold, Long Island, New York
- d. July 11, 1790; Litchfield, Connecticut
- Children
  - Oliver (see below)
  - Daniel II - b. February 11, 1737; Litchfield, Connecticut
    - m. Chloe Smith (c. 1735-1818)
    - d. April, 1814; Picton, Ontario
    - Children
      - Susan - b. March 10, 1756
        - m. Phineas Baldwin (d. Picton, Ontario)
      - Caroline - b. December 21, 1757
        - m. Henry Plumb
      - Anne - b. April 19, 1760
        - m. Oliver Dickinson
        - d. December 25, 1849
      - Mary - b. January 1, 1763
        - m. James Collins
      - Daniel III - b. February 25, 1765; Litchfield, Connecticut
        - m1. Anne Dickinson
        - m2. Anne Gardner
        - m3. Abigail Reece
        - d. December 29, 1824; Salisbury, Connecticut
        - Children
          - Kay   Norman   Daniel
          - Gardner   Henry
      - Stephen - b. December 18, 1766
        - d. February 14, 1768
      - Jeremiah - b. May 31, 1769
      - Nancy - b. 1771
        - m. _____ Ackley
      - Norman - b. February 23, 1773
        - d. young
      - William - b. 1777
        - d. 1777
      - Chloe - b. October, 1778
        - d. September, 1779
      - Rhoda - b. September 23, 17__
  - Abner - b. March 10, 1739
    - m. Eunice Gibb
    - d. 1795, Canada
    - Children
      - Mehitable - b. June 5, 1767

                    m. David, son of Lt. Ephraim and
                    Hannah Sanford Harrison
          Molly - b. April 6, 1743
             m. Sylvanus Bishop
          John - b. May 14, 1747
             m. Abigail Bissel
          Seth - b. December 18, 1749
             m1 Anna (1754-1800), dau of Zopher and
             Elizabeth Wadham Beach
             m2 Eunice (1751-1801), dau of Moses and Rachel
             Goodwin Seymour
             d. February 4, 1832; Litchfield, Connecticut
          Nathan - b. June 8, 1752
             m. Sally Smith
          Joseph - b. February 3, 1758; Litchfield,
             Connecticut
             d. August 24, 1775

Oliver Landon
    b. March 12, 1755; Litchfield, Connecticut
    m1. Aner / Arner Watkins (1754-March 18, 1800; Lansdowne,
    Ontario); May 2, 1776
    m2. Lois Loomis (May 27, 1761-July 20, 1825; Lansdowne,
    Ontario), dau of John Beach; September 13, 1801 or 1809
    d. January or June 29, 1820; Lansdowne, Ontario
    bur. Lansdowne Cemetery, Lansdowne, Ontario
    Children by Aner
        Joseph (see below)
        Benjamin - b. November 13, 1778; Litchfield,
            Connecticut
            m. pos Polly Cross (1777-1819)
            d. 1867; Lansdowne, Ontario
            Children
                Polly
                Samuel - b. 1803
                    d. 1837
        Oliver, Jr. - b. March 5, 1780; Litchfield,
            Connecticut
            m. Margaret, Canada
            bur. Lansdowne Cemetery, Lansdowne, Ontario
            Children
                Nathan   John   Joel
                William   Oliver III   Mary
                Amos   Margaret   Daniel
                Nancy
        William Henry - b. August 6, 1782; Litchfield,
            Connecticut
            m. 1802
            d. 1853; on board Lake Erie streamer
            bur. Lansdowne, Ontario
            Children
                Charles - m. Eleanor Yates
                    Children
                        Emeline   Lucy   Wellington
                        Clara   William   Charles E.
                Hiram
                Festus
                Henry
        Erastus - b. October, 1784; Litchfield, Connecticut
            m. Patience Plumb
            d. 1835; Lansdowne, Ontario

                          115

                    Children
                        Jeremiah   Anson   Erastus Jr.
        Luther - b. June 9, 1787; Litchfield, Connecticut
            d. 1829
        Daniel - b. December 5, 1792; Lansdowne, Ontario
            d. May 25, 1856
            bur. Lansdowne Cemetery, Lansdowne, Ontario
        Jesse - b. February 22, 1796; Lansdowne, Ontario
        Simcoe - b. August 30, 1799; Lansdowne, Ontario
            m. Mary Kyes
            d. 1862
            Children
                Edgar
                John B. - m. Alice Webster
        Children by Lois
            Lois - b. May 22, 1803; Lansdowne, Ontario

Joseph Landon
    b. April 9, 1777; Litchfield, Connecticut
    m1. c. 1800
    m2. Rebecca Elliott (1796-1891); August 2, 1819
    d. 1831; Lansdowne, Ontario
    Children
        Truman (see below)
        Antha
        Abner - b. February 3, 1804
            m1 Nancy Gray (1810-September 6, 1843); March
            2, 1826
            m2 Agnes Rogers Gorman, wid of John Gorman (c.
            1799-July 11, 1873)
            d. January 30, 1882
            Children
                Joseph Sawyer - d. young
                John Watkins - d. young
                Charlotte Ann - m. William Buck
                Samuel Gray - b. December 6, 1830
                    d. March 4, 1918
                Margaret - d. young
                Catherine - d. young
                Edwin Doty - b. February 14, 1843
                    m1 Emeline Landon (1822-1893), dau
                    of Charles Landon and Eleanor Yates
                    m2 Catherine Switzer
                    d. January 25, 1915
                    bur. Omar, New York
        Anna - b. 1805
            m. Henry Kyes; October 30, 1825
            d. November 13, 1854
            bur. Lansdowne Cemetery, Lansdowne, Ontario

Truman Landon
    b.c. 1810
    m. Caroline Burns (July 29, 1818-June 2, 1906), dau of
    Samuel Burns and Eliza Cassidy; 1840
    d. 1856; Orangeville, Ontario
    Children
        Joseph Sawyer - b. 1842; Clearville, Ontario
            m Harriet Ann Askins (1839-1920)
            d. May 1, 1886; Gosnell Cemetery, Highgate,
            Orford Twp, Ontario
            bur. Gosnell Cemetery, Highgate, Ontario

```
Children
    John - b. July 25, 1864
          m1. Matilda Jane Reddick
          m2. Alice
          d. February, 1943 or 1936; Edmonton,
          Alberta, Canada
    Truman - b. 1866
          m. Agnes Ford (1867-1938); 1888
          d. December 28, 1902
          bur. Gosnell Cemetery, Highgate,
          Ontario
    Eloda - b. 1869
          m. Abel Millar (1866-1946); 1891
          d. July 1, 1961
          bur. Gosnell Cemetery, Highgate,
          Ontario
    Abraham - b. 1872
    William - b. 1874
          m1. Robert Blue Mulholland
          m2. Anna Spence
          d. 1933
          bur. Gosnell Cemetery, Highgate,
          Ontario
    Herbert - b. 1876
    Amasa - b. May 4, 1879
          m. Rhea Wigle (1886-1956)
          d. November 10, 1963
    Ida - b. 1881
          m. William Scott (1882-1951)
          d. 1964
Margaret - b. 1843
Edna - b. 1845
      d. aft. 1896
William - b. 1850
Nancy - b. 1853
      m. Charles Holman (d. February 24, 1930)
      Children
          Truman
          Edna - m. Thomas Ford (1882-1973) of
                Duart, Orford Twp, Ontario
                Children
                        Neil      William    Altha
                        Lila      Clifford   Pearl
                        Joyce?    Truman?
          Lizzie - m. ____ Stritch of Detroit,
                Michigan
          Bertha - m. Joseph Lauzon of Woodslee,
                Essex, Ontario
          Ann - m. Charles Forsyth of Aldborough
                Twp. Elgin County, Ontario
          William - b. 1874
                r. Windsor, Ontario
                d. 1930
          Joe
          Albert
          George - r. Dearborn, Michigan


     James Landon's son Daniel I was born in 1714 in Southold,
Long Island, New York, but moved to Litchfield, Connecticut,
circa 1735. He took as his second wife Martha Youngs of
```

Southold. For some reason, their marriage appeared in both Southold and Litchfield record books.

Daniel Landon was made freeman in Litchfield in 1741, a voter in 1747, a grand juror in 1746, and a selectman in 1753. On November 5, 1745, Daniel I joined twelve others in the founding of the First Episcopal Society of Litchfield (later named St. Michael's Church) where he served as parish clerk for 45 years and to which he signed over title of 50 acres of land in 1747.

After the minister's death in 1771, Daniel and his family continued to meet regularly for services. According to J.O. Landon,

"Capt. Daniel Landon officiated as lay reader, being always anxious to promote the welfare of the Church. All his family attended with him through honor and dishonor..."

One Sunday morning, after the morning service at St. Michael's, Daniel I returned home and died. He was buried in West Burying Ground, Litchfield, Connecticut. Daniel drafted the verses of his own tombstone.

Sacred to the memory of
Daniel Landon of Litchfield
Who died July 11, 1790, aged 77
Who served as clerk to the Episcopal
Church in Litchfield forty years.

"His God he served with pious zeal
The sacred dome was his delight
For distant from this holy hill
He took his everlasting flight.

Lo here I leave this earthly clay
And fly beyond the ethereal blue
Unchained unto external day
To sing the praise of God anew."

Daniel had lived through some turbulent times. Anglicans were maligned, persecuted and harassed and their property was confiscated. Tories were killed by mobs or executed by local governments. On the other side, a number of massacres of patriots were carried on by Indians working for the Tories. Many of Daniel's children stayed out of it as long as they could. But when they watched their church being attacked by an angry mob, they probably realized that tough choices would have to be made.

Daniel II served as a private for the rebels in the Revolutionary War. Daniel II's uncle David Landon and son Seth also supported the colonists. A number of nephews also joined the rebels.

But several of Daniel II's sons and their families along with many other Landons did not support the fight for independence. Fearing retaliation for their support of the British, they fled to Canada. Abner built a saw mill in Oswegatchie and Asa fled to Augusta.

Despite his earlier rebel support, at 73 years of age, Daniel Landon II left Esopus, Ulster County, New York on foot bound for his eldest daughter Sarah Baldwin's home. Sarah's husband had received a 150 acre land grant on November 13, 1797 near Picton, Ontario. Daniel Landon III also settled there.

In the early days of the Revolution, Daniel I's son Oliver Landon was only 22 and Aner was only 21 years old and they were newly married. Since children were born to them throughout the war years, Oliver probably never fought for either side. But his lands were still confiscated. And when the new U.S. Federal Constitution was announced in October, 1787, it required all citizens swear allegiance to the United States. That was more than Oliver could do.

On October 16, 1787, Oliver left Litchfield and headed north into an area of Canada with no roads or trails. The family, including six sons from ten years to five months of age, traveled alone through the forest, arriving at what would become Lansdowne, Ontario on November 5, 1787.

At the time, Lansdowne was in the province of Quebec. Later it became part of Upper Canada and, finally, Ontario. When the town of Lansdowne on the St. Lawrence was laid out in June, 1788, was surrounded by 30 miles of wilderness. Oliver's land there came from a grant from Lord Dorchester of Quebec.

The first spelling of the town was Lansdown; with the final "e" being added after 1872. Some believe the town was named for the third Marquess of Lansdowne, Canada's Governor General from 1833-1888. But because of the dates, it was more likely named for an earlier member of that family.

Much of the information from that time came from a questionnaire circulated by Scotsman Robert Gourlay. A powerful group called the Family Compact controlled most land grants. In 1818, Gourlay called a meeting of pioneer farmers to address grievances. But the Compact had Gourlay arrested, tried and banished as a "seditious alien". Back in Britain, Gourlay published the results of his questionnaire (see Appendix).

The answers to Gourlay's questions gave an interesting view of conditions in early Lansdowne. The area had one government-assisted schoolhouse which also served as church for the Methodists and, at that time, for the Baptists and Presbyterians. There was no doctor and only one store. But Lansdowne did have three taverns.

In 1804, Oliver and his sons Joseph and Benjamin were granted 200 acres each by the crown. From that 1804 grant, Joseph owned a portion of Lot 12 Concession 2, Lansdowne Township. Oliver received Lot 14 Concession 2, Lansdowne Township. A deed dated 1795 and found in the library of Queens University, Kingston, Ontario showed Oliver conveying 200 acres to John McNeil. The Leeds County acreage was described as

"part of Lot II or one hundred acres on each side of the (King's) Road, for the valuable consideration of Seventy-five pounds Halifax."

A February 19, 1807 patent for part of lot "S 1-2 11" (southern 1/2 of lot 11), front concession of Lansdowne went to Oliver Landon. But there was also a document (R.G.I., C-1-3, Vol. 15 Page 485) which stated

"Oliver Landon of Lansdowne Township, Leeds County, Johnstown District, farmer, Land Board Certificate dated 12th November 1789, for the South half of Lot no. 11, in the front concession of the Township of Lansdowne. Fiat dated 18th February 1807."

When his first wife died, Oliver had nine sons and no daughters. He married second a widow Lois Loomis who already had two daughters. After their marriage, Lois presented Oliver with his first daughter who they also named Lois.

On 1804 land patent papers, Oliver Landon was listed as a "yeoman," a title which usually referred to a small farmer who cultivated his own land. Usually, a yeoman was someone belonging to a class of English freeholders below the rank of gentry.

In 1812, at age 57, Oliver disposed of all of his land, dividing most of it amongst his sons. At the same time, together with William Robinson, he built a dam and began a saw mill. They sold the mill to John Spencer in 1819. Then in 1818, Oliver Landon served as Township Assessor for Leeds County, Ontario.

Oliver Landon died on January 29, 1820. Oliver and his two wives, Aner and Lois, were buried side by side in the family plot in Lansdowne. His son William Henry died in 1853 in a fire on board the *Ocean Wave* steamer on Lake Erie.

Oliver's son Joseph Landon married first circa 1800, but his first wife's name has not been uncovered. At least one Landon researcher believed his wife was Polly Roone of Clearville, Ontario. Others have suggested her last name was Sawyer because that was later found in the family as a middle name. Others have made a case for the name Stone for the same reasons. Since Truman Stone was a neighbor of Oliver's, and since the name Truman also was carried down through the Landon family, a Stone family connection of some sort is possible.

Joseph farmed in the same area as his father. In fact, the land his father built the saw mill on was purchased from Joseph. He owned part of lot 12 Concession 2 of Lansdowne Township and sold 33 acres of it to Ephraim Webster in 1822. At his death in 1831, he was living on 39 1/4 acres of lot 4 of Concession 1.

Circa 1825, a letter to him was addressed to "Reverend Joseph Landon". He was also referred to as "Rev." in an 1822 agreement with Joel Stone and an 1830 letter from C. & J. McDonald. Then in the letters of administration of his estate, he was again addressed as "Reverend.

But that was just one of the "professions" Joseph Landon held. In fact, In First Settler..., Joseph was referred to as "one of the wheeler dealers of those early days." Through the years, Joseph was a storekeeper, township clerk (1805-1826), tax collector (1829), innkeeper (1816), fur buyer, potash entrepreneur and minister. His inn, the Sign of the Hart Inn, was located on lot number 12 and later became known as the McCormac Hotel.

He was even a "wheeler dealer" where his family was concerned. Land he purchased for 12 pounds 10 shillings in 1811, he sold to his father for 65 pounds in 1812. But his father did not lose on the deal. Oliver reserved the mill site and sold the rest of the land for 95 pounds.

Joseph's son Abner spent much of his life on forty acres of lot number 4 in the first concession of Lansdowne and, according to Mires, was considered a successful farmer. In 1840, Abner Landon was serving as a sergeant in the militia under Capt. Robinson. After his father held the office, Abner became Lansdowne Town Clerk.

Although Truman Landon I was born more recently (circa 1810) than his father, Joseph's son has been difficult to research. He probably arrived in Clearville in the early 1830's. Then, circa 1840, Truman married Caroline Burns and they settled in Clearville, Orford Township, Kent County, Ontario.

Truman was the first school teacher in Highgate, Ontario, but not in Orford Township. George Biggs taught the first school in Orford Township. It was situated at Clear Creek (Clearville) in 1827.

Truman was teaching in Highgate by 1839. While there, he was paid in produce and his additional duties included being school janitor and cutting all the school's firewood. Much later Highgate became a police village and was part of Orford Township until 1917.

In 1851 Truman was hired as teacher in Orangeville. Probably between 1839 and 1851, Truman taught somewhere else. But he must have been somewhere in the area, because in 1844 he witnessed the marriage of Jacob Ward and Nancy Burns and in 1846 the marriage of William Leetzel and Margaret Burns.

Truman was not living with his wife and children in the 1851 Orford Township census. Nor was he listed with them in 1861. However, since Truman's daughter Nancy was 8 years old in 1861, it could be assumed he was still living in 1853. At the time of the 1851 census, Truman was probably living in Orangeville, where he was teaching. Truman died circa 1856, possibly of consumption. He was only about 46 years old.

Joseph Sawyer Landon was born to Truman and Caroline Landon in 1842 in Clearville, Ontario. He married Harriet Ann Askins, daughter of William and Eliza Cassidy Askins.

Although Joseph Sawyer was primarily a farmer, he also had a love of baseball. In approximately 1862, he was one of the original members of the Slashers Baseball Team of Highgate, Ontario. They played with a rubber ball in those days and the Slashers were quite good. In 1870 they became the champions of Kent County.

Then in the early 1880's the Past Times Ball Club was organized from the best players in Kent County. Joseph Landon and his teenage son Truman II played for them. It was a rougher game in those days and the Past Times did not wear gloves, masks or chest protectors. Other Landons played on other ball teams as well.

Like his father, Joseph Sawyer Landon died while still in his forties. He died May 1, 1886 and was buried in Gosnell Cemetery, Highgate, Ontario.

Like his grandmother Caroline, Joseph Sawyer's son John Landon was an innkeeper. He owned at least one hotel and, perhaps two, in Canada before losing all his money. He took his family across the border to Michigan hoping to improve their situation. After first working on the railroad, John was able to open a hotel in Romeo, Michigan.

Romeo, north of Detroit, began as a trading post built on the site of an old Indian village as early as 1817. Then, in 1836, the town, which had been settled by Canadian lumbermen circa 1822 and New Englanders of 1826, had grown to thirty frame buildings.

After arriving in Romeo, John Landon's life began to fall apart again. The new hotel burned and John and his wife Matilda Jane Reddick Landon divorced.

After his divorce, John moved to Alberta, Canada where he remarried and operated a hotel at Landonville, near Vermillion. John Landon lived longer than either his father or his grandfather, dying at age 79 in Edmonton.

McKee Family

Thomas McKee
> b. pos Ireland
> m. Shawnee woman or white captive
> Children
>> Alexander (see below)

Alexander McKee I (Col.)
> b.c. 1735; western Pennsylvania
> m. Shawnee woman
> d. January 13, 1799; Thames River, Upper Canada
> Children
>> Thomas (see below)

Thomas McKee (Captain)
> m2 Therese Askin (February 10, 1774, bur. June 23, 1832; Sandwich, Ontario), dau of John Askin, Sr. and Marie Archange Barthe; April 17, 1797; Petite Cote, Upper Canada
> d. Spring, 1815; Lower Canada
> wll dtd. May 8, 1801
> Children by first wife
>> Marie Anne (see below)
>> James - b.c. 1790
>>> d. September 3, 1808; Detroit River
>>> bur. September 3, 1808; Amherstburg, Ontario
>> Catherine
> Children by Therese
>> Alexander II - b. aft 1797
>>> m. Felicity, dau of George Jacob and Mary Archange Chene dit Labutte

Marie Anne (Nancy) McKee
> b.c. 1796/97
> bpt. March 4, 1800; Sandwich, Ontario
> eng. but not m. - Spring, 1815

The Scottish MacKay chief was Sir Donald of Fair, who later became Lord Reay. In the 1600's, he was given permission by Charles I to raise a force of three thousand men to help Charles' sister Elizabeth and her husband the King of Bohemia, in a war against Austria. Then MacKay's Regiment became renown in the Thirty Year's War. In 1806, the Clan MacKay Society became one of the first clan organizations started to aid clan members.

The McKee / M'Ky / M'Kee / Mackay / MacKey family of this genealogy was established in the United States with Thomas McKee; probably born in Ireland, but possibly originally from Scotland; who appeared in American records in Pennsylvania on April 19, 1744. A William McKee, an Irish member of the Philadelphia, Pennsylvania Presbyteria in 1786, may have been a relative.

On the April 19, 1744 date, "Thomas M'Kee" was one of several who gave a deposition after looking into the suspicious deaths of John Armstrong, James Smith, and Woodward Arnold.

Thomas was a successful trader who had begun a trading post by 1749 (see Appendix). Rupp reported that

"McKee's fort or Trading house,(was) where Thomas Mckee, the Indian trader was stationed. this place was about twenty-five miles above Fort Hunter."

In the 1750's, Thomas McKee's fort was garrisoned according to "the exigencies of the times demanded it, and when the men were to be had." In fact, on July 1, 1756, William Clapham wrote to Gov. Morris that he was leaving twenty-four men at McKee's store under the command of an ensign.

It was necessary to have troops garrisoned at McKee's because of the increased Indian activity in the area. A letter from Conrad Weiser letter dated "Heidelberg; October 26, 1755; 11 o'clock Sunday night" and addressed to James Reed described one such incident.

"About one hour ago, I received the news of the enemy having crossed the Susquehannah, and killed a great many people, from Thomas McKee's down to Hunter mills."

An October 31, 1755 letter reported by Rupp described how friendly Indians "discovered a party of the enemy at Thos. Mckee's upper place."

Because of his marriage to either a Shawnee woman or a white captive and the placement of his post in Indian territory, Thomas became quite helpful to the governor in his dealings with the Indians. In December, 1755, Thomas was consulted by an emissary of Gov. Morris's concerning how to get the governor's "message to the Indians on the West Branch of the Susquehanna." The next year William Clapham wrote Gov. Morris that he "found Capt. McKee extremely useful" in dealings with the Indians. And Thomas was present at a 1757 conference with the Indians.

In October, 1755, Adam Terrance, Thomas Foster, "Mrs. Harris and Mr. McKee" and forty men went to the trading post of

"Captain McKee at New Providence in order to bury the dead, lately murdered on Mahahany creek; but understanding the corpse(s) were buried, (they) then determined to return immediately home."

Unfortunately, they were foolishly urged to visit other Indians at Shamoken before returning. While there they overheard Delaware Indians wondering if the English visitors had come to kill them. After the English left Shamoken, they were ambushed by "a good number of indians." Nine from the English party never returned according to a description written by Adam Terrance.

While Thomas' trading post flourished, other McKee families were living in Pennsylvania who could have been related to him. In 1751, Franklin County, Pennsylvania; an Alexander McKee lived in Peters Township, a John McKee in Lurgan Township, and Hugh and James McKee in Antrim Township. In 1750, a James McKee was on the tax rolls in Lebanon Township, Dauphin County, Pennsylvania, and a Widow McKee appeared on the rolls in East Pennsboro, Cumberland County, Pennsylvania.

A number of Pennsylvania McKees fought on the rebel side of the American Revolution, including Andrew, Gavin, George,

James, John, Samuel and William McKee. Any of them might have been related to Thomas Mckee of this genealogy. In fact, Andrew McKee (W3277) who enlisted in Cumberland County, Pennsylvania had a son he named Thomas. And George McKee (S22901) resided in Northumberland County, Pennsylvania, but had been born in August, 1754 in County Donegal, Ireland.

The Alexander McKee listed as a grand juror in Bedford County, Pennsylvania in 1771 may have been the son of the first Thomas McKee of this genealogy. Whether or not he was, Burton called Thomas McKee's son Alexander
"one of the foremost figures on the British side of the western theater during the Revolutionary War and long one of the most influential men in western Canada."

Alexander began his career as a young man serving as lieutenant with the Pennsylvania forces at the end of the Seven Years War. He began working with the Indian Department as George Croghan's assistant. Then in 1772, Alexander was appointed Deputy Agent of Indian Affairs at Fort Pitt (Pittsburgh). He served the department well and traded with the Indians, becoming highly regarded among the tribes. In the early 1770's Alexander McKee was married to a Shawnee woman and lived in a Shawnee village on the Scioto River in Ohio.

But in reality, McKee was a British sympathizer and when the American Revolution broke out, he was watched closely by the rebels. In fact, in 1777 he was imprisoned by General Hand.

After his pardon in March, 1778, Alexander joined with Loyalists Matthew Elliot and Simon Girty on their flight from the Fort Pitt area and sought refuge in Detroit. Alexander McKee's departure from Ft. Pitt had a devastating effect on the Americans who needed his influence with the Indians.

Upon his arrival in Detroit, his skills working with the Indians were quickly put to use. Alexander was first appointed a captain and interpreter in the British Indian Department. Later, he became Deputy Agent and, finally, Superintendent of Indian Affairs. He stood up for the Indians, urging John Johnson to forbid licensing traders who dealt in rum because unethical traders had been using excesses of liquor to defraud the Indians. In Fall, 1783, McKee objected to the confirmation of a deed in which the Ottawa Indians were relinquishing approximately seven square miles to Jacob Schieffelin, the Secretary of the Indian Department at Detroit. McKee contended that the purchase was being made "in a clandestine manner from a few drunken Indians who (were) not the real owners."

While Deputy Agent, Alexander McKee purchased all the land from Long Point on Lake Erie to Chenal Ecarte at the mouth of the St. Clair River for the Crown. The purchase was completed in May, 1790. And he purchased the land from the Indians from a mere 1200 pounds Quebec currency in goods.

On December 15, 1779, General Robert Prescott of Quebec ordered Alexander McKee, then Deputy Superintendent of Indian Affairs, to move to Amherstburg, since it was more centrally located then "the Western extremity of the Province," where he was living at the time. Prescott also ordered that Alexander's son Thomas McKee be given the duties of the "North Western district for which he was originally appointed superintendent."

In his role with the Indian Department, Alexander was able to incite the Indians against his enemies, the Americans, during the American Revolution; and to direct Indian operations in the Ohio Valley. He participated in Hamilton's capture of Vincennes in 1778, Bird's expedition against Kentucky in 1780, and the attack on Bryant's Station near Lexington, Kentucky in 1782. After the Treaty of Paris, British agents like McKee encouraged the Indians to protect the land to the north of the Ohio River against an American invasion. Colonels McKee and Elliott, backed by the British garrison at Ft.Miami, led the Indian opposition which lasted for over ten years.

Much of Alexander McKee's work was aimed at Major General Anthony Wayne's troops. McKee had a trading post on the Maumee (Miami) River which was the site of The Battle of Fallen Timbers (near present-day Waterville, Ohio) in August, 1794. Knowing the battle was about to take place, McKee had made his will the previous day. Even though McKee survived the battle, General Wayne was victorious and ordered the destruction of McKee's post in revenge.

While working with Lt. Gov. Simcoe, Alexander McKee attempted to formulate a plan for an Indian buffer state between American and British land. The state never came to be.

When the British removed from Detroit, McKee made his home on the Canadian side, where there were privileges to being an officer. A 1785 memorandum to a surveyor indicated that lots of land reserved for Captains Bird, Caldwell, Elliott, and McKee were six acres wide while all other lots were only four acres wide.

In the April 22, 1792 census for Petite Cote, "Col. McKay" had a three arpent by forty arpent farm with no one living on it. The farm was situated between the Gervais River and Turkey Creek, opposite Turkey Island and had been granted by Mr. de Sabrevoes.

Alexander also held lot 4, Malden township, Essex county circa 1794. His son Thomas held lots 15 and 16. Then on August 14, 1797, Col. McKee drew lot 5 on the east side of Russell Street at Sandwich, Ontario. At the same time Capt. Thomas McKee drew lot 6 on the west side of Bedford Street, Sandwich.

Alexander McKee became a member of the Land Board for the District of Hesse in 1789. He was appointed by Lord Dorchester. As an influential man, McKee's power was impressive. He was appointed judge of the Court of Common Pleas at Detroit in the late 1780's and was one of a group who agreed to support Rev. George Mitchell beginning in December, 1786 as the first pastor for the Protestants in the area. In July, 1792 Col. McKee was asked to support the legislative candidacy of David W. Smith. He was also the person John Askin contacted when he wanted "to change the boundaries between the Northern and Southern Battalion" and wanted to recommend men he thought would make good officers. He was still with the

Essex militia in 1796, at the approximate age of sixty-one years.

On January 5, 1799, John Askin wrote to Col. De Peyster that all his acquaintances in "the Quarter", such as Col. McKee from the Riviere a la Tranche and McKee's son Thomas who was married to Askin's daughter Therese, were alive and well. However, eight days later, Alexander McKee was dead from lockjaw.

At the time, negotiations with the Huron Indians to purchase Sandwich Township had been going on for about three years. With McKee's death, the negotiations were in trouble. However, Alexander's son Capt. Thomas McKee finally executed the deed in September, 1800.

Shortly after Alexander's death, Robert Richardson wrote to John Askin that he had heard that Alexander's son Thomas McKee was "left very handsomely provided for." In addition, Thomas McKee had married well. Therese was the daughter of John Askin, Sr. J.P. Prideaux Selby had performed the marriage on April 17, 1797 at Petite Cote. She was his second wife.

Despite the large inheritance from his father, Burton called Therese's marriage to Thomas, the most unfortunate marriage of all of Askin's children. In the beginning, things went well for Thomas. He achieved the rank of captain with the 60th Regiment. However, it may have galled him when, in June 7, 1791, on the Militia Roll appeared "Thomas McKee, the Colonels Son." It was probably hard to have been the son of such an influential, courageous man.

As late as August, 1799, Captain Thomas McKee was in negotiations with the Wyandotte Indians. Then in September, 1800, Capt. McKee was Superintendent of Indian Affairs. And even before his father's death, Thomas McKee was financially able to lease Pelee Island from the Chippewas and Ottawas in May, 1788, for 999 years at the rate equal to 3 bushels of corn a year.

Personally things were also going well for Thomas back then. Thomas and Therese were living at Petite Cote at the time and in an April 28, 1797 letter to her parents, Therese Askin McKee wrote
"I can now assure my loving parents that I am happy as it is possible to be with a husband who gives me every attention. He seems to love me more each hour and to anticipate my every wish."

But then her letters became more negative. Why or when things actually began to go wrong was hard to determine. On December 26, 1812, Therese was in Amherstburg and Thomas had "rheumatish in the Head." Then when Detroit was evacuated in the autumn of 1813, Thomas McKee fled with his family to Lower Canada in the wake of Proctor's retreating army.

On May 9, 1815, the McKees were in Montreal and Alexander Henry wrote to John Askin that Therese was suffering greatly and that Thomas was "deranged with liquor." McKee's career had been ruined by his drunkenness. Despite the early successes, he never attained a rank higher than captain. Through the years, his overindulgence with liquor had ruined Thomas McKee and brought about the loss of the estate he had inherited from his father. Upon Thomas' 1815 death, Therese was left penniless.

Of Thomas' children, his daughter Marie Anne (Nancy) by his first wife was supposedly baptized in Sandwich on March 4, 1800 at age 3 1/2 years old. Nancy was not mentioned in the will her father wrote in 1801, but she was still alive.

But life was not easy for young Nancy McKee. On January 31, 1807, James Askin of Sandwich wrote that "Poor Nancy McKee and Charles Brush were much burnt." James reported that Nancy's clothes had caught fire. While Charles Brush died, Nancy did survive.

In October, 1813, after taking refuge with her family from the war, Nancy and Jane Richardson left their families at the "Head [of] the Lake" and left "for York where they (would) be more comfortable."

In Spring, 1815, Nancy was engaged, according to her step-mother, to a "fine young man." At the time, Nancy and Therese McKee were staying with the George Hamilton family in what would become Hamilton, Ontario. Unfortunately, according to Burton, Nancy had not married by October, 1815 and Therese Askin McKee expressed worry about Nancy's financial future.

James McKee was about seven years old when his father Thomas married Therese Askin. Shortly after her marriage, Therese wrote to her father that "Little James" was very troublesome and asked her parents to send a spelling book for him. Sadly enough, James drowned in the Detroit River on September 3, 1808 at approximately eighteen years of age and was buried at Amherstburg by Rev. Richard Pollard.

Alexander II, also known as "the Younger" was the son of Thomas and Therese McKee. While a fugitive with his parents during the war, Therese McKee referred to him in a letter as Alick and wrote that his toe was "very bad."

Quaife claimed that during the War of 1812, Alexander McKee II was a second lieutenant in the First Lincoln Artillery Company, then a lieutenant in the Indian Department and, finally, on June 25, 1814, a captain. Quaife continued that since Alexander's parents "were married in April, 1797, he must have been a very youthful officer." Youthful indeed! Alexander McKee II would have had to have been a second lieutenant as early as age 15 and captain at age 17. Was that probable?

May Family

N.N. May
Children
James (see below)
Joseph (Capt.) - b. Warwickshire, England
m. Rebecca Knaggs (b. Maumee River bpt. March
1, 1778; Assumption, Sandwich, Ontario), dau of
George Knaggs and Rachel Schley
d. July, 1801; in shipwreck on Lake Erie

James May
b. 1756; Birmingham, Warwickshire, England
m1 Rose St. Cosme (1726-1797), dau of Peter Laurence St.
Cosme and Catherine Lootman dit Barrois; Detroit,
Michigan
m2 Margaret Deschamps / Descomps dit Labadie (1778-1850),
dau of Peter Deschamps / Descomps dit Labadie and Teresa
Gaillard dit Leonais; Detroit, Michigan
d. January 19, 1829; Detroit, Michigan
Children by Rose
Ann - b. May, 1785; Detroit, Michigan
bur. November 28, 1785
Geneveva - b. May, 1786; Detroit, Michigan
bur. June 17, 1786; Detroit, Michigan
Elizabeth - m. Gabriel Godfroy (July 3, 1783-1848),
son of Gabriel Godfroy and Catherine Couture;
April 27, 1808
Children by Margaret
Ann - b. December 2, 1798, Detroit, Michigan
m1 Peter Frances Audrain (bur. June 16, 1838),
son of Peter Audrain and Margaret Moore;
August 3, 1823
m2 James B. Whipple of Monroe, Michigan, wid
of Sophia Godfroy; November 2, 1843; Detroit,
Michigan
bur. September 19, 1871
Margaret - b. September 15, 1800; Detroit, Michigan
m. Lt. Edward Brooks, son of William Brooks
bur. January 1, 1844; Detroit, Michigan
Mary - b. September 7, 1802; Detroit, Michigan
d. November 7, 1802; Detroit, Michigan
Mary Ann - b. January 1, 1804; Detroit, Michigan
m. Louis Moran (b. March 18, 1797), son of
Louis Moran and Catherine Campau; August 6,
1823; Detroit, Michigan
James - b. December 8, 1805; Detroit, Michigan
bpt. January 19, 1806; Detroit, Michigan
m. Susanne Fournier (1813-1834), dau of
Frances Fournier and Mary Facer; january 7,
1829; Detroit, Michigan
d. April 18, 1813
Children
James Anthony - b. July 30, 1831;
Detroit, Michigan
Peter Benjamin - b. April 22, 1808; Detroit,
Michigan
bur. January 5, 1809; Detroit, Michigan
Teresa Augustina Charlotte - b. April 7, 1810;
Detroit, Michigan
bur. April 26, 1813; Detroit, Michigan

Charlotte Elizabeth / Caroline - b. October 29,
1813; Detroit, Michigan
   m. Alexander Daniel Fraser (b. Scotland);
January 3, 1829; Detroit, Michigan
Benjamin - b. April 10, 1816; Detroit Michigan
Samuel William - b. February 12, 1819; November 25,
1842
   m. Silence Cushing (b. February 27, 1827);
November 25, 1842
   d. aft 1883

The May surname meant "good, pleasant". This family
originated in Birmingham in Warwickshire, England, where
brothers Joseph and James May were born.

According to James May's son-in-law, the Honorable
Alexander D. Fraser, twenty-two year old May arrived in
Detroit from England in 1778. In his own journal, James May
related that it was a four day passage from Fort Erie, which
was on the Niagara River opposite Buffalo to Detroit. He
traveled on board the "brig-of war *Genl. Gage*". Because the
American Revolution was raging, military vessels were pretty
much the only ones able to get through on the Great Lakes.

According to his May's journal, the city of Detroit had
only about sixty families with about two hundred men and one
hundred women in it when May arrived. In the journal, he wrote
"They - the men - were chiefly bachelors. There was not
a marriage in the place for a number of years, until I
broke the ice (when he married Rose St. Cosme)."

James became a merchant and, in 1789, sold five thousand
pounds of live beef and fifty ewes to Lord Selkirk. According
to The Valley of the Lower Thames, in 1796, May owned *The
Swan*, a small sailing vessel used to deliver good up the
Thames River from Detroit.

Commercial vessels were important in the Great Lakes
region. In fact, it was on one such vessel that James May's
brother Joseph died. Joseph May served as a captain on the
lakes and was one of three crew members on John Askin's 28 1/4
ton vessel, *The Harlequin*, when it was shipwrecked in 1801.
Apparently everyone on board was lost. In October, 1801, John
Warren of Ft. Erie wrote Askin that parts of the wreck had
washed ashore at "Point Ebino," but that no bodies had been
recovered. However, at the end of the letter, Warren related
that one report he had received indicated that "Capt. May was
taken up and buried by some Indians."

Interestingly enough, when Joseph died, James May seemed
more upset about the loss of his slave than his brother in a
letter he wrote to Askin telling him the schooner was presumed
lost. May wrote
"The stroke is a very severe one for me, the effects of
which I shall feel for a long time; perhaps the rest of
my days. the loss of my Negro man, will probably be the
cause of loseing the negro woman, who ever since the
misfortune happened, has been delirious and is now very
Ill, in bed; being now deprived of two of the best
servants, in this country, my situation is very
distressing, unless you will condescend to let your Boy

George, remain with me until I can have time to look about for a servant ... should you be inclined to part with him, I would purchase [him] but cannot undertake to give a great price..."

May had a successful public career and became a colonel in the territorial militia, a justice of the peace and a marshall of the Michigan territory. In 1804 James May and Robert Abbott prepared the petition to Congress requesting territorial ship for Michigan. Quaife referred to him as "a man of energy and ability."

While James May was serving as Chief Justice of the Common Pleas Court in 1798, an interesting case was arbitrated by May concerning the five children of sailor Jesse Burbank and his common-law wife Mary Sutton. The couple had cohabited as man and wife for a little over a year. When they split up, there was dissention over what would become of all the children. May handed over two children to Burbank and three to Sutton.

May appeared on both sides of the Judge's bench. On July 8, 1790, James May and others petitioned Judge Powell to appoint a curator for Philip Dyean's estate. May was appointed. On October 7, he again petitioned the court for appointment of a guardian for Dyean's minor child.

Something legal was going on in December, 1798, when John Askin wrote to William Daly that because of late arrival of legal papers "Nothing whatever could be done in (his) demands against Mr. May for this term." Askin offered his support of Daly and added his hope that May would pay Daly without it coming to a lawsuit.

Then, when a man named Granchin owed him money, James May complained to Gov. Hamilton, who ordered Granchin to appear before him. In his journal, May related that
"being asked if he had anything to say against the debt, (Granchin) said no. (Hamilton) then ordered him to give (May) a negro wench in payment, and she served (May) twenty-five years."

Actually May had a number of slaves. In 1807, he again wrote Askin. In that letter he related that his "Negro Nobbin" had crossed over to Canada and was apprehensive about returning, fearing that May would whip him. In addition, May believed that someone was trying to persuade Askin's slave George to run away. Interestingly, George was the slave May had earlier attempted to purchase from Askin.

May owned a number of parcels of land too. In 1782, James May purchased a "tenement" from Chapman Abraham who, according to The Beth El Story..., was the first known Jewish settler in Detroit. In fact, in 1804, Askin recommended Todd and McGill property they needed to sell to May.
"The best prospect I see for the windmill is to sell it to Mr May and give him full time to pay otherwise he can not purchase. he is noted for immediately putting every thing he buys in best Order therefore the worst that can happen would be taking it back again when it would be worth double what it is today."

Navarre Family

Robert Navarre, son of Antoine Marie Francois Navarre and Jeanne Pluiette / Pleyette / Pluyette / Plugette
  b. 1709; Villeroy, Seine-et-Marne or Villeroy, Meaux, France
  m. Marie Lootman dit Barrois (1719-1799), dau of Francois Lootman dit Barrois and Marie Ann Sauvage (m. 1717); February 10, 1734; Ste. Anne Church, Detroit, Michigan
  bur. November 24, 1791; Detroit, Michigan
  Children
    Francois (see below)
    Marie Francoise - b. January 9, 1735; Detroit, Michigan
        m1. Lt. George McDougall (d. April 8, 1780; Montreal, Quebec); Detroit, Michigan
        m2. Jacques Campau (1735-1789), widower of Catherine Menard, son of John Louis Campau and Mary Louisa Robert; January 5, 1784; Detroit, Michigan
        Children by George McDougall
            George - b. October 19, 1766
            John Robert - b. June 30, 1764
                m1. Mary Archange Campau (bur. December 4, 1821; Sandwich, Ontario)
                m2. Geneveva Meny
                bur. July 24, 1846; Sandwich, Ontario
        Children by Jacques Campau
            Joseph - m. Adelaide Dequindre
            Jacques - m. Suzanne Beaubien
            Barnabie - m. Therese Cicotte
            Cecille - m. Thomas Williams
    Marie Anne - b. October 14, 1737; Detroit, Michigan
        m1. Jacques Baudry dit Desbuttes dit St. Martin (1733-1768), son of Jean Baudry dit Desbuttes dit St. Martin and Louisa Dayon or Adhemar St. Martin La Butte; October 28, 1760; Detroit, Michigan
        m2. Dr. George Christian Anthon (1734, Salzungen, Germany-1815, New York); August 13, 1770; Detroit, Michigan
        bur. October 1, 1773; St. Anthony Church, Detroit, Michigan
    Robert - b. November 25, 1739; Detroit, Michigan
        m. Mary Louis Archange de Marsac (1744-1796), dau of Francis Marsac and Teresa Cecilia Campau; December 13, 1762; Detroit, Michigan
        Children
            Francois - b. October 12, 1763; Assumption, Sandwich, Ontario
                m. Mary Suzor (1772-1826), dau of Louis Francis Suzor and Mary Joseph LeBeau; November 9, 1790; Detroit, Michigan
                bur. September 3, 1826; St. Antoine, River Raisin, Michigan
                Children

                    Robert   Julia   Joseph
                    David   Francis (2) Paul
                    Rosalie   Samuel   Mary
                    Magdelene Joseph   Oliver
                    Margaret
Robert - b. March 4, 1765; Brevoort,
    Southwest Coast of Detroit River
    m. Geneveva Bourdeau (1767-1828),
    wid Amable Cosme, dau of Joseph
    Bourdeau and Mary Louisa Clermont;
    April 14, 1809; Monroe, Michigan
    d. by 1829
    Children
        Robert - b. September 11, 1809
        Toussaint - b. october 23, 1810
Jacques - b. December 15, 1766, Detroit,
    Michigan
    m1. Basile LaPointe (1784-1819), dau
    of Jean Baptiste Audet dit LaPointe
    and Catherine Gouyou; November 5,
    1800; St. Antoine, River Raisin,
    Michigan
    m2. Mary Ann Vessiere dit Laferte
    (b. 1779), dau of Louis Vessiere dit
    Laferte and Catherine Esprit dit
    Champagne; May 3, 1823; Detroit,
    Michigan
    Children
        Francis   Peter
        Jean Baptiste Jacques
        Malildor?   Joseph
        Elizabeth
Isidore - b. August 19, 1768; Detroit,2
    Michigan
    m. Mary Frances Labadie (1774-1836),
    dau of Alexis Labadie and Mary
    Frances Robert; June 18, 1795;
    Detroit, Michigan
    bur. August 22, 1835; St. Antoine,
    River Raisin, Michigan
    Children
        Mary Ann   Agatha
        Isidore   Catherine
        Monica   Anthony
        Adelaide   Gregory
        Mary   Francis Xavier
Marie Louisa Archange - b. July 23, 1770;
    Detroit, Michigan
    m. Francois Dominic Godet dit
    Marentette (1763-1808), son of
    Francis Godet dit Marentette and
    Jane Parent; October 20, 1788;
    Assumption, Sandwich, Ontario
    bur. May 15, 1851
Anthony - b. May 26, 1772; Southwest
    Coast of Detroit River
    bur. April 19, 1812; Detroit,
    Michigan
Charlotte - b. April 10, 1774; Southwest
    Coast of Detroit River

bur. March 3, 1852; Grosse Point,
Michigan
Peter - b. December 3, 1775; Southwest
Coast of Detroit River
m. Magdelene Cavalier dit Rangeard
(bur. February 8, 1810), dau of Jean
Baptiste Rangeard and Magdelene
Parent
bur. April 27, 1808; St. Antoine,
River Raisin, Michigan
Children
Peter - b. January 18, 1807
Mary Magdelene - October 18,
1808
Simon - b/d. 1777
John Mary - b. October 23, 1778;
Southwest Coast of the Detroit River
Mary Ann - b. September 20, 1780;
Detroit, Michigan
bur. September 4, 1866; Grosse
Pointe, Michigan
Mary Catherine - b. September 4, 1782;
Detroit, Michigan
m. Lt. Henry Bergaw Brevoort
(January 13, 1775-1858), son of
Henry Brevoort and Esther Bergaw;
January 15, 1811; Detroit, Michigan
d. December 4, 1868; Detroit,
Michigan
Children
Mary Ann Brevoort - b. February
17, 1812
Monique/Monica - b. January, 1784;
Detroit, Michigan
bur. December 19, 1785; Detroit,
Michigan
Peter - b. February 8, 1787; Detroit,
Michigan
r.c. 1807, mouth of the Maumee River
Monique/Monica - b. August 13, 1789;
Detroit, Michigan
m. William Macomb (d. 1826; Grosse
Pointe, Michigan), son of William
Macomb and Sarah Dring; Detroit,
Michigan
bur. November 4, 1813; Detroit,
Michigan
Joseph - b. August 3, 1748; Detroit, Michigan
bur. August 8, 1748; Detroit, Michigan
Marie Catherine - b. July 14, 1749; Detroit,
Michigan
bur. September 7, 1751; Detroit, Michigan
Bonaventure Pierre - b. October 7, 1753; Detroit,
Michigan
bur. September 29, 1764; Detroit, Michigan
Mary Catherine - b. April 12, 1757; Detroit,
Michigan
m. Alexander Macomb (b. July 27, 1748; May 4,
1773; Dunturky, Ballymure Co., Antrim,
Ireland; d. January 19, 1831; Georgetown,

m. Alexander Macomb (b. July 27, 1748; May 4,
1773; Dunturky, Ballymure Co., Antrim,
Ireland; d. January 19, 1831; Georgetown,
Washington, D.C.), son of John Macomb and Jane
Gordon; Detroit, Michigan
d. November 17, 1789; New York
Children
    Maj. Gen Alexander, Jr. - b. 1782
    John Navarre - m. Christina Livingston
    Jane - m. Robert Kennedy
    Catherine
    William
    Sarah
    Robert
    Anne
Jean Marie Alexis - b. September 21, 1763;
Southwest Coast of Detroit River
m. Archange Godet (bur. August 17, 1834; St.
Antoine, River Raisin, Michigan), dau of Rene
Godet dit Marentette and Catherine Campau;
January 22, 1787; Detroit, Michigan
bur. May 22, 1836; St. Antoine, River Raisin,
Michigan
Children

Alexis	Magdelene	Catherine
Peter	Alexis Platt	Joseph

Francois Marie Navarre dit Utreau
b. November 19, 1759; Detroit, Michigan
m. Marie Louisa Godet dit Marentette, dau of Rene Godet
dit Marentette and Catherine Campau; February 26, 1781;
Detroit, Michigan
Children
    Susanne - b. December 8, 1782; Detroit, Michigan
    bur. December 9, 1782; Detroit, Michigan
    Francis Xavier - b. January 21, 1784; Detroit,
    Michigan
    Robert - b. September 8, 1785; Detroit, Michigan
    m. Susanne Moore (b. April 28, 1797; Detroit,
    Michigan), dau of Louis Moore and Mary Moreau;
    1815; St. Antoine, River Raisin, Michigan
    Children
        Moses - b. May 17, 1815; St. Antoine,
        River Raisin, Michigan
        Joseph - b. January 27, 1817
        Frances - b. January 29, 1819; St.
        Antoine, River Raisin, Michigan
        Children

Francis	Elizabeth
Hubert	Joseph
Honorius	Frances
Maria	James

        Daughter - b./d. July, 1820
    James - b. April 7, 1788; Detroit, Michigan
    m. Catherine Couture, wid of Peter Fortier,
    dau of Jean Baptiste Couture and Catherine
    Linfant; August 20, 1814
    Peter - b. March 28, 1790; Detroit, Michigan
    m1. Catherine Suzor

m2. Geneveva Robert (1799-1827), dau of
Isidore Robert and Agatha Reaume; September
13, 1825; St. Antoine, River Raisin, Michigan
m3. Catherine Bourdeau (b. February, 1804; St.
Antoine, River Raisin, Michigan), dau of
Joseph Bourdeau and Agatha Reaume
Children
    Felicity - b. March 31, 1815; St.
    Antoine, River Raisin, Michigan
    m. Moses Abntaya; August 4, 1834
    d. September 22, 1888
    Daughter - b. February 17, 1827; St.
    Antoine, River Raisin, Michigan
      bur. February 19, 1827; St. Antoine,
      River Raisin, Michigan
    James - b. December 6, 1832; St. Antoine,
    River Raisin, Michigan
    Oliver Benjamin - b. September 21, 1839;
    St. Antoine, River Raisin, Michigan
Mary Archange - g. July 13, 1792; Detroit, Michigan
    m. Reuben Kelsey
    bur. December 14, 1820; St. Antoine, River
    Raisin, Michigan
Anthony - b. October 24, 1793; Detroit, Michigan
    bur. January 10, 1795
Anthony - b. April 4, 1796, Detroit, Michigan
Mary Louisa - b. March 20, 1798; St. Antoine, River
    Raisin, Michigan
    m. Dominic Godet
    bur. May 15, 1851; Detroit, Michigan
Alexis - b. February 14, 1800; St. Antoine, River
    Raisin, Michigan
    m. Mary Ann Cadoret (b. September 13, 1811),
    dau of Nicholas Cadoret and Amable Huyet dit
    Champagne; September 9, 1833
    r. Presque Ile, near Monroe, Michigan
Geneveva - b. January 23, 1802; St. Antoine, River
    Raisin, Michigan
    m. Jean Baptiste Lacelle (b. September 18,
    1796), son of Jean Baptiste Lacelle and
    Catherine Rivard; February 15, 1825
Archange - b. February 4, 1806; St. Antoine, River
    Raisin, Michigan
    m. Jean Baptiste Bouvier (b. 1797; Detroit,
    Michigan), son of Jean Baptiste Bouvier;
    September 13, 1825; St. Antoine, River Raisin,
    Michigan

    The Navarres of this genealogy were descendants of the
noblemen of the Navarre region of France and Spain, and the
Bourbon and Burgundy regions of France. The Navarre region was
an inland province of northern Spain and southern France
transversed by the Pyrenees Mountains. Over time the area was
ruled by the Vascones, Romans, Visigoths, Moors, and
Charlemagne's Franks; all before the 9th century. After
finally getting their first King, Garcias Ximenez in 860 A.D.,
things remained calm in the area for several centuries.

    Beginning in the 11th century, the Navarre Region was
united with Castile, Leon, Sobrarve and Aragon. The area was
then divided again and reorganized yet a third time, before

Joanna of Navarre married Phillip, King of France in 1284, uniting the crowns for a short period.

When Catherine of Navarre was about to assume the crown of Navarre, a distant relative seized the throne of Spanish Navarre, leaving only the French Navarre for Catherine.

Catherine's daughter Jane married a Bourbon who then claimed the title of King of Navarre through his wife (see Appendix). The family continued through Jean Marten, Jean, Antoine and Antoine Marie Francois Navarre before the birth of Robert Navarre of this genealogy.

Robert Navarre was born at Villeroy, France in 1709. In History of Wayne Co. and the City of Detroit, Michigan, Navarre was described as a man of superior education, more than ordinary education for his time. He may have been educated in Paris.

Navarre was sent to Ft. Pontchartrain of Detroit by Ives Jacques Huges Pean, Sieur de Livaudiere Baron de Palude, as Royal Notary and, according to a French document presented by Quaife, "sub delegate of the Intendant of New France" for the French government. He arrived in 1730. Although the man officially in charge was the military commandant, Navarre was the highest ranking civilian at the fort.

On February 10, 1734, Robert married Marie Lootman dit Barrois at Ste. Annes in Detroit. The Lootman family was originally from Holland. According to Dennissen, in 1665 Willibrord Lootman / Lotham dit Barrois went to Canada as Secretary, Councillor and General Agent of the "compagnie des Indes" (East India Company). As a linguist, he was the official interpreter for Portuguese.

Then Denissen reported that Willibrord's son Francois Barrois was the first of the family who settled in Detroit. But Tanquay said that Francois was the son of Antoine Barrois and grandson of Jean Barrois, a surgeon, in Berri, France.

Reuben Thwaites pointed out his was a perfect example of confusion caused by name changes and sobriquets. The Lootmans, who migrated from Holland to Berri, France received the sobriquet "le Berrois", later corrupted to "Barrois". Upon removing to Canada, the "Lootman" was dropped. The Detroit branch of the family used variations and surnames became "Lotham", "Lothman dit Barrois" and "Barrois-Lothman."

Father Pierre Potier first included "Navarre" in the 1743 census of French in Detroit. In 1747, Navarre received a land grant west of the fort, on Private Claim 22. The September 1, 1750 census listed his family as containing Navarre, 1 woman, 1 girl over 15, 1 boy under 15, and 1 girl under 15. He had 45 arpents land under cultivation with 1800 sheaves of wheat, 300 sheaves oats, 7 arpents of land in corn, 3 horses, 4 oxen, 10 cows, 4 hogs and 50 poultry.

According to History of Wayne County and the City of Detroit, Michigan, as notary, Robert Navarre was

"record keeper, the lawyer, the general scrivener, the surveyor, tithe gather, tax collector, treasurer ... and perhaps, the school teacher of the settlement."
He was notary for all legal forms including real estate deeds and marriage contracts. As a trustee, he kept all of Ste. Anne Church's financial books. His signature of "Navarre" appeared on all public documents between 1734 and 1760. He traveled a great deal, probably because of his position. As judge, Robert Navarre decided what to do about delinquents and bad debts, and listened to squabbling citizens. When Commandant Sabrevois of Detroit granted land to Louis Gervais in 1749, Navarre witnessed the transaction. Even a French manuscript describing the siege of Pontiac was written by Navarre. A French document reported that no matter of local importance was taken up and discussed "without the approval of Navarre".

Robert Navarre was very good at his job. And even after the British took control, Capt. Campbell wrote to Col. Henry Bouquet that Navarre would continue to act in his old employment..." Two additional notaries, Gabriel Legrand and Philippe Dejean were appointed by the English, but neither spoke English well. In a later letter Campbell wrote that Navarre was
"an excellent man (who had) undertaken to furnish us with twenty thousand weigh of flour at least one hundred Bushes of Peas as much Indian corn as we shall want..."

As a reward for his service, the French King granted Navarre land near the fort, next to Cadillac's estate. He retired as notary in 1762 and remained on his farm until his death in 1791.

Navarre's children married well. Daughter Marie Catherine married Alexander Macomb. According to "History of Westchester Co. (New York)," the Macomb family descended from the "Mac Coombies" of Scotland who emigrated and settled first in Antrim co., Ireland. In 1785, Alexander and Marie Catherine removed to New York, where they built a great mansion and where Alexander became a land speculator. Their son Alexander Macomb, Jr. served as Chief of the Army for the United States following the War of 1812.

Mary Frances, daughter of Robert Navarre I, married Lt. George McDougall, a Scottish member of the Royal American Regiment. Backed by his influential in-laws, McDougall was able to receive a land grant for Hog Island (Belle Isle). During the American Revolution, he served as captain with the 84th Regiment. He served in Detroit until 1778 when he was sent to Charleton Island. He became so ill that he had to go to Montreal to ask permission to sell his commission. He died there in 1780.

After his death, "Marie Magdougale" offered to sell her family's interest in Hog Island for 500 pounds. But the offer was refused. Their sons, Lt. John Robert and George, Jr., took over the interest in Hog Island (Belle Isle). According to Quaife, George McDougall, Jr., was a lawyer "of eccentric temperament" who was "regarded by his contemporaries as somewhat abnormal mentally." Eventually he was disbarred and ended up as lighthouse keeper at Fort Gratiot on the St. Clair River.

Mary Frances' second husband was Jacques Campau who owned the house Major Rogers and his men took refuge in during the Battle of Bloody run in 1763. But that occurred prior to his marriage to Mary Frances.

In 1772, Robert Navarre II received four arpents of land on the river from the Potawatomis. The land, near modern 23rd Street had been part of the Potawatomi village cemetery. Records indicated the land was given so that Navarre could "cultivate the same light a fire thereon, and take care of (the Indian) dead." As namesake and eldest son, he took care of most of the legal business in the area of Detroit.

Mary Catherine, one of Robert Navarre II's daughters, married Henry Brevoort, a member of an early Dutch family from New York. After serving in the army in the lower Mississippi Valley, Brevoort was ordered to Detroit in 1802. There he assumed command of the *Adams*, built at River Rouge, Michigan. Then during the War of 1812, Brevoort commanded the navy of the Great Lakes. After his capture in 1813, he was banished from Detroit by General Proctor. He served with Commodore Perry and received a silver medal from Congress in 1823. Later, he became Indian Agent at Green Bay, Wisconsin. And through his wife, Brevoort was able to claim a portion of the land originally owned by her father.

Although Robert Navarre I was a highly educated man, he apparently did not feel it necessary for his children to also be well educated. In fact, according to <u>History of Wayne Co.</u> <u>and the City of Detroit, Michigan</u>, at age 17, son Francois could not write and probably never learned.

Descendant of Francois settled in Monroe, Michigan on the Raisin River and fought gallantly in the Indian Wars. On December 27, 1816, his son Alexis Navarre petitioned for

Pattinson Family

Unknown
    m1 ?
    m2 ?
    Children
        Richard (see below)
        Hugh

Richard Pattinson (Capt.)
    m1 Judith de Joncaire dit Chabert (1783-1804, Assumption, Sandwich, Ontario), dau of Philip Daniel de Joncaire dit Chabert
    m2 Ellen Phyllis (Felicity Eleonora / Nelly) (b. April 17, 1788, Detroit d. Riviere a la Tranche bur. October 15, 1813; Assumption, Sandwich, Ontario), dau of John Askin and Archange Barthe; aft 1804
    d. by February 28, 1818
    wll dtd. December 31, 1817; Albany, New York
    wll pro March 4, 1818; Albany, New York
    Children by Judith
        Mary Ann - b. August 8, 1803; Assumption, Sandwich, Ontario
    Children by Ellen Phyllis
        Ellen Phyllis (Felicity Eleonora) - b. February 22, 1811
            bpt. April 13, 1811; Assumption, Sandwich, Ontario
        Archange Ann - b. July 14, 1813; Riviere a la Tranche, Ontario
            bur. April 25, 1814; Assumption, Sandwich, Ontario
    Children by Unknown
        ?Richard?

According to John Askin's papers, a 1st Lt. Mark Pattison was with the Royal Regiment of Artillery as late as 1793. On August 17, 1791, he had a fine imposed on him by the Detroit Commissioners of Police. But no reason was given for the fine. Then in 1795 John Askin and Alexander Grant paid the expenses of "Mrs. M. Pattinson's" school. The total expense for the school was over thirty-five pounds, a large amount for the time.

It could not be determined if there was a relationship between these people and the Richard Pattinson of this genealogy. But Richard Pattinson did have a brother Hugh. In fact on September 26, 1795, they both signed the purchase of the peninsula of Lower Michigan.

Richard had arrived in Detroit from Montreal circa 1793 and engaged in what Burton called "a ruinous course of competition for the Indian trade." Whether it really was ruinous or not, all other indications were that Richard was very prominent in the Indian trade.

He served as a grand juror in Sandwich, Ontario on July 8, 1800 and continued to be actively involved in trade. But in 1806, Richard took on a different sort of cargo when he was hired to deliver troops to Chicago, Illinois. Although he was unable to fulfill his contract because of problems with his ship, he was still running a vessel in the Detroit area as late as September, 1812.

At the same time, Richard was raising oxen to sell on his property on the Thames River. In July, 1809, John Askin, Sr. went to Sandwich to see Pattinson and to purchase an American Ox from him.

Throughout his life, Richard Pattinson remained intensely pro-British. In 1796, after the American Revolution, "Rt. Pattinson" became one of those residing in Detroit who chose to remain a British subject. He moved to the south side of the river shortly thereafter.

Actually, Richard Pattinson was one of the very early settlers on the southern shore. Although the lots in Sandwich were snatched up quickly, the owners did not begin building right away. In order to encourage building, on August 19, 1797, the government decided that settlers who built the first houses would receive twenty-four additional acres to the rear of the township. Richard was one of the first four. All collected their bounties on March 5, 1798. Richard's original lot was lot 1 on the east side of Russell Street.

Then he became even more involved in real estate. Having been a landowner in old Detroit; after the 1805 fire, Richard drew a donation lot. In March, 1806, he offered his father-in-law 200 pounds for 500 acres of land in southern Ontario. John answered that he would sell it to Pattinson for 300 pounds. Askin later wrote that he really suspected Pattinson was acting on someone else's behalf.

Circa 1808, John Williams mortgaged lot number 8 in Camden to Richard Pattinson. And in 1813, Richard indicated he was interested in purchasing the Smith farm for 200 pounds.

Richard took Ellen Phyllis (Felicity Eleanora / Nelly), John Askin, Sr.'s youngest daughter, as his second wife after the death of Judith, his first wife, in 1804.

When Ellen and Richard married, Richard already had a daughter and together they had at least two more children of their own. On May 10, 1811, John Askin, Jr. wrote to his father "Madelaine joins me in wishing Mr. & Mrs. Pattinson joy on the Birth of a Daughter." That child was named Ellen Phyllis. Their next daughter Archange Ann was born July 14, 1813 at Riviere a la Tranche (Thames River).

But that was after the outbreak of the War of 1812. Before that, as early as 1807, Richard Pattinson was a captain in the Eighth Infantry. Once the war arrived, Richard found himself in the middle of it. Col. Duncan McArthur's American troops raided and confiscated a large quantity of flour from Capt. Pattinson's place on the Thames River. When Proctor evacuated Detroit in the Fall of 1813, Richard and his family fled from General Harrison's oncoming army.

According to Burton, General Harrison was gratefully remembered by the captured city as a kind man. In fact, John

Askin wrote that he appeared "very indulgent to the British under his authority."

But while Richard's family fled in the wake of Proctor's retreating army, Ellen died at the home of George Jacob (her brother Charles' father-in-law) on the Thames River near Moraviantown.

After Ellen's death, Mary Pattinson went to live with a Mrs. Park. Richard & Ellen lived with John Askin, Sr. and his wife at the time Askin wrote to his other children that "the last child (Archange was) with a good nurse at river Thames. we thought it unsafe to remove her at this Season. I requested Mr Brush to write Mr. Pattinson, as I do not wish to keep up any Correspondence Except with you, when permitted by the Commanding Officer of Detroit so to do."

A grieving Pattinson eventually returned to Sandwich, but for only a short time. He then removed to Montreal where he died by February 28, 1818, just five years after his young wife. In his will (see Appendix), he referred to himself as being sick.

Reddick Family

George Washington Reddick
  b. c. 1828; Hastings County, Ontario
  m. Berthina / Pertina Salome Porter (May 27, 1837; North
  Umberland, Ontario d. January 3, 1888; Detroit, Michigan
  d. 1901; Hastings County, Ontario
  Children
        Matilda Jane (see below)
        Annette (Nettie) - b.c. 1868; Kent County, Ontario
          m. Lawson
          d. 1899; Detroit, Michigan
        Mary Abigail (Minn) - b. Kent County, Ontario
          d. age 61

Matilda Jane Reddick
  b. April 27, 1865; Kent County, Ontario
  m. John H. Landon (b. July 25, 1864 d. February 16, 1943;
  Edmonton, Alberta), son of Joseph Sawyer Landon and
  Harriet Ann Askins
  div.
  d. 1924, Romeo, Michigan
  Children (see Landon)

The Reddick / Rettick family of Hastings County, Ontario
had some engaging facets to it. One researcher wrote that the
family could not have been English since she had not found the
name under any variation in any English surname book. However,
they very well might have been English. For instance, the
family could have originated in Reddish in the parish of
Manchester. Through the centuries, that town has also been
spelt Redytch / Redich / Reddiche. Or they might have come
from Redditch, which meant "reedy ditch", in Worcestershire,
England.

There were also several families in England who bore the
name "Reddit / Reditt. James and John Redditt, born circa 1798
and 1800 respectively, originated in Necton County, England.
James Redditt died on December 2, 1885 in Richmond Hill,
Canada. Curiously enough, the name George was found frequently
in their family as well as in the Reddick family of this
genealogy.

Or the family may have been of Scottish origin. According
to The Scotch-Irish Families of America, "Redick" was the name
of a border clan in the Dumfries and Kirkcudbright area in the
late 1500's.

So despite what one researcher wrote, the family very
likely could have originated in the British Isles, and, in
particular, in England. The fact that so many Reddicks
supported the British side during the American Revolution
further supported that premise.

For example, on June 12, 1798, Peggy Redick appeared in
records requesting land as daughter of a member of the United
Empire Loyalist. She received two hundred acres. And Philip
Riddick requested lands as a settler on July 1, 1797. He
received two hundred acres. An Elizabeth Reddick married Jacob
H. Merkley on October 30, 1823 at Williamsburg, a loyalist

center. In fact, several George Reddicks appeared in a listing of children of Loyalists living in Ontario. Philip Reddick of Ameliasburgh and Adam Reddick of Williamsburgh both had sons named George.

However, it would be surprising to find out the Reddick family of this genealogy was related to one of the Loyalist families of Canada, since the earliest member of the family recorded here was George Washington Reddick. It would seem highly unlikely that a Tory family would name their son after the great Revolutionary War General and America's first president.

There were Reddicks who fought on the side of the rebels. For instance, William Reddick of Pennsylvania (W9620/BLWT 40674-160-55) who fought in the Revolution, and his wife Margaret might have named a child after George Washington. According to an abstract of his Revolutionary War pension file, William and Margaret had a number of sons, including their first named Richard (b. 1786) and their third named William (b. 1790) who could have been the father of George Washington Reddick (see Appendix).

While the January, 1925, New England Genealogical and Historic Register had a note which mentioned George Washington Cowdery (b. December 13, 1808), son of Dr. Jonathan Cowdery and Elizabeth Reddick, no connection between Elizabeth Reddick and the Reddicks of this genealogy could be found. The two George Washingtons were probably simply a coincidence.

George Washington Redick (b.c. 1821), son of Hamilton Redick, settled in Pulaski County; Indiana. And a George W. Reddick, a Quaker born in Pennsylvania circa 1839, was the nephew of George above and also apparently settled in Indiana. Who would have expected the Reddick name to attract so many unrelated George Washingtons?

The George Washington Reddick of this genealogy married Berthina / Pertina Salome Porter of North Umberland, Ontario. Although Berthina died of consumption in Detroit on January 3, 1888, the death certificate was not filed until September 30, 1889. Her husband George died twenty-three years after Berthina.

Their daughter Matilda Jane Reddick became the first wife of John Landon, son of Joseph Sawyer Landon and Harriet Ann Askins. But John had a wanderlust about him. Before their divorce, John and Matilda operated a hotel in Romeo, Michigan from 1900 to 1905. After their divorce, John removed to Alberta, Canada.

Richardson Family

Robert Richardson (Dr.)
  b. Scotland
  m1 Mary Madeline Askin (d. January 10, 1811), dau of John Askin, Sr.; January 24, 1793
  m2 Ann McGregor, dau of Gregory McGregor; August 8, 1811
  d. 1832, Amherstburg, Ontario
  Children by Madeline Askin
    John (see below)
    Jane - b. May 19, 1794; Queenston, Ontario
      m. Capt. Robert Rist of 37th Regiment; January 15, 1816
      d. October 31, 1831
      bur. Butler Burying Ground, Niagara, Ontario
    Robert II - b. September 10, 1798; Queenston, Ontario
      d. June 7, 1819; Amherstburg, Ontario
      bur. Christ Church Burying Grounds
    William - b. January 7, 1801
      m. Jane Cameron Grant, dau of Commodore Alexander Grant (b. August 29, 1799) and Therese Barthe; February 11, 1834
      d. Brantford, Ontario
      Children
        James - r. London
    James A. - b. January 19, 1803
      d. August 18, 1828; drowned Lake Erie
    Charles - b. March 26, 1805
      m1. Elizabeth Euretta Clench (1808-September 28, 1835), youngest dau of Col. Ralph Clench of Butler's Rangers; April 2, 1827
      m2. Jane Clark, dau of William Clark of Niagara, Ontario
      d. 1847
      Children by Elizabeth Clench
        Elizabeth Magdalene - b. May 31, 1828
          d. June 3, 1828
        John Beverly Robinson
      Children by Jane Clark
        Jeanie - d. young
        Kate - d. young
    Alexander - b. February 15, 1808
      d. August 18, 1828; drowned Lake Erie
    George - b. August 25, 1810
      d. February 3, 1811
  Children by Ann McGregor
    George McGregor - b. July 4, 1812
      m. Mary Nelles, dau of Col. Robert Nelles; March 2, 1836
      Children
        Robert - m. Minerva Hindershott
        Emily - m. Fanning
        William Lock
        Abran
    Henry Wellington (tw) - b. August 12, 1816
      d. December 21, 1841; Amherstburg, Ontario
    David Johnston (tw) b. August 12, 1816
      m1. Margaret Watson of Windsor, Ontario; January 22, 1844

m2 Sarah Mercer of Sandwich, Ontario; 1856
d. 1885
Children by Margaret Watson
    Robert Watson - b. November 26, 1844
    Theresa Ann Grace
Children by Sarah Mercer
    Mary Mercer
    Neville Peto
Ann - b. June 2, 1818
    m. William G. Duff, Jr., son of William G.
    Duff, Sr.; June 4, 1842
    d. March 23, 1869
Catherine Grace - b. August 31, 1820
    m. never
    d. December 3, 1841; Amherstburg, Ontario
Therese Louisa - b. october 6, 1822
    m. Capt. John Neville Peto of Royal Canadian
    Rifles, son of Rev. James Peto, Vicar of
    Preston near Faversham, Kent, England; July 4,
    1848
Robert Harvey - b. March 3, 1825
    m. never
    d. c. 1851; Grasshopper River, Missouri

John Richardson (Maj.)
    b. October 4, 1796; Queenston, Ontario
    m. Maria Caroline (b.c. 1808 d. August 16, 1845)
    d. May 12, 1852, New York

According to <u>American Surnames</u>, the admiration of the British people for Richard the Lion-Hearted led many to name their sons after him and from it came the frequently found Richardson surname.

Richardsons of early Ontario included Loyalist Asa Richardson and his sons Henry and William. A Thomas Richardson was also listed as a Loyalist. When the French Revolution began to affect the fur trade in the Detroit area, according to Russell, a John Richardson of Montreal wrote
    "The Returns from the indian country are very, very
    bad... The war injures the Country most seriously in
    every point of view."
But whether he was related to the Richardson family of this genealogy was not determined.

Dr. Robert Richardson was a native of Scotland who arrived in Upper Canada in 1792 and served as assistant surgeon to Simcoe's Rangers. Madeline Askin, daughter of John Askin, Sr. and his Indian consort, met Dr. Richardson and the couple married January 24, 1793. The ceremony was performed by Rev. Robert Addison. They had eight children.

Richardson was stationed at Queenston and St. Joseph Island. While Richardson was at Queenston, it was merely a village five to six miles from Niagara Falls. But later Queenston would become the grave site of Sir Isaac Brock, a hero of the War of 1812. Madeline was able to accompany her husband there and stayed with her brother-in-law Robert Hamilton at least part of the time. The area had been settled by former soldiers from Butler's Rangers and Loyalists. It became the first seat of government for Upper Canada.

While in Queenston, Madeline wrote to her father that
Robert would "always guard as one of his highest duties, the
welfare of your daughter." And in 1799, Robert wrote his in-
laws from Fort Erie that "Madelaine and the children have
enjoyed perfect health all this winter..." But supposedly when
he went to St. Joseph Island, Madeline went to stay with her
parents. Robert Nichol wrote to John Askin, Sr. in 1801 that
"Dr. Richard and his Family arrived last night at Ft. George
on their way to St. Joseph's where they (were) to be
Stationed. You will therefore have a visit from them in a
short time ..."

A letter written by Dr. Richardson from St. Joseph Island
on August 6, 1801 reported to John Askin that
"I by no means think St. Josephs so bad as we had every
reason to believe ... We have got comfortable lodging
belonging to the Girl that lives with Mr Frero At the
rent of thirty dollars pr annum ... Madelaine frets a
little some times about (John, who was with the senior
Askin)."
So obviously, for at least part of the time at St. Joseph,
Richardson's wife was with him.

When the Rangers were disbanded in 1802, Dr. Richardson
became post surgeon at Amherstburg. That same year he was
appointed Western District Court Judge, a post he held until
his death. But in 1807, Richardson was in Amherstburg and on
June 27th Askin reported that Richardson was "very unwell and
still weak."

His father-in-law thought well enough of him to call him
a "deserving man" and, in September, 1809, John Askin wrote to
Isaac Todd attempting to secure the position of Barracks
Master at Amherstburg for Richardson.
"He is an excellent good character, much liked, but
so loaded with a large Family that not withstanding
the utmost of economy, & great Sobriety, his income
as Surgeons mate to the Garrison, District Judge
which fetches him little or nothing, and his present
practice does not furnish near sufficient to keep
pace with his absolute necessary expenses."
He lost both his wife and youngest child in a short interval
in 1811. After their deaths John Askin, Jr. said
"Poor Richardson always shewed himself a good Husband
& tender Father, he has met with a severe loss its
true ..."
But to the Askin family his grief apparently seemed short
lived; for after his remarriage, John Askin, Jr.'s wife wrote
how
"surprised (she) was ... to hear that Dr. Richardson
was paying court to Miss McGregor in three months after
poor Madelaine's death, and now ... I hear that they
were married ... I think he might have had more respect
for his wife's memory."

Despite his youth, Robert Richardson II became a
provincial marine midshipman at the outbreak of the War of
1812. He was only 14 years old at the outbreak of the war.
Robert II volunteered for General Winchester's successful
expedition at the Raisin River. His father proudly reported
that Robert had "behaved like a little hero on the field and

147

has borne his wound like a man." But then Robert II received a severe wound to his knee at the battle at Frenchtown on January 22, 1813. Although his father wrote on February 7, 1813, that Robert was out of danger and that "his health improves and his leg, I think will be saved;" the wound eventually led to his death in 1819. The legislature gave him a pension from January 22, 1813 through December 31, 1816.

On February 19, 1811, Alexander Askin wrote to his brother Charles about attending
"the funeral of the Doctor's youngest [George] who died of the same complaint as its poor mother [Madeline]. Jane was pretty well reconciled, but the poor Doctor quite dejected."

Robert I's daughter Jane took over after Madeline's death since the rest of the family was primarily men. Richardson wrote that at times he had to be away nights and days.
"Tis true My Daughter has behaved in the most praise worthy and exemplary Manner, but she is little more than a child herself, and certainly not fit to be so often left entirely alone."
He admitted that the primary reason he married again so quickly was for Jane's sake.

William Richardson became the postmaster at Brantford. And Henry Wellington Richardson became a barrister. Their brother James became the registrar of Kent. In 1828 he and his half brother Alexander drowned together in Lake Erie. Charles Richardson was appointed "cornet" of the Queens Light Dragoons in 1822. Afterwards he removed to Niagara where he practiced law and held a number of elected offices.

John Richardson was Robert I's and Madeline's second child and eldest son. He was born in Queenston while his father was stationed there. In 1798, John's mother wrote to her father from Ft. Erie that "John walks everywhere and is as fat as ever." He spent most of his childhood at his grandfather's home. While at St. Joseph Island, John's father wrote to John Askin, Sr. who was keeping his family for him
"I hope John is a good boy and attentive to his Gran Papa. Madlaine frets a little some times about him, but I am perfectly easy myself as I am certain he is with his best frinds (sic), next to ourselves."
On November 9, 1801, grandfather John Askin, Sr. was billed by teacher James May for educating several children, including John Richardson.

As a member of the Miami Company on September 9, 1789, John was there when the division of the company's debts was made. At the beginning of the War of 1812 he volunteered for the Forty-first Regiment. During the war he was captured during Commodore Perry's defeat of Barclay's fleet on September 10, 1813.

Supposedly John I's son, John Richardson II, was captured at the Battle of Thames on October 5, 1813. However, since John I was born in 1796, he was only 17 years old at the time. Any son of his would have to have been little more than an infant. Could John Richardson I have been captured on September 10, 1813; and then again on October 5, 1813?

One of the positions John Richardson I held after the war was Superintendent of Police. But after being relieved of his police duties, John began to write in earnest.

In 1847 he published his <u>Eight Years in Canada</u>, which Casselman described as "well-written". In it Richardson described his career in Canada. His next publication, <u>The Guards in Canada or the Point of Honor</u>, was written as a defence of his character and discussed the duels in which he had participated. Apparently he participated in several duels including his first one in Paris and several in Canada.

His writings were very patriotic in nature, but John was unable to sell enough of them to feed himself. Sometime circa 1850 Richardson removed to New York City where he wrote <u>Hardscrabble or the Fall of Chicago</u> and its sequel <u>Waunangee or the Massacure of Chicago</u>. Other titles included <u>The Canadian Brothers</u>, <u>Westbrook, or the Outlaw</u>, and <u>The Monk Knight of St. John</u>. Despite the quantity of writing, the books were all published with poor quality materials.

John Richardson died at his residence at 113 West Twenty-ninth Street, New York City; on May 12, 1852. When he died, it was discovered that he had been living in virtual poverty. According to Casselman, he died of "erysipelas," a streptococcal inflammation of the skin. In John's case, medical help was sought too late. He was "taken outside the city for burial."

His obituary appeared in the <u>New York Journal</u> on May 14, 1852. It read
"Died - On the 12th inst. Major John Richardson, late of H.B.M. Gordon Highlanders aged 53 [actually 55] years. His friends are invited to attend his funeral, without further invitation, from the Church of the Holy Communion, corner 6th Avenue and 20th Street, this day at two o'clock, P.M."

149

Robertson Family

Unknown
  Children
    William (see below)
    Samuel (Capt.) - m. Catherine Askin (b.c. 1763),
        dau of John Askin; by 1779
      d. aft 1779; Detroit, Michigan or Montreal,
        Quebec, Canada
      Children
        William II - b. by 1782
        John - b. by 1782
        David - m. pos Peggy McDonald, September 30, 1792;
            Detroit, Michigan
        dau

William I
    b.c. 1760, Scotland
    m1 Cornelia Eleanor Brooks (b.c. 1780, d. 1800); January
      26, 1798; New York City, New York
    m2 Jane Dunlop Ogilvie / Ogilvy (d. December 13, 1806;
      London, England), mot of John Ogilvie; betw 1800-1803
      separated August, 1803
    d. December, 1806; London, England
    Children by Cornelia
        Elizabeth Lucy - m. Henry Ronalds

The Robertson family (Clan Donnachaidh) originated with
the Earls of Athol who were descended from King Duncan of
Scotland. Alexander, son of Robert, captured one of the
murderers of James I. The crest given him as rewarded by James
II had a hand supporting a regal crown and a chained wild man
representing that first Robertson.

According to The British Regime in Michigan and the Old
Northwest 1760-1796, a number of Robertsons were in the Great
Lakes region in the early years. In a 1763 deposition, Chapman
Abraham reported that before Pontiac's attack on Detroit's
garrison in 1763, a Capt. Robertson / Robson / Robinson,
ship's officer; and Sir Robert Davers were murdered, according
to Burton, while "taking soundings at the head of St. Clair
River." They had been previously warned not to venture too far
from the fort.

In 1783, another Capt. Robertson was so concerned that
Indians were about to attack, he used traders to guard his
post at Michilimackinac. He claimed to be threatened by
Ottawas and Chippewas who had been encouraged to desert their
families and attack. Then in the British Regime in Michigan
and the Old Northwest, 1760-1796, Nelson Russell reported that
the same Capt. Robertson was so concerned about his unpaid
bills that on July 10, 1783 he wrote
    "I am sorry & ten times so that I ever came here, to be
    obliged to cringe & borrow Rum from Traders on account of
    Government ... it is my Lot to be here at this juncture
    & no Friend to attempt to give me common assistance."
In 1784 Capt. Robertson began repairs to Michilimackinac's
pickets, wharf, and road. He may have been the Capt. Daniel
Robertson called by Quaiffe "a beginner in trade" at Mackinac
in 1783.

A Margaret Robertson from Scotland married Daniel Sutherland, a Scottish merchant, on September 1, 1781, in Montreal, Quebec. Sutherland was the senior member of the firm of Sutherland and Grant who traded as early as 1785 with Donald McKay. In 1790 Sutherland became a partner in the Northwest Company. His 1800 waterworks partnership failed. But circa 1817 and 1818 Sutherland became Postmaster General for British North America, a position he held until 1827. Margaret Robertson Sutherland died in Quebec after 1831.

Loyalists who emigrated to Canada included Robertsons named James, Daniel, Donald, Joseph, Prince, Neil, Thomas, and William. On May 28, 1799, Robert Nichol of Queenston wrote to John Askin that "Prince Robertson's acct (was) inclosed." He was probably the same Prince Robertson in early Loyalist records. But he was also obviously connected with John Askin who became personally and economically connected with many of the Robertsons of this genealogy.

William Robertson I of this genealogy was a merchant, judge, office holder, politician, and militia officer who was born circa 1760 in Scotland. He settled in Detroit in 1782, the same year that his brother Samuel died.

William became clerk to John Askin, Samuel's father-in-law, and became his partner on July 1, 1784, receiving 600 pounds a year until the partnership was dissolved in 1787.

According to The British Regime in Michigan and the Old Northwest, 1760-1796, in 1788 Robertson said Detroiters were "Wholly illiterate, and if we except five or six Canadian families ... there will not be found twenty people nor half the number, who have the least pretensions to education, or can even write their name or know a Letter of a Book."

Although the partnership with Askin was dissolved, William Robertson continued as a successful merchant, particularly in the fur trade. His brother David went to work for him in 1788.

Dissatisfaction with the government began when it forbade sailing private vessels, but refused to provide enough government troops for hauling merchandise. In addition the settlers in the region were required to pay the King 15 shillings to each of the few barrels that did get through, seriously effecting both merchants and traders. And William Robertson was one of those who criticized the government vehemently.

William Robertson I acted as financier, patron, and customer to Robert Hamilton (see Appendix) in the late 1780's. From 1791 or 1792 to 1795, William was in London, England, lobbying for increased business when the French Revolution brought about a depreciation of fur prices.

When he returned from London, he became involved in a new partnership with John Askin, Sr. and settled in Montreal after stopping in Philadelphia, Pennsylvania. Together Askin and Robertson owned a salt spring and supplied the garrison at Amhersburg with corn.

In addition to mercantile interests, William Robertson found himself appointed to the Land Board for the District of Hesse in 1789 along with Alexander McKee and Alexander Grant, and as judge to the Common Pleas Court in 1780. But Detroiters, including Robertson, did not approve of merchants becoming judges and presented the governor of Quebec with a petition urging the appointment of a lawyer to the post. As a result, William Dummer Powell, a lawyer, was appointed to the judgeship.

Despite the loss of his judgeship, William's political interests continued. For example, in David Smith's 1792 listing of election expenses was the notation for 103 pounds 3 shillings 11 pense paid to William and David Robertson "for sundry articles furnished by them" and paid for by a Mr. Dolsen

And his public service did not stop there. Sir John Johnson recommended him to seats to the legislative and executive councils of Upper Canada. The appointments were made in early July, 1792. But on November 4, 1792, William resigned both positions. Although he might have gone to England at that time, it was more likely he was already in England when the appointment were made and simply did not return from England to accept it.

After living first in England and then in Montreal, William returned to Detroit in 1801. His wife had died the year before, leaving him so inconsolable, he cut his stay in Detroit short and returned to London.

But he did not find any peace there either. On February 23, 1803, his nephew John described William Robertson's voyage to London in a letter. John wrote
"He is fast vergeing towards his grave by his former ill habit (of drinking alcohol) and am afraid will hardly live to see my brother. On his passage home he made a new will, leaving his Daughter on 5000 pounds, a trifling legacy to a friend or two and the remainder of his fortune to an Irish Catholic Priest who had been sometime acquainted with him in Quebec and went in the same Vessel with him to England. This will was wrote by the Priest and dictated by himself. the Captn and Mate witnessed it. it was from them his Sister received this information who happened accidentally to be on a visit to London from Scotland at the time they arrived. She used every means in her power to recover her brother from his sad state but in vain ... Her daughter and husband set off for the same purpose. thy brot him as far as Liverpool on their way down to Scotland the villain of a priest followed and persuaded my uncle they were taking him to Edinburg to put him in Bridewel as a Lunatick (after they made their escape) the Priest and him in continual debauch. his poor daughter is also there and only a servant woman to attend her."

Concerned about his uncle's welfare, William Robertson II hurried to London. He wrote to Askin about what he found when he arrived.
"I reached London ... just three days after my Uncle was married to Mr. Ogilvy's mother. I hope this will prove a

fortunate circumstance for him, from the good character given of her and her influence over him, I am in hopes she will be able to reclaim him from that dreadful habit he had. I did not find matters so bad as they were said to have been. that there was such a person as a parson who went over with him who had his passage and other Experiences paid, and who was also fond of the bottle I believe was true, but nothing more ...

But the marriage did not prove to be the salvation for which his nephew had hoped. In August, 1803, the couple separated. Robertson blamed it on her extravagance, but he was still drinking. Isaac Todd deplored the condition to which "the immoderate use of liquor" had reduced Richardson. In November, 1805 Archange Meredith wrote that "the unfortunate Wm. Robertson ... lives in the vicinity of Billinsgate in a miserable ale house." After Isaac Todd visited William I in London in 1806, Todd wrote to John Askin that
"William Robertson is not only a sot & blackguard but infamous as a Liar & Rogue. Among other of his bad conduct his poor bror is Starving. He will not pay him what he owes. indeed my friend I begin to think we were all deceived in him & that he never was an honest man."
William Robertson died later that year.

David Robertson was William's youngest brother. He appeared in Detroit as William's junior partner in 1788, And in 1790, when William went abroad, David was left with the business. Although the partnership was dissolved when William returned from Scotland; while he was running the business, David was awarded the contract to supply food to the Upper Canada garrisons.

Despite the dissolution of the partnership, the brothers continued to do business together. Quaiffe advised that on September 26, 1795, they purchased shares in the "Michigan Peninsula." That year they also appeared as claimants to the estate of John Askwith (see Appendix). Together they were owed over 79 pounds in 1794 for household items such as hinges, candles, and green tea. Alone, the Askwith estate owed "David Robertson, Taylor" was 2 pounds 4 shillings.

David Robertson was also connected to John Askin. On September 30, 1792 he may have married Peggy McDonald, Askin's servant. And in 1790 and 1791, David appeared on Askin's militia roll. In fact, on the 1791 roll, David Robertson was listed as a merchant.

Samuel Robertson was the second of William I's brothers, but the first to arrive in the Detroit River area. Quaiffe related that Samuel had been a sailor in his youth in Scotland. In 1774, after he arrived in the New World, Samuel was sent to Detroit by Phyn and Ellice, a London firm, to command a vessel for merchants in the fur trade.

And like his brothers, Samuel was also connected to the John Askin family. In 1778 he married John's 15 year old daughter Catherine. While discussing the marriage, John wrote that "once past fifteen (one) cannot marry too soon." And John was pleased with his new son-in-law. In April of that year he wrote about the marriage

"I don't remember if I mentioned to you that I had a Daughter came up from Montreal last year, where she has been for several (years) past in a Nunnery. She was married this winter to Capt. Robertson, a Match which pleases me well, as I never was acquainted with a more industrious, Sober, Honest man, a fine prospect, perhaps to be a grand father next year."
And in another letter Askin wrote
"Kitty is married to a very worthy man, who has been Master of my Vessel this several years past."
And finally, on June 14, 1778 John wrote
"I believe Capt. Robertsons marriage will make him consent to pass some years in this Country ... He could have the command of a Kings Vessel on these leakes but it realy is not worth his acceptance, not will he take it."

Samuel's duties kept him busy. Quaiffe related that in early 1778, Capt. Robertson sent George McBeath to Prairie du Chien "to urge them to refrain from further war like activities." In a May 8, 1778 letter John Askin wrote to Isaac Todd that
"Major DePeyster has taken my Vessill into the Service, Robison (Robertson) I believe will be ready to sail with her by the 10th."
Then on June 6, 1778, John Askin, while at Michilimackinac wrote to John Baptiste Barthe at Sault St. Marie that Samuel had arrived, but left the same day "to examine the coast along the French River" where Askin had decided to build a house. In 1779 Samuel visited Milwaukee.

And shortly after that Gov. Sinclair had Samuel Robertson arrested at Mackinac and sent to Montreal for trial. But he died supposedly before the trial could be held. Three years after his dearth his wife married Robert Hamilton (Appendix).

Samuel and Catherine Robertson had two sons, James and William. Both boys were sent to England for their education after their mother married Robert Hamilton. In August, 1792, Uncle William Robertson wrote from London that William II was learning well in multiplication, writing and Latin and that John was also advancing. On May 20, 1794, Catherine wrote her father John Askin that her husband Robert was taking "three more of (her) boys for their education" in Scotland. They would have been Robert, George, and Alexander Hamilton. In the same letter Catherine mentioned that "William and Johnny" Robertson were still in school.

In 1803 John Askin wrote to Robert Nichol that William Robertson II was "a most worthy man whose honest Character (he) esteemed much" and that John was "a most Dutifull fond child."

Their grandfather seemed concerned about the brothers, possibly because he thought they had been left out of William Robertson I's will. But a July 27, 1803 letter from William II to his grandfather must have eased John Askin's concerns. William II reported that William I had given his brother John and him 2000 pounds Halifax credit at the "House of Parker Gerard, Ogilby & Co."

While overseas. William II went to visit his grandfather John's native town of Strabane, Ireland. He also visited the Meredith and Mercer families who were in England at the time.

Both William II and John Robertson returned to Canada and were in the Battle of Queenston in the War of 1812. Charles Askin recorded that William in particular behaved gallantly. Charles added that after the battle he and John Robertson took a leave of absence together on a "mountain near Queenston."

Several later Robertsons in the Detroit / Windsor area may have been descendants of this Robertson family. In The Valley of the Lower Thames, 1640-1850, Hamil reported that in 1828 charges were filed against Surveyor-General Iredell for receiving bribes and giving the best lands to "Mr. Robertson" and Matthew Dolsen but the Mr. Robertson was not further identified.

Later, in 1832, Dr. Alexander R. Robertson was a petitioner for lots in Chatham. He and his wife Euphemea, the daughter of Joseph Eberts appeared in Chatham records at least through 1841. Dr. Robertson had an apothecary shop there.

Viller / Villier / Viler / Villar Family

Louis Viller dit St. Louis I
   b. 1708; Lorraine, France
   m. Marie Josephene (Josette) Morin (b. St. Ours bur.
   September 6, 1793; Sandwich, Ontario), dau of Peter Morin
   and Marie Josephene Daunet; August 22, 1746; Detroit,
   Michigan
   bur. December 23, 1765; Detroit
   Children
      Louis II - b. June 8, 1747; Detroit
      m. Charlotte Reguindeau dit Joachim; January
      9, 1775; Sandwich, October
      bur. June 3, 1826; Sandwich, Ontario
      Marie Louise - bpt. October 4, 1751 or 1754;
      Mission of the Hurons, Assumption Church,
      Sandwich, Ontario
      m. Thomas Pageot
         Children
            Madeline - m. Capt. Laurent Bondy (March
            21, 1771 - 1813); November 21, 1791;
            Assumption, Sandwich, Ontario
               Children (see Bondy)
            Marie Archange - m. Gabriel Douaire de
            Bondy (b. 1762), son of Joseph Douaire de
            Bondy and Marie Josephene Gamelin;
            November 17, 1787; Assumption Church,
            Sandwich, Ontario
      Francois - bpt. January 1, 1753; Assumption Church,
      Sandwich, Ontario
      Marie Anne - m. Francois de Rouillard / Drouillard
      (b. 1740), son of Jean Baptiste Drouillard dit
      Argentcour (1707-1756) and Elizabeth Rapin of
      Riviere des Prairies; January 13, 1766
      Jeanne - m. Rene Theodore Duroseau, dau of Antoine
      Duroseau and Louise Marchand;July 22, 1769;
      Assumption Church
      Marie J. - m. Michael Roy, son of Certain Roy and
      Marie Parent of Montreal; September 24, 1777
      Pierre

One relative of this family might have been Louis Claude
Hector de Villars, France's Minister of War from November 26,
1715 to September 24, 1718. Another could have been Louis de
Villers, who arrived with Rochambeau's Expedition to help the
colonies during the American Revolution.

Louis Viller dit St. Louis I migrated from Lorraine,
France to Canada, and served as an ensign with the French
troops in Detroit. According to Thwaites, he was called St.
Louis because of his great piety. But by August 22, 1746, when
he married Marie Josephene Morin, he had found his way to
Detroit, where, according to The Windsor Border Region, "St.
Louis" obtained land three arpents by forty arpents on the
south side of the Detroit River. His land abutted was below
Sandwich, Ontario and his brother-in-law Louis Morin's three
arpents and the two families worked their land together.

On February 24, 1750 "Big St. Louis" sold flour to the
mission. In the September 1, 1750 census, Louis' family

included 1 woman, 1 boy under 15, and 2 girls under 15. They
had 10 arpents of land under cultivation, 2 of them in corn;
300 sheaves of wheat; and 150 sheaves of oats. The family
owned 2 horses, 2 oxen, 4 cows, 4 hogs, and 35 poultry.

When their son Francois was baptized at the Huron mission
in 1753, Francois Janis and Marguerite La Durantaye were named
his godparents. Pierre Morin and Marie Louise Becquemont
served as godparents for Marie Louise Viller.

Louis Viller dit St. Louis was a soldier whose July 10,
1756 successful action on the Oswego River was reported in the
journal of Louis Antoine de Bougainville.
   "With four hundred men he attacked a convoy of three or
   four hundred bateaux, each with two men, and three
   companies of soldiers ... Villiers put them to fight and
   knocked off a great number, and would have knocked off a
   lot more were it not for the poor quality of the
   tomahawks furnished by the King's Store, took twenty-four
   scalps and killed or wounded in their flight, according
   to his estimate, about three hundred men."
De Bougainville recorded that the Menominee tribe, or "Wild
Oars people" were with M. de Villiers during the attack on the
English bateaux. Then, on July 15, 1756, de Bougainville
reported that
   "M. de Regaud (de Vandreuil) left ... with M M de Levis,
   de Courte Manche and de Ligneris to take command of the
   camp of M. de Villiers where the indians and the
   Canadians who have been sent daily are supposed to go.
   The body which constitutes this camp will be an army of
   observation, if they lay siege to Oswego ... (The
   Menominees were thanked) for their zeal in coming despite
   the smallpox, eulogies of their valor in M. de Villier's
   last stroke ..."

By the 1768 census the family had grown to 4 boys and 4
girls. But by July 18, 1782, the family was down to Louis,
Marie, 1 young or hired man, and 2 girls, and the family owned
33 arpents of cleared land.

Francois Janis and Marguerite La Durantaye were
godparents of Louis and Marie's son Francois. Pierre Morin and
Marie Louise Becquemont were the godparents of Louis and
Marie's daughter Marie Louise Viller.

According to The Windsor Border Region, Marie Louise
Viller was the first known white child baptized at the Huron
Mission of the Assumption at La Pointe de Montreal. However,
she was not the first white child born on the Detroit River's
south side.

Louis Viller dit St. Louis II remained a British subject
when the Americans took control of Detroit. And Louis II or
one of his brothers may have been the "St. Louis" John Askin
referred to in an April 8, 1801 letter which read
   "I will make Enquiry if St. Louis is come. however it
   will not answer any purpose unless you are here when he
   comes, for to put him in prison is only throwing good
   money after bad."

Erskine / Arreskin Family of Scotland

Source: Woodward, Frank E. "The Erskine Family of Bristol, ME"
        and
Douglas, Sir Robert. Peerage of Scotland: Containing Historical and Genealogical Account of the Nobility of that Kingdom, from Their Origin to the Present Generation...

Henricus de Erskine
     alive 1220 and 1226
     Children
          Johannes (see below)

Sir Johannes (John) de Erskine
     Children
          John (see below)
          William - r. Ayrshire

John Erskine of Erskine
     alive 1296
     Children (see below)

Sir John Erskine of Erskine
     alive 1309
     Children
          William (see below)
          Mary - m1 Sir Thomas Bruce, bro of King Robert I
               m2 Sir Ingran Morvile
          Alice - m. Walter, High Steward of Scotland
               Children
                    Jean - m. Hugh, Earl of Ross
          Agnes - m. Sir William Livingston

Sir William Erskine of Erskine
     d. 1329
     Children
          Robert (see below)
          Adam of Barrowchan
          Sir Alan
          Andrew
          Sir Archibald

Sir Robert Erskine
     m1 Beatrix, dau of Sir Alexander Lindsay of Crawford, wid of Archibald Douglas
     m2 Christian, dau of Sir John Menteeth, Lord of Arran, and Elyne (dau of Gratney, the Earl of Marr), wid of Sir Edward Keith
     d. 1385
     Children by Beatrix
          Thomas (see below)
          ?Malcom
          Sir Nichol
          Alan

```
Muriela - m. Sir Maurice Drummond
Elisabeth - m. Sir Walter Oliphant of Aberdalgy

Thomas Erskine
    m1 Johanna Barclay
    m2 Janet Keith, dau of Sir Edward Keith and Christian
    Menteeth
    d. 1419
    Children
        Robert (see below)
        John Erskine of Dunn
        Elisabeth - m. Duncan Wemyss of Leuchars
        Christian - m. Sir John Haldane

Robert Erskine of Alway, Earl of Marr
    m. dau of Robert, Lord of Lorn and Innermeath
    d. 1453
    Children
        Thomas (see below)
        Janet - m. Walter Steward of Levenax, 1421, by
            dispensation
        Elisabeth - m. Sir Henry Douglas of Lochleven

Thomas, Lord Erskine and 2nd Earl of Marr
    m. Lady Douglas, dau of James, Earl of Morton, granddau
    of King James I
    d. by December 6, 1494
    Children
        Alexander (see below)
        Elisabeth - m. Sir Alexander Seton
        Mary - m. Sir William Livingston
        Muriela - m. William, 2nd Earl of Marischal

Alexander, Lord Erskine and 3rd Earl of Marr
    m1 Christian, dau of Sir Robert Crichton of Sanquhar
    m2 Helen, dau of Alexander, Lord Home
    Children
        Robert (see below)
        Agnes - m. Sir William Menteeth of Carse
        Alexander
        Walter of Over Donottars
        Christian - m. Sir David Stewart of Rosyth

Robert, Lord Erskine and 4th Earl of Marr
    m. Isobel, dau of Sir George Campbell of Loudoun
    d. 1513
    Children
        John - (see below)
        Robert - d. young
        James - m. Catherine Stirling
        Alexander - parson of Monnybreck
        William
        Catherine - m. Alexander, 2nd Lord Elphinston
        Margaret - m1 John Haldane of Gleneagles
                m2 George Home of Lundies and Argaty
        Elisabeth - m. Sir James Forrester of Torwood
        Janet - m. John Murray of Touchadam

Sir John, Lord Erskine and 5th Earl of Marr
    m. Lady Margaret Campbell, dau of Archibald, 2nd Earl of
    Argyll
```

d. 1552
Children
    Robert - m. Lady Margaret Graham
        d. 1547
    Thomas - d. 1551
    John (see below)
    Alexander of Gogar
        Children
            Thomas, Earl of Kellie
    Sir James Erskine of Tillibody
    Elisabeth - m. Walter Seton of Touch
    Margaret - m1 King James V
        m2 Sir Robert Douglas of Lochleven
        Children
            James Stewart

Sir John, Lord Erskine and 6th Earl of Marr
    m. Annabella, dau of Sir William Murray of Tullibardine
    d. October 29, 1572
    Children
        John (see below)
        Lady Mary - m. Archibald, 8th Earl of Angus

John Erskine, Earl of Marr
    b.c. 1558
    m1 Anne, dau of David, Lord Drummond
    m2 Lady Mary Stewart, dau of Esme, Duke of Lennox
    d. December 14, 1634; Stirling, Scotland
    Children
        John (see below)
        James, Earl of Buchan
        Henry
        Sir Alexander - d. 1640
        Sir Charles of Alva - d. 1663; Edinburgh, Scotland
        Sir John - m. Margaret Inglis
        Sir Arthur of Scotscraig
        William - d. 1685
        Lady Mary - m. William, Earl of Marischal
        Lady Anne - m. John, Earl of Rothes
        Lady Margaret - m. John, Earl of Kinghorn
        Lady Catherine - m. Thomas, Earl of Haddington

John, 8th Earl of Marr
    m. Lady Christian Hay, dau of Francis, Earl of Erroll
    d. 1654
    Children
        John, 9th Earl of Marr
            m1 Lady Mary Scott, dau of Walter, Earl of
            Buccleuch
            m2 Lady Mary Mackenzie, dau of George, Earl of
            Seaforth
            d. September, 1668
            Children
                Charles   Barbara   Sophia
                George   Jean
        Sir Francis
        William Erskine
        Lady Elisabeth - m. Archibald, Lord Napier
        Lady Mary

Most Askin / Askins / Areskine / Eriskyne / Irskyn / Arreskin / Erskines were a branch of the Scottish house derived from the barony of Erskine on the Clyde River in Refrewshire headed by Henricus / Henry of Erskine in 1220. It was known that Henricus, proprietor of the barony of Erskine on the Clyde, was succeeded by his son Johannes who witnessed a charter of Alexander III in 1252.

Sir John Erskine, great grandson of Henricus, received a grant of land in Largs, Ayrshire, Scotland. The family had been one of historical importance. In the early 1300's, a Christina of Marr was probably an early ancestor of this family. Her sister-in-law was the wife of Robert Bruce and Christina, as owner of Rum, Eigg, Vest and Barra Islands, had the means to assist Bruce raise a force to fight when Bruce's wife and daughter were taken prisoner by Edward.

In 1327 Sir John's only son William was a part of an expedition to England led by Randolph and Douglas. William was knighted under the royal banner, but died shortly thereafter.

William's son, Sir Robert Erskine, served as Chamberlain of Scotland from 1350-1357 and again in 1363; and became ambassador to France in 1358. The King also awarded him the castle at Stirling and Sir Robert eventually became sheriff of the area. He first married Beatrix, the daughter of Sir Alexander Lindsay of Crawford. They may have been the parents of Malcolm, progenitor of the Erskine family of Kennoull.

Secondly, Sir Robert Erskine married Christian, the widow of Sir Edward Keith and the daughter of Sir John Menteeth and his wife Elyne, the daughter of Gratney the then Earl of Mar.

Thomas, son of Sir Robert and his first wife took as his own second wife Janet Keith, the daughter of Thomas' stepmother by her first husband. "Thomas de Erskyne, knight" received a grant of lands in "Cultrehone and Tulchgorme, in Stirlingshire" in 1368 and the barony of Dun in Forfarshire in 1376. In 1384, Thomas fought an expedition of English. And that same year he was named ambassador to England, a post he also held in 1392.

Thomas and Janet had Robert who became Lord Erskine and John, who became progenitor of the Erskines of Dunn. Robert was later in the Battle of Homildon in 1402. In 1421 he was appointed to negotiate the release of King James I and finally became a hostage himself for James' ransom in 1424. At the death of Alexander, Earl of Marr, the title went to Robert.

Robert's son Thomas received a charter for lands at Daluotte in Lennox in 1459 and supported James III even though James had confiscated Thomas' castle of Stirling.

The next Lord Erskine was a favorite of King James IV, having been caretaker of the King in his youth. As a reward, Alexander Erskine was named privy-councillor, governor of Dunbarton Castle, and holder of a number of charters.

His son Robert, the 4th Earl of Marr fell in 1513 during the Battle of Flodden. And Robert's son John was sent as ambassador to France in 1515. Later John was entrusted with keeping his future son-in-law, young King James V and appointed governor of Stirling Castle where the young king lived. John's service to his king continued until his death in 1552.

Sir John, the next Earl of Marr also acted as a regent. After the birth of James VI in 1566, Queen Mary gave custody of him to the Earl of Marr, then residing in the castle in Edinburgh. Several times he saved the young King from danger.

Circa 1570, after Mary, Queen of Scots was imprisoned by her cousin Queen Elizabeth I of England; Sir John Erskines served as regent. In fact, he was part of a proposal to release Mary and return her to Scotland in order to be executed. But before negotiations could be completed, the Earl of Marr died in 1572.

His son John also supported King James VI along with whom he was raised. In 1595 the King entrusted John with his son Prince Henry. John served as ambassador to England in 1601 and accompanied James when he succeeded Elisabeth on the English throne in 1603. As a reward for his loyalty, John was named to the privy-council and was installed as Knight of the Garter.

The 8th Earl of Marr lost control of the castle of Edinburgh in 1638. Although he was appointed as a privy-councillor for life, John purchased an estate in Ireland which he lost in the Irish rebellion.

Rea / Rae Family

James Rea

> d. prob 1758
> Children
>> Alice - r. Dungannon
>>> m. John Erskine
>>> Children
>>>> John Askin
>>>> William
>>>> Robert
>>>> Mary
>>>> Sarah - m. pos Campbell
>> Richard - d. by 1792; New York

Among the variations of the name were Reah / Rhe / Ray / Rhea / Rae / Rea / Wray / Raye / Reay. A dragon's head appeared on the family crest.

One possibility was that the name stemmed from Greek mythology where the goddess Rea was the mother of other gods.

According to <u>Peerage of Scotland...</u>, the Lord of Reay was descended from Walter, chamberlain to the bishop of Caithness by whose daughter he had a son named Martin. The family used the surname M'Ky / MacKay. Martin had Magnus who, in turn, had Morgan and Farquhar. But they used the surname Macky. The Reay family originated in northern Scotland.

And then, Le Van Spicer's work on the Rea family looked at Alexander Rea who was born circa 1700 in Northern Ireland, but was of Scottish descent. Le Van Spicer believed him to be a member of the McRea clan who settled in New Jersey.

The Rea family in this genealogy may have been related to either the McRea or the Reay families. What is known about the family was reported by John Askin, primarily in a 1793 letter in which he described his childhood and referred to his mother as "Alice Rea," the daughter of a clergyman. But then in a May 26, 1801 letter, Askin wrote to James Ersken "of Drimcan near Dunleer County of Leith, Ireland", that he was brought up by his "Grandfather John Rae" within a mile and half of Dunghannon, Ireland. So even Askin used two different spellings for his mother's family name.

But obviously, all spellings were not related to Askin. While according to Quaife, a Dr. Ray, the only prisoner taken alive from La Balme's expedition, was sent to Detroit and a Joseph Reah was employed by the Indian Department before 1783; they were probably not related to John Askin.

John Askwith

John Askwith was clerk for John Askin, Sr. But he may also have been Askin's indentured servant. On November 7, 1793, Askwith wrote in a letter to Margaret Jervis, mother of his apparently illegitimate daughter Fanny.
"I wish my time was out tomorrow I wou'd immediately go on board the last Vessel that sails, as this is at present perhaps the most miserable place in all Canada ... I do not mean to stay one day longer in the Place than the expiration of my agreement, for I never detested any place so much ..."

Unfortunately, Askwith did not live long enough to leave. Just two years later, in November, 1795, Margaret Jervis wrote Askin that she had heard that Askwith had "died in affluant circumstance" and wanted to make a claim on Askwith's estate for her daughter Fanny
"who he (had) always acknowledged; by letters in (Jervis') possession and publicly ... to be his Daughter'"
But there was no money for Fanny. When Askin settled the estate he reported that Askwith owed

1521 pounds	3 shillings	1 pense	mortgage
11	15	0	Meldrum & Park (h o u s e h o l d items)
13	8	8.5	James Donaldson (tavern bill)
11	6	4.5	Dr. Thomas Smith (tavern bill)
79	10	6.5	W i l l i a m & David Robertson (household items & food)
499	15	6.25	John Askin

Unfortunately the sale of his estate, minus auction expenses, only brought

188 pounds	13 shillings	3 pense	Personal property
194	16	0	One 75 by 53 foot lot inside the fort.

Baudry / Dusault Genealogy

Touissaint Toupin, Sieur Dusault
  b. 1616
  m. Margaret Boucher (b. 1634)
  bur. Chateau Richer, August 10, 1676
  Children
        Francis - b. 1641
              d. Quebec
        Jean Toupin, Sieur Dusault - b. December 15, 1648;
              Quebec, Quebec
              d. Quebec, Quebec
              Children
                    Unknown
                          Children
                                Louis Joseph Toupin - b.
                                February 16, 1735; Quebec,
                                Quebec
                                r. 1759; Detroit, Michigan
                                m. Louisa Margaret Baudry
                                Desbuttes dit St. Martin;
                                January 11, 1762; Church
                                of the Huron, Sandwich,
                                Ontario
                                bur. July 7, 1810; Raisin
                                River
                                Children
                                      Jean Francis Dusault -
                                            b. August 11,
                                            1762; Sandwich,
                                            Ontario
                                            m. Mary Jane
                                            Raoul; November
                                            4, 1783

Archange St. Martin

Source: **Marriage Register for the Western District of
the Province of Upper Canada**

Province of Upper Canada
Western District
      I Angus Mackintosh of Detroit merchant do solemnly swear
in the presence of Almighty God that I did publicly intermarry
with Archange St. Martin at Detroit aforesaid on the
seventeenth day of June One thousand seven hundred and eighty
three, and that there is living issue of the said marriage,
Duncan Mackintosh born on the Twenty fourth day of September
One thousand seven hundred & Eighty five, Alexander Mackintosh
born on the Twenty third day of August One thousand seven
hundred and Eighty Seven, Anne Mackintosh born on the first
day of April One Thousand seven hundred and Ninety, Archange
Mackintosh born on the Twenty fifth day of April One Thousand

Mackintosh born on the Twenty fifth day of April One Thousand Seven hundred and Ninety three & Isabelle Mackintosh born on the seventeenth of March One thousand seven hundred and ninety five.

signed Angus Mackintosh

I Archange St. Martin do solemnly swear in the presence of Almighty God that I did publicly intermarry with Angus Mackintosh of Detroit Merchant on the seventeenth day of June... [rest as above].

signed Archange St. Martin

Source: The Refuges of 1776 from Long Island to Connecticut.

Thomas Brush
    b. 1610, England
    emigrated 1653
    r. 1656; Southold, Long Island
    m. Rebecca, dau of John and Mary Conklin / Conkling
    d. 1675
    Children
        Thomas - m. Sarah
            r. Huntington, Long Island
            wll dtd. April 5, 1698
            wll pro. April 26, 1699
            Children
                Thomas   Rebecca   Sarah
                Richard   Jacob   Susannah
                John   "Timithy" Elizabeth
                Mary   Martha
        Richard - b.c. 1635, England
            r. Huntington, Long Island
            m. Johanna / Hannah, dau of John Corey / Cory
            d.c. 1711
            Children
                Thomas
                    Children
                        Thomas
                            Children
                            Maj. Jesse - b. 1752
                            m. Dorothy (c.
                            1751-1835), dau
                            of   Zephaniah
                            Platt
                            Children
                                Jesse - bc
                                1775
            Robert - b. June 30, 1685

Crean Brush

Source: Records of the Governor and Council of the State
of Vermont. Vol 1.

In Council, Bennington June 17, 1778

To Nathaniel Robinson, Esqr:
    You are hereby Authorized & Impowered to settle with
the Committee appointed by a former County committee in
the County of Cumberland to Lease the estate of Crean
Brush (who is deserted over to the Enemy) and after
allowing them a reasonable Reward for their Services, to

receive the money arising from said Leasings, and pay the Same into the Treasury of this State.

By order of the Govr. & Council
Thomas Chandler, Jur., Sec'y

According to volume 1 footnotes, Crean was born in Dublin in 1725 and was educated as a lawyer. He held a military position before emigrating to New York City in 1762. He served as deputy secretary of the province of New York and, in 1764, became a licensed attorney for the king's courts. In 1771 Brush moved to Westminster, Vermont, where he had numerous land holdings from New York land grants. In February, 1772, Crean was appointed clerk of Cumberland County. He was a member of the New York Colonial Assembly from early 1773 to its dissolution in 1775 and wrote for a Tory newspaper. When the war came, Brush joined British General Gage at Boston. Seizures he made in the name of General Gage bordered on robbery and he was required to make a hasty escape. His allies, the British, captured him and jailed him from April 12, 1776 through November 15, 1777, when he escaped. With both the British and the Americans hunting him, in May 1778 Brush "with a pistol, besmeared the Room with his Brains."

Will

Source: New York Calendar of Wills

1863 (V82)   VEDDER, Jacobus, of Schonectady, Albany Co.,
1762   yeoman. Wife Maria, brothers Harmen
Vedder,
July 1   Johannis Har. Vedder, sister Antje, wife
Septbr. 6   of Harmanis Peeck, son of Johannis Peeck,
             Harmanis Franse, son of Nicolaes Van den
             Bogert, children of dec'd sister Suffia
             Pieters, vizt: Harmanis Pieters and
             Marghariet, wife of James Seuter, da. of
             dec'd sister Lydia, vizt. Margariet van
             Sleyck, children of bro. Arent Bradt
             vizt: Harmanis and Margrieta, widow of
             Cornelis van Dyck, do. of sister Batseba,
             vizt: Andries Burn, Catoleyn Burn and her
             grandchildren, i.e. children of dec'd son
             Samuel Burn and of Jacomeyn; Margrieta,
             wife of John Brown. Real and personal
             estate. Executors the wife and bro.
             Johannis har. Vedder. Witnesses Thomas
             Brower Bancker, John van Sice and John
             Sanders.

Newspaper Article

Taken directly from the June 18, 1896 Highgate Monitor
Newspaper.

There lives in Highgate, an old lady who is said to
be the first white woman born in Orford Township. She was
the daughter of Samuel Burns Sr. and was born at
Clearville, July 29th 1818. Her brother Samuel Burns Jr.
married Catherine Johnston, daughter of Francis and Sarah
(Chittick) Johnston of Enniskill County Fermanagh,
Ireland.

Caroline lived at Clearville for 22 years, then she
married Truman Landon and they lived in the area till
1851. Truman taught the school on Con. 4 south of
Highgate 1838-1839.

In 1851 Mr. & Mrs. Landon then moved to Orangeville
but in 1856 he died and she and her small family moved
back to Orford to live there.

She now [1896] lives with her daughter-in-law Mrs.
Joseph Landon in Highgate.

Truman & Caroline Landon had 3 girls and 2 boys,
Joseph, Margaret, Edna, William and Nancy.

In 1896 only Edna and Nancy are living but many
Highgate residents will remember her son Joseph Landon.

Nancy Landon is Mrs. Truman Holman, Highgate.

Mrs. Caroline Landon has two sisters living Nancy
(Burns) Ward and Elizabeth (Burns) Arnold.

Mrs. Landon is now about 78 years old, has 25
grandchildren, 18 great grandchildren and has now resided
in Highgate for 24 years.

Oliver Landon's Answers to Robert Gourlay's Questionnaire

Source: Truman Landon's _First Settler..._

1. Township of Lansdown, situated on the River St. Lawrence, in width 6 miles in front and rear, in depth, 16 concessions or ranges of lots about one and a quarter mile in length, and about 80 rods in width.

2. This town was laid out in June 1788 as was Leeds above and part of the township of Yonge below, at that time a wilderness of 30 miles, and first Lot taken up and first settled under the patronage of Lord Dorchester of Quebec, by Oliver landon, whose family then was a wife and six boys, with a gift of 200 acres of land, called Lord Dorchester's Bounty; The same man now living in this town with nine sons, six sons wives, nineteen grandsons, and twelve granddaughters, and also three daughters with two children, being thirty one grandchildren, and total 59 of his family. Inhabitants in front of this township, 205. Houses 36 and all in the 1st and second concessions.

3. One schoolhouse, and for public worship, Methodist every Sabbath, and occasionally, Baptists and Presbyterians, but no settled preachers.

4. Medical practitioners, none.

5. Schools, one assisted by Government, 25 pounds and by people 45 pounds annually.

6. Stores, one.

7. Taverns, or inns, three.

8. Mills, one saw mill.

9. Soil composed of sandy loam and clay, and the surface level, and well watered with small streams and springs, and may be considered as an excellent township for wheat and grass, as well as oats, pease and flax, potatoes etc. All kinds of produce flourish, but much depends on the husbandry of the land.

10. Timber; oak, pine, ash, maple birch, beech, walnut, hemlock, black spruce, alder, willow, and elder. Apples and plums together with cherry will thrive here.

11. Minerals, no discovery.

12. But one quarry of building stone, and obtained by digging, and that with ease, and of good quality.

13. Bricks have been made here, and the materials abundant, are worth about six dollar's a thousand.

14. Limestone has not been discovered in this town but abundantly supplied in the township of Leeds adjoining.

15. Blacksmith work; axes 10 s., horse shoeing 10 s., chains per pound, 1 s., 3 d. masons, 5 to 10 s. carpenters the same and boarded.

16. Laborers; from 120 to 150 dollars per year. 5 s. per day in haying and harvest and boarded. Women per week, 5 shillings housework and spinning.

17. Mowing grass 2 s. 6 d. per acre. Reaping 3 s. 6 d., cradling 2 s. board and lodging.

18. Clearing and fencing five acres (for the harrow and seed, for this is the way for the first crop) 15 dollars per acre, not boarded.

19. Present price of good work horse from 50 to 70 dollars; good saddle horse sometimes 100 dollars; cows from 16 to 30 dollars, according to size; oxen from 70 to 100 dollars; sheep 10 s. to 15 s.

20. Average crop of wool from sheep in spring, 2 lobs to 5 lobs, price of wool from 2 s. to 6 s. per lb.

21. Cattle will do well in the woods at large, if in good order, from the first of April; but the grass in fields is not a support until the month of May. Time of taking in to feed from 15th Nov. to 25th Dec. most general Dec. 1st.

22. The ordinary time of snows fit for business is three months, and that generally steady, and much to the advantage of the laboring teamster, as well as for the convenience and pleasure of life.

23. We commonly begin ploughing about the 15th of April, for spring crops, and mostly have in out spring seed in the month of May; winter wheat, last of August and 1st of September. Reaping wheat the month of Aug. 1st half; oats and peas, last half.

24. It is common to sow one bushel of wheat on new land, if early, and 1 1/4 on old land; with respect to the quantity, much depends on tillage, from 20 to 40 bushels per acre.

25. The pasture enclosed is common and natural to white clover and English spear grass, and on moist land, of which this town abounds, yields an abundance very great. Cows will produce 120 lobs. of cheese, and 80 lobs of butter in the season; and oxen are raised from six to seven around the girth, and will weigh from 600 to 1000 pounds, 60 to 100 weight of tallow. Butter per pound, 1 s. 3 d.; cheese 7 1/2 d., the market good; valuable mills that never fail; 7 1/2 miles of good road.

26. Cropping on shares is various, and little done here; manure serves well on all lands, but is mostly applied around the stable, where made.

27. Land is rented at four dollars per acre; this is the worth annually.

28. Price of wild land; at the first settlement, it was sold at 5 pounds per 200 acres, and has gradually risen to one

dollar per acre at a distance from the settlement; but on the road or river it may be valued at three dollars per acre, and that without any improvement; in the center of town from three to six dollars per acre.

29. The quantity of land for sale, 50,000 acres.

30. The main road leading through this town from the province of Lower Canada is at present quit passable for wagons in summer and sleighs in winter and will not need great expense to keep it so.

31. The principle impairment which prevents this township from being settled is the want of spirited and industrious men, who having money, might apply it with safety and profit.

Witness by us the first settlers,

Oliver Landon   Joseph Landon
Benjamin Landon   Oliver Landon, Jr.
and six others*

*The six others were not named in Truman Landon's book. He related that it also was not in the original 1822 account.

Letter from Thomas McKee to Edward Shippen

Source: Rupp, I. Daniel. The History and Topography of Dauphin, Cumberland, Franklin, Bedford, Adams, and Perry Counties. Gilbert Hills. Lancaster, Pennsylvania. 1846.

I desire to let you know that John Shecalemy, Indian, is come here in the afternoon and gives me an account that there is great confusion amongst the Indians up the North Branch of Susquehannah; the Delawares are moving all from thence to Ohio, and want to persuade the Shanoies along with them, but they decline going with them that course as they still incline to join with us. The Shanoies are going up to the town called Teaoga (Diahoga) where there is a body of the Six Nations, and there they intend to remain. He has brought two more men, some women and some children along with him, and says that he intends to live and die with us, and insist upon my conducting him down to where his sister and children are at Canestogo, and I am loath to leave my post as his Honor was offended at the last time I did, but can't help it. He desires me to acquaint you that his sister's son was killed at Penn's creek in the scrimmage with Capt. Patterson. This with due respect from yours, &c.

Early Navarre Genealogy

Sources: <u>Navarre, or Researches after the Descendants of</u>
<u>Robert Navarre whose Ancestors Are the Noble Bourbon of France</u>
<u>and some Historical Notes on Families who Intermarried with</u>
<u>Navarres.</u>
                          and
              <u>Arbre Genealogique de la Famille Navarre.</u>

```
       Jean d'Aragon
   (John II, King of Navarre)

        Eleanor        m.    Gastonde Foix
    (Queen of Navarre)        |
      crowned 1479            |
                              ?
                       ┌──────┴──────┐
  Francois Phoebus              Catherine  de  Navarre   m.   John
  D'Albret                                                      │
  (King of Navarre)                              ┌──────────────┘
     crowned 1482                                │
                                        ┌────────┴──┐
                          Jane D'Albret m. Antoine de Bourbon
                          (Queen of Navarre) (King of Navarre)
                             crowned 1554  │    crowned 1554
                                           └────────┐
                        Perett Barat  m.  Jean Navarre   Henri IV
                                1572                     (King of
                                  │                       France)
                                  └───────┐
                        Jane Lefebre/Lefavre m. Martin Navarre de Villeroi
                                    1593
                                     │
                          Susanne LeClef m. Jean Navarre
                                  1623
                                     │
               Marie Lallemant m. Antoine Navarre du Plesses en Bois
                          1665
                            │
   Jeanne Pluiette/ m. Antoine Marie Francois Navarre
   Pleyette/Pluyette/
   Plugette              │
                   Robert Navarre
```

Will of Richard Pattinson

Source: <u>New York Calendar of Wills</u>

1373	PATTINSON, Richard, of Montreal, Lower Canada.
1817	Children Mary Ann, Richard, Ellen Phyliss,
Decbr 31	halfbrother Hugh Pattinson, Mrs. Archange Askin
1818	and her da Mrs. Therese McKee, Dr. William

Caldwell of March 4 M o n t r e a l ,   F e m a l e
Benevolent Society of Montreal, of which Mrs.
Aird is treasurer, Jasper Tough. Real estate
in Upper Canada, in Indiana and Michigan,
personal property. Executors Robert Gillespie,
George Moffat, both of Montreal, merchants,
and William Gilkson of Glasgow, Scotland,
merchant, with George Jacobs of Sandwich, John
Askin and James Gordon of Amherstburg, Upper
Canada, as agents. Witnesses H. Bleecker, J.W.
Rockwell and Jas. Van Ingen. Will made,
executed and proved in Albany. Recorded ut
supra, p. 346.

William Reddick

```
          William        m.          Margaret
          Reddick    Sept., 1784   Trump / Tramp
     enl. Philadelphia              b.c. 1766
     r. Aug. 8, 1818;           r. Marion Co. Indiana;
     Clermont Co., Ohio             Nov. 22, 1838
          b.c. 1760
     d. Marion Co.
     Indiana; Oct. 3,
          1831
```

Richard	?	William	Joshua	Helia
b. 1786		b. 1790	b.c. 1806	b.c. 1802

Lucinda	Rachel
b.c. 1810	b.c. 1812

Headstone of Maria Caroline Richardson

Here Reposes, Maria Caroline, the Generous-Hearted, High-Souled, Talented and Deeply-Lamented Wife of Major Richardson, Knight of the Military Order of Saint Ferdinand, First Class, and Superintendent of Police on the Welland Canal during the Administration of Lord metcalfe. This Matchless Wife and This (Illegible) Exceeding Grief of Her Faithfully Attached Husband after a few days' illness at St. Catharines on the 16th August, 1845, at the age of 37 years.

Hamilton Family

Robert Hamilton
    b. 1749
    m1 Catherine Askin Robertson (d. 1796), dau of John
    Askin, Sr., wid of Capt. Samuel Robertson; 1785
    m2 Mary Herkimer McLean (d. January 26, 1808), wid of
    Neil McLean
    d. March 23, 1809; Queenston, Ontario
    Children
        Robert - 1786
            m. Mary Biggar, c. 1808
            d. 1856; Queenston, Ontario
        George - b. 1788
            m. Maria Jarvis
        Alexander - b. 1790
            m. Hannah Jarvis
        dau

On April 23, 1808, Robert Hamilton was residing in
Queenston and wrote John Askin about
    "the sad Evil which befell (his) family in the course of
    (the) winter."
His second wife Mary Herkimer Hamilton had died on January 26,
1808. He related that his
    "young folks have suffered a sad Loss but ... God has
    given them a new constitution ... I hear regularly from
    my Boys in Schenectady. My Youngest is still with me, but
    goes to Niagara next month where he has already two
    Brothers. My little Girl will go to Kingston to her Aunts
    for sometime, till of fitt age to go to a publick school
    at Quebec ... I come now to the oldest of whose Marriage
    you perhaps have heard ... I ceased opposition & let him
    have his own way. The Girl he has married seems extremely
    well disposed to make him happy, & probably may be more
    successful than one taken from a higher Grade ..."

Then on March 29, 1809, John Askin wrote to his friend
James McGill
    "I most sincerely regret the loss of that worthy Man my
    Friend Mr. Hamilton, he is a great loss not only to his
    Family but to his Country."

Robert Hamilton's son George was the founder of Hamilton,
Ontario, Canada.

No history of this region would be complete without details pertaining to Cadillac. While the importance of his family in the history of the area was of little consequence, Cadillac's own significance to the area was immeasurable.

Cadillac Family

Jean Laumet / de la Mothe, Seigneur of Cadillac of Launay and Montet et Conseiller du Parliament de Toulouse
    m. Jeanne de Pechagut / Jane De Malenfant; June 25, 1687; Quebec
    Children
        Antoine (see below)

Antoine Laumet de la Mothe Cadillac
    b. March 5, 1656 or 1658; St. Nicholas de la Grave, Upper Garonne, France
    bpt. March 6, 1656 or 1658
    m. Marie Therese Guyton (b. April 9, 1671, Quebec), dau of Francois Guyton; June 25, 1687; prob Nova Scotia, Canada
    r. 1694, Michilimackinac
    d. 1730; Castelsarrasin, France
    bur. October 16, 1730; Church of the Fathers of the Carmelite order
    Children
        ?Judith, b. 1689, Port Royal
            became Ursuline nun November 2, 1711; Quebec
        Magdalene - b. Quebec or Mount Desert Island or Arcadia
            became Ursuline nun
        Antoine de la Mothe Cadillac fils - b. April 26, 1692; Quebec
            d.c. 1730
        Jacques - b. March 16, 1695; Quebec
        Pierre Denis - b. June 13, 1699; Quebec
            bur. July 4, 1700; Quebec
        Marianne - b. June 7, 1701; Quebec
            bur. June 9, 1701; Quebec
        Child - b. 1702/3
        Marie Therese - b. February 2, 1704; Detroit, Michigan
            m. Noble Francois de Pouzargues; February 16, 1729; Castersarrasin, France
            d. February, 1753; Castelsarrasin, France
        Jean Antoine - b. June 19, 1707; Detroit Michigan
            bur. April 9, 1709; Detroit, Michigan
        Marie Agathe - b. December 28, 1707; Detroit, Michigan
        Francois - b. March 27, 1709; Detroit, Michigan
            d. aft 1730
        Rene Louis - b. March 17, 1710; Detroit, Michigan
            bur. October 7, 1714; Church of the Recolets, Quebec
      ? Joseph

Literature Cited

Brown, George; David, M. Hayne; and Francis Halpenny (eds.). Dictionary of Canadian Biography. University of Toronto. Toronto. 1979.

Burton, Clarence M. and M. Agnes Burton (eds.). History of Wayne County and the City of Detroit, Michigan. Vols 1 & 2. S.J. Clarke Publishing Co. Detroit. 1930.

Casselman, Alexander Clark. Richardson's War of 1812: With Notes and a Life of the Author. Historical Publishing Co. Toronto. 1902.

Coldham, Peter Wilson. American Loyalist Claims: Abstracted from the Public Records Office, Audit Office Series 13, Bundles 1-35 & 37. National Genealogical Society. Washington, D.C. 1980.

Connecticut Daughters of the American Revolution. Connecticut Revolutionary Pensioners. Genealogical Publishing Company. Baltimore. 1982 Reprint of 1917.

Day, Mrs. C.M. Pioneers of the Eastern Townships: A Work Containing Official and Reliable Information Respecting the Formation of Settlements with Incidents in Their Early History and Details of Adventures, Periols and Deliverances. John Lovell, printer. Montreal. 1863.

Denissen, Christian (comp.). Navarre, or Researches after the Descendants of Robert Navarre whose Ancestors Are the Noble Bourbon of France and some Historical Notes on Families who Intermarried with Navarres. Detroit.

Douglas, Sir Robert. Peerage of Scotland: Containing Historical and Genealogical Acount of the Nobility of that Kingdom, from Their Origin to the Present Generation: The Public Records, "Antient" Chartularies, the Charters and other writings of the Nobility, works of Our Best Historians etc. George Ramsay and Co. London. 1813.

Etten, William J. A Citizen's History of Grand Rapids with program of the Campeau Centennial. A.P. Johnson Co. 1926.

Field, James Bird. Progenitors and Descendants of Our Grandfather Seldon Field 1793-1857. Will H. Green Pub. np. nd.

Field, Osgood. "Matthew Field of London, Mercer; His Family and Arms" New England Historic and Genealogical Record. July, 1894.

Galbraith, John Kenneth. The Scotch. Houghton Mifflin Co. Boston. 1964.

Grehan, Ida. Irish Family Names: Highlights of 50 Family Histories. Macmillan Publishing Co., Inc. New York. 1973.

Hall, Theodore Parsons. Family Records of Theodore Parsons Hall and Alexandrine Louise Godfroy of "Tonnancour", Grosse Pointe near Detroit, Michigan. Wm. C. Heath Printing Co. Detroit. 1892.

Hamil, Fred Coyne. The Valley of the Lower Thames 1640-1850. University of Toronto Press. Toronto. 1951.

Hamilton, Edward P. (trans.) Adventure in the Wilderness: The American Journals of Louis Antoine de Bougainville (1756-1760). University of Oklahoma Press. Norman, OK. n.d.

Hamilton, William. The MacMillan Book of Canadian Place Names.

Handlin, Oscar. A Pictorial History of Immigration. Crown
     Publishers. New York. 1972.
Hanna, Charles.   The Scotch-Irish Families of America.
     Genealogical Publishing Co. Baltimore. 1968.
Heldman, Donald P.   Archaeological Investigations at French
     Farm Lake in Northern Michigan, 1981-82: A British
     Colonial Farm Site.   Mackinac Island Park Commission.
     Mackinac Island, Michigan. 1983.
Horsman, Reginald.   Matthew Elliott, British Indian Agent.
     Wayne State University Press. Detroit. 1964.
Jacobson, Judy.   Southold connections: Historical and
     Biographical Sketches of Northeastern Long Island.
     Clearfield Co., Genealogical Publishing Co. Baltimore.
     1991.
Keffer, Marion Christena. "Migrations to and from Ontario /
     Michigan". Families.
Kenton, Edna (ed.). The Jesuit Relations and Allied Documents:
     Travels and Explorations of the Jesuit Missionaries in
     North America (1610-1791). Albert & Charles Boni. New
     York. 1925.
Laforest, Thomas J.   Our French Canadian Ancestors. LISI
     Press. Florida. 1983.
Landon, Fred.   Western Ontario and the American Frontier.
     Ryerson Press. Toronto. 1941.
Landon, James Orville. Landon Genealogy: The French and
     English Home and Ancestry. Clark Boardman Co., Ltd. New
     York. 1928.
Landon, Truman B.   The First Settler: Genealogy of Oliver
     Landon, His Ancestors and Descendants. np. 1979.
Lefebvre, Georges. The Great Fear of 1789. Pantheon Books.
     New York. 1973.
Le Van Spicer, Florence (comp.).   Genealogical Record the
     Campbell-Rea Families. Pluid Printing Parlor. Eugene,
     Oregon. 1973.
Lucas, Sir Charles (ed.).   Lord Durham's Report on the
     Affaires of British North America [1912]. 3 Vols.
     Augustus M. Kelly Pub. New York. 1970.
McNaught, Kenneth.   The History of Canada.   Praeger
     Publishers. New York. 1970.
Marcus, Dr. Jacob R. The Beth El Story: With a History of the
     Jews in Michigan before 1850 by Irving I. Katz. Wayne
     State University. Detroit. 1955.
Massicotte, E.Z. (ed.).   Canadian Passports 1681-1752.
     Polyanthos. New Orleans. 1975.
Massicotte, E.Z. and Regis Roy. Armorial du Canada Francais.
     Genealogical Publishing Co. Baltimore. 1970 Reprint.
Mather, Frederic Gregory. The Refugees of 1776 from Long
     Island to Connecticut.   Genealogical Publishing Co.
     Baltimore. 1972.
Matthews, C.M. Place Names of the English Speaking World.
     Charles Scribner's Sons. New York. 1972.
Michigan Ghost Towns. Gendon Publishers. Sterling Heights,
     Michigan. 1970
Mires, Maynard H.   A Short History of the Landon Family in
     America. Village Press. Concord, New Hampshire. 1978.
Munro, R.W. Highland Clans and Tartans. Octopus Book Ltd.
     Hong Kong. 1977.
Neville, Dr. George A.   "Returns of the Asylum at William
     Henry for Loyalist Invalids. Families. Vol. 16 No. 3.
Old United Empire Loyalists List. Genealogical Publishing Co.
     Baltimore. 1969.

Palmer, Gregory. Biographical Sketches of Loyalists of the American Revolution. Meckler Publishers. Westport. 1984.

Parkens, Almon Ernest. The Historical Geography of Detroit. Kennikat Press. Port Washington, NY. 1970 Reprint of 1918.

Payette, B.C. The Northwest. Payette Radio Limited. Montreal. 1964.

Pioneers of the Eastern Townships: A Work Containing Official and Reliable Information Respecting the Formation of the Settlements; With Incidents in their Early History and Details of Adventures, Perils and Deliverances. John Lovel Printers. Montreal. 1863.

Quaife, Milo M. (ed.). The John Askin Papers. Vol 1, 1747-1795. Vol. 2, 1796-1820. Detroit Library Commission. Detroit. 1928.

Records of the Governor and Council of the State of Vermont - June, 1778. AMS Press. New York.

Romig, Walter. Michigan Place Names. Wayne State University Press. Detroit. 1986.

Rupp, I. Daniel. The History and Topography of Dauphin, Cumberland, Franklin, Bedford, Adams, and Perry Counties. Gilbert Hills. Lancaster, PA. 1846.

Russell, Donna Valley (ed.). Michigan Census 1710-1830: Under the French, British, and Americans. Detroit Society for Genealogical Research, Inc. Detroit. 1982.

Russell, Donna Valley (ed.). Michigan Voyagers. Detroit Society for Genealogical Research, Inc. Detroit. 1982.

Russell, Nelson Vance. The British Regime in Michigan and the Old Northwest 1760-1796. Porcupine Press. Philadelphia. 1978 Repr of 1939.

Schoolcraft, Henryh R. Narrative Journal of Travels Through the Northwestern Regions of the United States Extending From Detroit Through the Great Chain of American Lakes, to the Sources of the Mississippi River: Performed as a Member of the Expedition Under Governor Cass: In the Year 1820. Albany. 1821.

Scott, Kenneth and Rosanne Conway (comp.). Genealogical Data from Colonial New Haven Newspapers. Genealogical Publishing Co. Baltimore. 1979.

Sims, Clifford Stanley. The Origin and Signification of Scottish Surnames. Avenel Books. New York. 1964.

Sketches of the City of Detroit, State of Michigan: Past and Present, 1855. Detroit, Michigan. 1855.

Smith, Elsdon C. American Surnames. Chilton Book Co. New York. 1969.

Soboul, Albert. The French Revolution 1787-1799: From the Storming of the Bastille to Napoleon. Vintage Books. New York. 1984.

Stewart, George R. American Place-Names. Oxford Press. New York. 1971.

Swift, Esther Munro. Vermont Place names. Stephen Green Press. Vermont. 1977.

Taylor, Philip. The Distant Magnet: European Emigration to the U.S.A. Harper & Row. New York. 1971.

Tepper, Michael (ed.) New world Immigrants: A Consolidation of Ship Passenger Lists and Associated Data from Periodical Literature. 2 Vol. Genealogical Publishing Co. Baltimore. 1980.

Territorial Papers: Michigan Territory.

Thwaites, Reuben Gold (ed.). The Jesuit Relations and Allied Documents: Travels and Explorations of the Jesuit

Missionaries in New France 1610-1791. Vols 68, 69, 70, and 71. Pageant Book Co. New York. 1959.

United Empire Loyalist's Association of Canada (Toronto Branch). Loyalist Lineages of Canada 1783-1983. Generation Press.

Vexler, Robert I. (comp.). Detroit: A Chronological & Documentary History, 1701-1976. Oceana Publications, Inc. Dobbs Ferry, New York. 1977.

Virkus, Frederick Adams (ed.). The Compendium of American Genealogy. Institute of American Genealogy. Chicago. 1939.

Wallace, W. Stewart. The United Empire Loyalist: A Chronicle of the Great Migration. Glascow Brooke Company. Toronto. 1922.

Walton, E.P. (ed.) Records of the Governor and Council of the State of Vermont. 2 vols. J. & J.M. Poland. Montpelier, Vermont. 1973.

White, Virgil D. (abstract). Genealogical Abstracts of Revolutionary War Pension Files. 4 vol. National Historical Publishing Co. Waynesboro, Tennessee. 1990.

Whyte, Donald. Dictionary of Scottish Emigrants to Canada before Confederation. Ontario Genealogical Society. Toronto. 1986.

Woodward, Frank Ernest. "The Erskine Family of Bristol, ME" NEHGR. January, 1920.

Index of Names